Governance and Public Management

Series Editors
Robert Fouchet
Universite Aix Marseille
France

Juraj Nemec
Masaryk University
Czech Republic

IIAS
International Institute
of Administrative Sciences

IIAS Series: Governance and Public Management
International Institute of Administrative Sciences (IIAS) *–Improving Administrative Sciences Worldwide*

Website: http://www.iias-iisa.org

Governance and Public Management Series
The *Governance and Public Management* series, published in conjunction with the International Institute of Administrative Sciences (IIAS), brings the best research in public administration and management to a global audience. Encouraging a diversity of approach and perspective, the series reflects the Institute's conviction for a neutral and objective voice, grounded in the exigency of fact. How is governance conducted *now*? How could it be done better? What defines the law of administration and the management of public affairs, and can their implementation be enhanced? Such questions lie behind the Institute's core value of *accountability*: those who exercise authority must account for its use – to those on whose behalf they act.

More information about this series at
http://www.palgrave.com/gp/series/15021

Andrea Lippi
Theodore N. Tsekos
Editors

Local Public Services in Times of Austerity across Mediterranean Europe

palgrave
macmillan

Editors
Andrea Lippi
Department of Political
and Social Sciences
University of Florence
Firenze, Italy

Theodore N. Tsekos
Department of Business
and Public Administration
Technological Education
Institute of Peloponnese
Kalamata, Greece

Governance and Public Management
ISBN 978-3-319-76224-1 ISBN 978-3-319-76225-8 (eBook)
https://doi.org/10.1007/978-3-319-76225-8

Library of Congress Control Number: 2018935122

Printed on acid-free paper

This Palgrave Macmillan imprint is published by the registered company Springer International Publishing AG part of Springer Nature.
The registered company address is: Gewerbestrasse 11, 6330 Cham, Switzerland

Acknowledgments

This book was made possible thanks to the support and advice of many colleagues and institutions and, therefore, we are very grateful to everyone who contributed to this endeavour.

The research that resulted in the present publication was made possible by the financial support of the European Cooperation in Science and Technology programme through the Local Public Sector Reforms: An International Comparison—LocRef project. Particular thanks go to the LocRef chairs, Sabine Kuhlmann and Geert Buckaert, for ensuring a very fruitful working environment for research and scientific dialogue. Sincere gratitude also goes to the academic coordinator of the LocRef project, Christian Schwab, who played a vital role in facilitating our research and discussion.

The LocRef's Working Group 1, aiming at analyzing the "external" reorganisation of the municipal sector, was the framework for our work. We have benefited largely from the time, energy and enthusiasm invested on our common research from each of its members. The WG1 co-chairs, HellmutWollmann, Ivan Koprić and the late Gérard Marcou, played a key role in providing coordination and support at all stages of the research cycle.

Finally, we would like to thank Robert Fouchet and Juraj Nemec, the editors of the Palgrave IIAS series Governance and Public Management, for reading the manuscript and providing very useful comments that helped in improving the quality of the book.

University of Florence
Firenze, Italy
Andrea Lippi

Technological Education Institute
of Peloponnese
Kalamata, Greece
Theodore N. Tsekos

Contents

1 Introduction: Local Public Services in Times of Austerity 1
Andrea Lippi and Theodore N. Tsekos

2 Importing or Constructing Austerity? Global Reforms and Local Implementation as a Case of Policy Transfer 25
Andrea Lippi and Theodore N. Tsekos

3 Greek Municipalities Before and During the Austerity Era: Imposed Policies, Local Resistance and Unsuccessful Reforms 49
Theodore N. Tsekos and Nikos K. Hlepas

4 The Biggest Loser? Local Public Services Under Austerity Measures in Portugal 73
Patrícia Silva and Filipe Teles

5 Spanish Local Government and the Austerity Plan: In the Eye of the Perfect Storm 95
Carmen Navarro and Esther Pano

6 In the Shadow of Austerity: Italian Local Public Services and the Politics of Budget Cuts 115
Giulio Citroni, Andrea Lippi, and Stefania Profeti

7 **Austerity Measures and Local Public Services in Cyprus: Coping with Challenges Old and New and Reinforcing Historical Continuities** 141
Andreas Kirlappos, Philippos Philippou, and Kalliope Agapiou-Josephides

8 **Local Public Services and Austerity Measures in Croatia: Adaptations of the Resilient Social Model Through the Central-Local Power and Blame Games** 167
Ivan Koprić, Mihovil Škarica, and Romea Manojlović Tomań

9 **The Bumpy Road of the Externally Transferred Austerity Agenda in Albania and Its Fragmentary Effects on Local Public Services** 193
Visar Dizdari, Arjeta Troshani, and Elvisa Drishti

10 **Conclusions: The Direction and Entity of Austerity in Mediterranean Local Public Services** 217
Andrea Lippi and Theodore N. Tsekos

Index 243

Notes on Contributors

Kalliope Agapiou-Josephides holds a PhD in Political Science from Paris I Panthéon-Sorbonne University. She is a Jean Monnet Chair Holder (2001) and Assistant Professor at the Department of Social and Political Sciences, University of Cyprus. Her research focuses mainly on different aspects of European Integration and its impact on human rights and democratisation, women and politics. Her work has been published in English, French, German and Greek. She has been conducting and leading cross-national and transnational research, edited books, published articles, book chapters and research studies for international organisations (e.g. European Parliament, Council of Europe). She has served/is serving on the Board of a number of EU-related agencies/centres, namely, as Chair of the Management Board of the European Institute for Gender Equality, Vilnius, Lithuania, and as Deputy President of the European Inter-University Centre for Human Rights and Democratization, Venice, Italy.

Giulio Citroni is Associate Professor of Political Science at Università della Calabria (Italy). He is engaged in a number of national and international research projects on local government, governance and administration (MSCA Rise, Prin 2015) and he is a member of the Citygov research group on local governance. His works on local public service delivery and the politics of local government reforms have been published on the Public Management Review, Local Government Studies and European Political Science Review. He is the Co-founder and present President of *Associazione Sottosopra*, engaged in the development of deliberation and participation in political organisations.

Visar Dizdari is full-time Lecturer of Sociology and Social Research at the Faculty of Educational Sciences, Department of Psychology and Social Work, University of Shkodra “LuigjGurakuqi”, Albania. From 2016, he has been Head of Psychology and Social Work Department. He has a BA in Sociology from the University of Tirana and an MA in Social Research Instruments from the University of Florence. He defended a PhD degree in Methodology of Social Sciences in 2014 at the Department of Political and Social Sciences, University of Florence, discussing his thesis in Phenomenological Sociology. His main areas of interest and expertise include the social research method, theoretical sociology, social problems and social policy.

Elvisa Drishti is a PhD student, Faculty of Economy, Department of Business Administration, University of Shkodra “Luigj Gurakuqi”, Albania. She is attending her PhD studies in Labour Market Economics at the Birmingham Business School, UK. Her studies are focused on the performance of the Albanian labour market in general and on non-standard employment, wage equation estimation and the effects of the non-ability factor on employability. In March 2013, she joined the Department of Business Administration of the Faculty of Economy at the University of Shkoder. As an Assistant Lecturer, she is engaged in teaching Basic Statistics for the Social Sciences, Research Methods for Business Students and Econometrics. Her post-graduate studies include a Master of Sciences degree in European Economics Studies at the University of Tirana, Albania, in collaboration with University of Bamberg, Germany, and a Master of Business Administration at the Oxford Brookes University, U.K.

Nikos K. Hlepas is Associate Professor of Regional and Local Government, Department of Political Science and Public Administration, at the National and Capodistrian University of Athens.

Andreas Kirlappos holds a PhD in Political Science (University of Cyprus, 2015). He has participated as Cyprus’s delegate to the Cost Action IS1207 – Local Public Sector Reforms: An International Comparison i.e. Political Leaders in European Cities – Second Round and Local Public Sector Reforms (WGIII). His research interests and publications focus, among others, on Local Government and Public Administration, the impact of the crisis on Local Government, Decentralisation, Europeanisation and Cohesion Policy.

Ivan Koprić holds a PhD and Tenured Professor of Administrative Science and Local Governance at the Faculty of Law, University of Zagreb, President of the Institute of Public Administration in Zagreb, Croatia, and Editor-in-Chief of the international scientific journal *Croatian and Comparative Public Administration*. His current work is focused on administrative reforms at the central and local levels and their evaluation, European Administrative Space in the multi-level context, decentralisation and improving local democracy. His recent books include *Evaluating Reforms of Local Public and Social Services in Europe: More Evidence for Better Results*, Palgrave Macmillan, 2017 (with H. Wollmann and G. Marcou) and *European Administrative Space: Spreading Standards, Building Capacities*, NISPAcee, 2017 (with P. Kovač).

Andrea Lippi is Associate Professor of Political Science at the University of Florence. He holds a Ph.D. in Sociology and Social Research at the University of Trento and is Associate Professor at the Department of Political and Social Sciences, University of Florence. He is a member of the Citygov research group on local governance and his research interests include local public services, local governance, evaluation, public sector reforms, policy instruments and political legitimacy. He is engaged in a number of research groups and his works have been published in journals such as *Policy Sciences*, *European Political Science Review*, *Local Government Studies* and *Public Management Review*.

Romea Manojlović Tomań is Assistant Professor of Administrative Science at the Faculty of Law, University of Zagreb, Croatia, and is Executive Editor of the international scientific journal *Croatian and Comparative Public Administration*. Her recent books include *Quality and Performance Management in Public Administration* (in Croatian; with I. Koprić and J. Džinić). Her areas of interest include public management, local self-government, European administrative space and human resources management.

Carmen Navarro is Lecturer at the Department of Political Science, University Autónoma of Madrid, where she focuses her research and teaching activities on local government and public policy. Her specific research interests are local government institutions and local leadership. She is a member of international networks for research on local government and policies, including, among others, the European Mayor Project (first and second rounds), the International Metropolitan

Observatory, Municipal Assemblies in European Local Government, Second Tier of Local Government in Europe, Local Government Reforms: An International Comparison and Local Autonomy Index.

Esther Pano is Associate Lecturer in the Department of Constitutional Law and Political Science at the Barcelona University. She is also the coordinator of the project "Local Government Observatory" held by the Fundació Carles Pi i Sunyer (http://www.pisunyer.org/), a non-profit organisation devoted to gather and analyse data regarding the operation and performance of local institutions. She is currently a member of the GREL (research group in local politics, www.ub.edu/grel). Her research interests are related to empirical institutional analysis, local government and those questions connected to institutional design, both from a political perspective and from an organisational point of view.

Philippos Philippou is a PhD candidate at the Department of Social and Political Sciences, University of Cyprus, with a background in English (University of Cyprus) and European Studies (King's College London). He works as a Training Officer at the Cyprus Academy of Public Administration (CAPA). His research centres on the impact of European Integration as well as the financial crisis on the Republic of Cyprus Public Administration with a particular focus on the L&D function.

Stefania Profeti is Associate Professor at the University of Bologna, where she teaches Administration and Public Policies and Organisation Theory. She is a member of the Citygov research group on local governance. Her research interests include public services, local governance, administrative reforms, regionalism and EU Cohesion policy. She has recently published in several journals, including *European Political Science Review*, *Local Government Studies*, *Public Management Review* and *West European Politics*. Since 2015, she is Co-Editor of *Rivista Italiana di Politiche Pubbliche* (*Italian Journal of Public Policies*).

Patrícia Silva holds a PhD in Political Sciences with a thesis researching party patronage and party government in the Portuguese context. She is a post-doctoral researcher at the Governance, Competitiveness and Public Policies Research Centre of the University of Aveiro. Her main research interests are political parties, the politicisation of the recruitment of appointed elites, territorial governance and local public sector reform.

Mihovil Škarica holds a PhD and is Assistant Professor of Administrative Science at the Faculty of Law, University of Zagreb, Croatia. He has published a dozen scientific and other papers. His recent book is *Inter-municipal Cooperation and Local and Regional Development* (in Croatian; with I. Koprić and B. Milošević). His work is related to the institutional, organisational and developmental issues of local government and multi-level governance, especially with regard to inter-municipal cooperation and local public services.

Filipe Teles is Assistant Professor at the Department of Social, Political and Territorial Sciences at the University of Aveiro, Portugal. He is a member of the Research Unit on Governance, Competitiveness and Public Policy, where he has developed research work on governance, local administration and territorial reforms. His most recent book was published in 2016: "Local Governance and Inter-municipal Cooperation" (Palgrave, UK). Subsequently, he co-edited a volume, out in 2018, for the same publisher: "Inter-municipal Cooperation in Europe: Institutions and Governance".

Arjeta Troshani is a professor at the Faculty of Economy, Department of Tourism, University of Shkodra "Luigj Gurakuqi", Albania. She was Dean of the Economic Faculty at the University of Shkoder from 2008 to 2016. Prof. Troshani is a Professor of Marketing with 23 years of experience in teaching and research on different topics related to the field of Economics and specifically on the challenges of transition countries. She is the author of several articles related to sustainable economic development and marketing of tourism products, mainly in Western Balkan and specifically in Northern Albania. She has had several international teaching experiences in universities such as Vienna University of Economics and Business (WU), Austria, North Carolina Central University, East Carolina University, University of North Caroline at Pembroke, USA, Sarajevo University etc. In addition, Prof. Troshani has been very active in attracting funds from different academic EU projects at the Economic Faculty of Shkoder University, in the field of teaching quality, creating links between enterprises, public administration and university and the reform of Higher Education in Western Balkan.

Theodore N. Tsekos is Associate Professor of Public Administration, Department of Business and Public Administration, and Director, Research Laboratory for European and National Governance and Economic Integration (RELENGE) at the Institute of Technological Education, Peloponnese.

List of Contributors

Kalliope Agapiou-Josephides Department of Social and Political Sciences, University of Cyprus, Nicosia, Cyprus

Giulio Citroni Department of Political and Social Sciences, University of Calabria, Cosenza, Italy

Visar Dizdari Faculty of Educational Sciences, University of Shkoder "Luigj Gurakuqi", Shkoder, Albania

Elvisa Drishti Faculty of Economy, University of Shkoder "Luigj Gurakuqi", Shkoder, Albania

Nikos K. Hlepas Department of Political Science and Public Administration at the National and Capodistrian, University of Athens, Athens, Greece

Andreas Kirlappos Department of Social and Political Sciences, University of Cyprus, Nicosia, Cyprus

Ivan Koprić Faculty of Law, University of Zagreb, Zagreb, Croatia

Andrea Lippi Department of Political and Social Sciences, University of Florence, Firenze, Italy

Romea Manojlović Tomań Faculty of Law, University of Zagreb, Zagreb, Croatia

Carmen Navarro Department of Political Sciences and International Relations, Autonomous University of Madrid, Madrid, Spain

Esther Pano University of Barcelona, Barcelona, Spain

Philippos Philippou Department of Social and Political Sciences, University of Cyprus, Nicosia, Cyprus

Stefania Profeti Department of Political and Social Sciences, University of Bologna, Bologna, Italy

Patrícia Silva Research Unit in Governance, Competitiveness and Public Policies (GOVCOPP), University of Aveiro, Aveiro, Portugal

Mihovil Škarica Faculty of Law, University of Zagreb, Zagreb, Croatia

Filipe Teles Research Unit in Governance, Competitiveness and Public Policies (GOVCOPP), University of Aveiro, Aveiro, Portugal

Arjeta Troshani Faculty of Economics, University of Shkoder "Luigj Gurakuqi", Shkoder, Albania

Theodore N. Tsekos Department of Business and Public Administration, The Peloponnese Institute of Technological Education, Kalamata, Greece

Abbreviations

AAM	Association of Albanian Municipalities
ALL	Albanian Lek (Currency)
ANAFRE	National Association of Parish Councils
ANMP	National Association of Municipalities – Portugal
ASEP	High Commission for Public Personnel Selection – Greece
ASWM	Act on Sustainable Waste Management – Croatia
ATO	Optimal Territorial Unit for Service Management and Delivery – Italy
ATR	Administrative and Territorial Reform – Albania
BDI	Bancad'Italia, Bank of Italy
CAF	Central Autonomous Funds, Greece
CAPA	Cyprus Academy of Public Administration
CDS-PP	Conservative Centrist Democrats-Popular Party – Portugal
DP	Democratic Party, Albania
EC	European Commission
EDP	Excessive Deficit Procedures
ECB	European Central Bank
EMU	European Monetary Union
EPP-CCE	European People's Party Group, Albania
ERM	European Regulatory Mechanism
EU	European Union

EYDAP/EYAT	State-Owned Public Water Suppliers and Sewerage and Wastewater Treatment System Operators for Athens and Salonica, Greece
FODSA	Solid Waste Management Agency
GDP	Gross Domestic Product
GoA	Government of Albania
HUGO	Croatian Association for Waste Management
HDZ	Croatian Democratic Union
HRADF/TAIPED	Hellenic Republic Asset Development Fund
HRK	Croatian Kunas (Currency)
IMF	International Monetary Fund
INSTAT	Albanian Institute of Statistics
ISTAT	Italian Institute of Statistics
IRI	Italian National Agency for Economic Development, Ceased at the Beginning of the 1990s
L&D	Learning & Development
LGO	Local Government Organisation
LGS	Local Governments
LGU	Local Government Unit, Albania
LPS	Local Public Service
MBT	Mechanical Biological Treatment – Croatia
MIPA	Ministry of Innovation and Public Administration – Albania
MSLG	Ministry of State for Local Government, Albania
MSLI	Ministry of State for Local Issues – Albania
MoU	Memorandum of Understanding on Specific Economic Policy Conditionality
MTFS	Ministry of Finance, Greece
NSRF	National Strategic Reference Framework – Portugal
NPM	New Public Management
NIMBY	Not in My Backyard
NGO	Non-Governmental Organisations
OECD	Organisation for Economic Co-operation and Development
OSCE	Organisation for Security and Co-operation in Europe
PAEL	Local Economy Support Program – Portugal
PAYT	Pay as You Throw
PIGS	Portugal, Italy, Greece and Spain

PIIGS	Portugal, Ireland, Italy, Greece and Spain
PA	Public Administration – Italy
PD	Democratic Party – Italy
PDL	Liberty People Party – Italy
PM	Prime Minister
PPP	Public Private Partnership
PSD	Social Democrats Party – Portugal
RAT	Territorial and Administrative Reform Law – Albania
ROC	Republic of Cyprus
RWMC	Regional Waste Management Centres – Croatia
SAP	Social Assistance Program – Albania
SDP	Social Democrats Party – Croatia
SHSSH	Albanian State Social Service
SMI	Socialist Movement for Integration – Albania
SNDP	Special Needs and Disabilities Pension – Albania
SP	Albanian Socialist Party
STAR	Support to Territorial and Administrative Reform, a Project Implemented by the United Nations Development Programme and Funded by the United States Agency for International Development
STAR2	A Project Developed in Continuity of the Results of Its Predecessor, STAR
SYRIZA	Greek Left Party
TAR	Territorial and Administrative Reform, Albania
Trojka	EU, European Central Bank, International Monetary Fund
UCM	Union of Cyprus Municipalities
USAID	United States Agency for International Development
VAT	Value Added Tax
WB	World Bank
WSA	Water Service Areas – Croatia

List of Figures

Fig. 4.1	Central government transfers and local government expenditures (% of variation). (Note: Percentage of variation of expenditures excludes expenses yet to be reimbursed. Source: Carvalho et al. 2015)	80
Fig. 4.2	Local government revenues: taxation and transfers (2003–2015). (Source: Authors' compilation, based on municipal budgets available at DGAL [http://www.portalautarquico.pt/pt-PT/dgal/])	81
Fig. 5.1	Evolution of excessive deficit procedures (EDP) in Spain and Eurozone (% GDP) (1995–2016). (Source: Delgado et al. 2017. https://www.bde.es/f/webbde/SES/Secciones/Publicaciones/InformesBoletinesRevistas/NotasEconomicas/T2/fich/bene1702-nec6.pdf)	96
Fig. 5.2	Evolution of public debt by subsector of public administration. (Source: Based on data from the *Banco de España*)	97
Fig. 6.1	Municipal budgets for local public service. (Source: ISTAT)	132
Fig. 9.1	Primary deficit in absolute and relative value to GDP. (Source: Open Data Albania 2017)	202
Fig. 9.2	National local government units funding by source. (Source: Ministry of Finances 2017b)	211
Fig. 9.3	Disaggregation of LPS transfers (by year). (Source: Ministry of Finances 2017b)	212

List of Tables

Table 1.1	Observed countries and LPSs	15
Table 4.1	Local government revenue (% of GDP)	77
Table 4.2	Subnational government expenditure by economic function (as % of expenditure)	82
Table 4.3	Subnational debt	82
Table 4.4	Transfers to non-profit organizations, as % of local government expenditures (2010–2015)	84
Table 4.5	Local public enterprise sector (2011–2016)	90
Table 5.1	Local government expenditure and revenue	108
Table 5.2	Austerity measures in municipalities with more than 500 inhabitants and their potential impact	109
Table 7.1	Annual state grant to Municipalities 2009–2017	149
Table 7.2	State budget: annual transfers to local authorities, including community councils–district offices 2008–2016	150
Table 7.3	Examples of reductions in Municipal budget revenues	151
Table 7.4	Reductions in municipal personnel	152
Table 8.1	Local budgets changes (2008–2014)	171
Table 8.2	Equalization grants for decentralized functions (2008–2014)	171
Table 8.3	Revenues of local budgets stemming from borrowing (2008–2014)	172
Table 10.1	Mix of tools for the seven countries	229
Table 10.2	Policy transfer and impacts compared	233

CHAPTER 1

Introduction: Local Public Services in Times of Austerity

Andrea Lippi and Theodore N. Tsekos

The Rise of Austerity and Its Impact on Local Public Service

Local Governance in Europe has recently undergone dramatic retrenchment due to the fiscal consolidation adopted by the central governments because of the economic crisis and the consequent decline of fiscal capacity. From 2010 to 2014 a wave of financial cutbacks and limits on public expenditure was enacted by most of the Eurozone central governments (Lodge and Hood 2012). These measures envisaged reductions of provisions and resources as well as new arrangements implemented to save costs (e.g. central budget supervision, reorganization, privatization, and program termination) (Kickert et al. 2013).

A. Lippi (✉)
Department of Political and Social Sciences, University of Florence, Firenze, Italy
e-mail: lippi@unifi.it

T. N. Tsekos
Department of Business and Public Administration, Technological Education Institute of Peloponnese, Kalamata, Greece

A. Lippi, T. N. Tsekos (eds.), *Local Public Services in Times of Austerity across Mediterranean Europe*, Governance and Public Management, https://doi.org/10.1007/978-3-319-76225-8_1

This retrenchment severely affected local policies across Europe and particularly degraded their core business: the public services. As demonstrated by a recent research (Wollmann et al. 2016), public services increasingly became a crucial and strategic core of local governance in Europe. In recent years, local authorities have managed a large percentage of the public expenditure on producing and delivering public services to citizens. Hence the steering of services at local level became of major importance for the public sphere, on the one hand, and for citizens' rights—insofar as citizens' proximity to local power enhances transparency, public scrutiny, and participation—on the other (Wollmann 2014). Accordingly, the public services (ranging from welfare services—health and social services—to public utilities—water provision, waste collection, transport) may now be considered a crosscutting and significant key to understanding the extent of the retrenchment and its detrimental impacts. As a result, the Local Public Service (LPS) will be the unit of analysis adopted in this book to reflect on austerity policy and look for recommendations.

A large body of studies have recently focused on austerity policies and their capacity to solve problems (Reinhart and Rogoff 2009; Hood 2010; Pollitt 2010; Schaefer and Streeck 2013; Hood and Himaz 2017), as well as their impact on specific and strategic areas like welfare (Leon et al. 2015) and employment. This book focuses on the public services for two reasons. Firstly, because the importance of austerity for public service provision has often been neglected by scholars in favor of its economic and sociological impact. Secondly, because the public services are also a good lens through which to consider the center/periphery (government and governance) relation (reduction of autonomy, upscaling, recentralization) due to the crisis and fiscal consolidation (Wollmann 2016).

Nevertheless, this consequence is not homogeneous across the European Union. If on the one hand it is evident that the economic crisis has impacted harshly on almost all the European countries, ranging from Iceland to Romania, and affected also consolidated economies in the Eurozone, like Germany and Denmark, on the other we know that there is a significant difference among European areas (Kitson et al. 2011). Southern Europe—and more precisely the Mediterranean area—has suffered decidedly more than Central or Eastern Europe from both the crisis and the following therapy. Scholars argue that Mediterranean countries have combined low economic growth with low-performing public sectors (Verney 2009; Hopkin 2012; Ongaro 2014), especially in regard to the capacity to implement New Public Management (henceforth NPM) reforms in recent decades (Kickert 2007; Di Mascio and Natalini 2015) Additionally, we believe that there are two further important reasons for considering Mediterranean Europe.

Firstly, public services are managed and delivered by local authorities to a greater extent than in central and northern Europe. As well known, this prominently concerns the so-called Napoleonic arrangement (Kickert 2011; Kuhlmann and Wollmann 2014; Kuhlmann and Bouckaert 2016), a highly traditional, fragmented, and innovation-resistant pattern of local government that at the same time is of great importance in the national politics of southern Europe (Sotiropoulos 2006; Kickert 2007; Ongaro 2010).

Secondly, the EU member states as well as the non-EU member states (or EU candidates) suffered the economic crisis and the following neoliberal stream of measures in a manner more sweeping and homogeneous than in other parts of Europe, where some countries were affected more specifically and dramatically than others, with a strong variance (e.g. Ireland compared with the United Kingdom). By contrast, in Southern Europe the crisis dramatically affected all the countries, and austerity increasingly spread like a contagion (Verney 2009). Time and space influence this phenomenon. The Mediterranean area, more specifically than 'generic' Southern Europe as a whole, experienced a stream of coercive or mimetic isomorphism imposed by supranational authorities and agencies: from 2010 to 2014 a permanent agenda of retrenchment became the core of policy making across the Mediterranean area, spilling over from country to country (step by step, first to Greece, then to Portugal, Spain, Italy, Cyprus and so on). The above-mentioned underpin the fact that in the context of austerity the Mediterranean region has ceased to be only a geographical entity and becomes more of a unit for political analysis.

Finally, time and space are variables that shed light on a further important aspect (Overmans and Noordegraaf 2014). A recent study on the relation between fiscal austerity and local governance (Silva and Bucek 2014) has shown the scattered and variable impact of fiscal retrenchment on local governance across the European countries. The aforementioned book is a precursor, because it highlights some recurrent features, like centralization, stricter regulation, the shift of competences and resources from the local to the central government, the introduction of budgetary supervision, and a move back from networking to hierarchy. All these impacts create strong disparities among countries according to the institutional profile and intergovernmental relations. The main result was that the conception of austerity was probably the same, but its implementation at local level was differentiated and sometimes contradictory: 'many responses to a similar overall external pressure', as Silva and Bucek put it in the conclusion.

This is the starting point of this book. Austerity travelled across Mediterranean Europe as a global discourse that took place at local level (Christensen 2012) due to (or in spite of) local factors and center-peripheries dynamics. There is a lack of knowledge about the concrete variance and its factors far from macro-economic indicators and political discourse. The goal of this book is to take the evidence a step forward. The intention is to investigate *how* many (and *what*) responses took place to the similar input and because of what factors. In other words, we want to understand (according to the stream of study on comparative studies in the public sector (Kuhlmann and Bouckaert 2016)) if there are regularities in the way that the Mediterranean countries adopted and implemented the austerity measures and how these latter impacted on local government and LPS management and delivery.

Hence, the book addresses three main research questions:

(i) What kind of austerity policies affected the Mediterranean LPS? Were they similar or different? Is there a common pattern and who promoted them at supranational or domestic level?
(ii) How were austerity measures adopted and implemented in terms of strategies, instruments, and organizational arrangements in the LPS? What domestic factors favored or disfavored this adoption at central or local level?
(iii) What impacts really affected LPS management and delivery and what were the political and social reactions?

The book is intended for scholars, researchers, and students, and it makes recommendations to policy makers in the fields of local governance, public policy and public administration, political science, and geography. The collection of chapters describes the Mediterranean perspective on fiscal austerity within and externally to the Eurozone. In what follows we describe the aims, background, and research design of the book. The general relevance of fiscal politics is discussed in the section 'The Rise of Austerity and Its Impact on Local Public Service', while the section 'The Politics of Fiscal Austerity' scrutinizes the geography of austerity on public services, and the section 'The Geography of Austerity: Why Does Mediterranean Europe Matter?' focuses on the impact on the Mediterranean public services.

Finally, the interpretative approach, aims, and research design, including the structure of the book, are respectively described in the sections 'Austerity's Impacts on the Mediterranean Public Services' and 'How Is Austerity Transferred to the Mediterranean Local Public Services?'.

The Politics of Fiscal Austerity

Austerity may be defined as 'a form of voluntary deflation in which the economy adjusts through the reduction of wages, prices, and public spending to restore competitiveness' (Blyth 2013). It usually follows historical trajectories of crisis for a long time, but the recent crisis is considered to be the 'second great contraction' putting states in a permanent condition of inadequacy. It is widely agreed among scholars that 'this time it is different' (Reinhart and Rogoff 2009). The overlapping troubles involving banks, economic performance, and fiscal decline (Di Mascio and Natalini 2015: 130–132) set new and challenging policy agendas. They created a condition whereby policy making is now permanently addressed in light of a perpetual and self-reproducing financial, political, and cognitive 'premise of weakness' that frames the representation and the decision making (Pierson 2001). This condition is labeled the new politics of *debt management by consolidation* (Streeck 2013: 2), a transformation 'in the direction of a State that is "leaner," less interventionist, and, in particular, less receptive to popular demands for redistribution than was the case for States of the post-war period' (ibid.).

Above all, austerity implies a potential and radical change in the public sector and in cross-level interactions. More specifically, it can alter the delivery of public services to citizens and the mission of the welfare system (Léon et al. 2015). Austerity is more than a concept; it is furthermore a package of measures to be implemented according to the international agreements and, regarding EU member states, supranational directives by the EU institutions (Pollitt 2010). As a consequence, financial downsizing directly or indirectly pertains to a potential reduction of resources and rights in service provision. It involves service management and delivery (e.g. cuts in service provision, capital spending freeze, limits to service frequency, quality requirements, outlets, and timing, etc.) as well as the institutional and organizational background (e.g. rescaling and upscaling of functions, central budget supervision, postponing procurement, transfer of costs to private capital, and privatization, etc.) (Kickert et al. 2013). All in all, every provision oriented to fiscal retrenchment unavoidably involves the public service because it extends beyond the services customarily delivered by the welfare state (like social assistance and health care) to include other important ones like public utilities and transport. The public service is specifically affected by all the measures. This is the case on the demand side (i.e. a downsizing of provisions and services) and on the supply side (i.e. measures on public employees like early retirement without hiring, salary reductions or freezes).

Hence, the importance of austerity policies is wider than their financial nature, and it concerns the fate of both political systems and citizenship. In particular, austerity affects the political responsiveness of the governors and the expectations of the governed. Put briefly, it does not merely concern a limited set of fiscal measures but has effects on society as a whole, and creates the premises for the '*politics of fiscal austerity*' (Posner and Bloendal 2012: 27).

In the worst scenario, the deterioration of public finance in the rich post-war democracies can influence (and undermine) their democratic nature, influencing their politics in terms of expectations, roles, and cognitive frames. According to the idea that the latest economic crisis is more incisive and pervasive, Schaefer and Streeck (2013: 16–18) have argued that the fiscal crisis can trigger specific dynamics deriving from the fiscal retrenchment approaches, and they state that these programs rapidly involve all the politics and the democratic society. The external shock triggers domestic reactions at political, institutional, and social levels.

Indeed, Schaefer and Streeck claim that the 'austerity State' ran into a contradiction between the market logic and that of citizenship. These two logics are in conflict, and the ensuing impact on democracy can be potentially detrimental. This scenario is perhaps overemphasized, but there is no doubt about the expected and often indirect impacts on democracy deriving from austerity measures: 'this is because an economic crisis limits governments' capacity to spend and it involves a general decline in citizens' wealth' (Morlino and Quaranta 2016: 2). It can therefore promote changes in the quality of democracy that do not directly concern financial aspects: it can have a negative effect on equality as well as on the allocation of resources. More precisely, it can encompass a decline of legitimacy at national level and many resistances at local ones, often resulting in the political questioning of the European unification perspective and the democratic process itself (Bosco and Verney 2012; Mayer 2013; Streeck 2013; Teperoglou et al. 2014; Morlino and Raniolo 2017). Therefore, the austerity measures that occur in times of crisis call for broader adjustments and generate further (sometimes unexpected) changes (Peters et al. 2011).

The Geography of Austerity: Why Does Mediterranean Europe Matter?

After the 2008 crisis, austerity became a global phenomenon extending from the United States to Australia and from the Mediterranean to the Baltic countries with a different intensity, severity, and combination. There is no common pattern of austerity policies across the world; rather, there are specific areas in which austerity took place in a different way and to a different extent. Also the timing varied greatly. Some countries were forerunners, while others delayed their interventions according to their proactive or reactive attitude. The geography of austerity spread across the world influencing all countries more or less profoundly, but in particular the European ones, which were more engaged in welfare provisions and LPS (Kitson et al. 2011). It triggered an isomorphism (following coercive measures imposed by supranational agencies) in adopting austerity measures that rapidly had an impact (or had to be implemented) at local level. There is abundant evidence that in the vast majority of cases, instead of boosting competitiveness and development, these provisions shrank household income and thus reduced economic growth and increased unemployment. In addition, sharp drops in Gross Domestic Product in many cases caused a higher debt-to-GDP ratio, thereby increasing the debt burden (Batini et al. 2012; Ball et al. 2013; Whitfield 2013; Matsaganis and Leventi 2014; Miller and Hokenstad 2014; Sommers et al. 2014; Monokroussos and Thomakos 2015).

As the financial crisis in 2008 mutated from a problem affecting private institutions to a problem of sovereign debt (in most cases partly because of the transfer of private debt to the public sector), it seemed necessary to adopt measures to tackle it, as well as international agencies and supranational institutions.

The global financial crisis spread across the world and involved the European Union in particular. After 2010 it affected in particularly severe manner the Mediterranean countries (initially, the so-called PIIGS: Portugal, Greece and—the non-Mediterranean—Ireland and at a later stage Spain and Italy as well), which were performing very badly financially—with the exception of Ireland—mostly because of their public indebtedness and their loss of economic competitiveness. The crisis in the 'Old Southern Four' (Portugal, Italy, Greece, and Spain) seemed more radical and more severe than in Ireland, beyond the economic significance of the public debt and the external deficit. Consequently, there ensued a stream of provisions to prevent their default (Verney 2009). The bailouts of Greece, Ireland, and Portugal took place in 2010, while Spain and Italy's bailout was in 2012 and that of Cyprus in 2013; but more stringent austerity measures generally spread across the Mediterranean area after 2010–2011. Accordingly, the sovereign debt crisis also involved other peripheral countries like Croatia while strong recommendations were made by the IMF also to EU candidates like Albania. In 2014 even inertial governments decided to adopt severe measures to tackle the financial crisis with cutbacks and retrenchment. In other words, austerity measures became the mainstream prescriptions for all countries that were not performing well or at (presumed) risk of default.

Fears regarding the political consequences of the crisis affecting the 'Old Southern Four' stressed the triggers of the crisis itself (Verney 2009). On the one hand, there was a potential divide in the Eurozone between the Northern countries and the Southern ones. On the other hand, there were fears of a contagion between the 'old four' Eurozone member states and the other European countries, both Eurozone members and countries not part of the Eurozone or not yet EU member states like Turkey and Albania. The permanent public deficits, the inefficient and corrupt public sectors, the untrustworthy public accounting practices, and the economies in recession of all the Mediterranean countries suggested that a chain reaction was likely. Here, the advent of Economic and Monetary Union stressed once again the 'Southern Question' existing on the Community's agenda since the 1990s (Hlepas and Getimis 2010; Moury and Freire 2013; Di Mascio and Natalini 2015). Austerity was thus manifest as a case of *policy transfer* from some geographical and institutional places to others.

For all the Mediterranean countries, the crisis highlighted already-existing problems in economic competitiveness and financial performance. The 'Old Southern Four' were perceived as a source of vulnerability and as an infected body spreading the contagion, even though many other countries were in trouble to a similar extent. High public indebtedness made them particularly weak with respect to financial turmoil, so that they lost the confidence of creditors. As a result, austerity was considered as a necessary, radical, and ultimate therapy (Verney and Bosco 2013).

The Troika composed of the European Commission (i.e. the Commissioner in charge of Economic and Financial Affairs), the European Central Bank, and the International Monetary Fund intervened in three countries (Greece, Portugal, and Ireland) with a very prescriptive approach, which included dictating a set of 'recipes' on how to (re-)organize the public sector. More indirectly, countries like Italy (and partially Spain) that could no longer borrow money from the European Stability Mechanism (ESM) 'received' a letter from the European Central Bank (ECB) Governor that targeted a wide and specific range of reforms. The letter literally dictated the 'contents and timing of reforms of the public sector in Italy—hence making it manifest that a different configuration of actors entered the decision-making opportunities with different roles and powers' (Ongaro 2014: 16).

As a matter of fact, a 'theory of change' (Weiss 1995) affected financial stakeholders and EU policy makers: the idea that the spread of the economic crisis was due to the financial weakness and low accountability of unreliable governments. Consequently, policy against the financial crisis had to deal with bad performers so as to prevent the further spread of the crisis. In this case, there is a matter of space and time.

Regarding space, the problem was seen by international policy makers as mainly concentrated in geographical areas where financial reliability was lower and economic productivity was decreasing. For this reason, Mediterranean Europe was subjected to supranational pressure and conditionality to improve its performance more than Eastern or Northern Europe. Mediterranean States suddenly appeared in deep trouble and unable to cope with their public debt or improve their economic productivity. At the same time, the public sector in the Mediterranean area was deemed extremely inefficient and resistant to innovation, with a high degree of corruption. The slow (and sometimes biased) implementation of the NPM (Sotiropoulos 2004; Kickert 2007; Ongaro 2008) was seen as a further indicator of the low reactivity and scant capacity to cope autonomously with problems.

Austerity's Impacts on the Mediterranean Public Services

Austerity nominally targets excessive public debt and affects public services through spending cuts. Therefore, public services bear the most significant consequences of austerity policies. As a result, they constitute the most appropriate field for studying the conditions, the content, and the impact of such policies.

In the first place, fiscal rebalancing does not mean spending cutbacks alone. Some of it can derive from tax increases. Both tax hikes and public expenditure reductions can decrease public debt (and can have counter-cyclical effects), although in the former case—mostly if public spending is well prioritized and planned—essential public services can be more or less preserved. In this case, and from a purely public service point of view, fiscal rebalancing can be achieved with minimal negative effects. The impact of tax hikes on aggregate demand and the market has to be subject to a different kind of analysis.

However, while austerity policies may contain a balanced mix of both tax increases and spending cuts, the politically dominant economic ideas assume that the latter are more effective than the former (Alesina and Ardagna 2010; Leigh et al. 2010; Alesina and Giavazzi 2015; Attinasi and Metelli 2016). The '*tax rises bad, spending cuts good*' approach has been extensively challenged and criticized (Ball et al. 2013; Hein and Truger 2013; Krugman 2015; Monokroussos and Thomakos 2015; Sen 2015). It has even been described as a 'mantra lacking sound theoretical or empirical basis' (Van Reenen 2012: 58). Despite such criticisms, policy makers are heavily influenced by these ideas, which seem, however, to be expressed only by a minority of economists. As Amartya Sen puts it, 'very few professionally trained economists were persuaded by the direction in which those in charge of European finances decided to take Europe' (Sen 2015). Therefore, one can conclude that the austerity policies mix is defined by following political imperatives rather than sound technical economic evidence and analysis.

As a result, and to the extent that neoliberal ideas influence political power (Hall 2011; Clarke and Newman 2012), fiscal policies heavily depend on spending cuts rather than tax rises. This dependence produces direct effects on the public services. In the United Kingdom, for example, 70% of the rebalancing concerns a fall in public expenditure. Consequently, it is estimated that by 2018 British public services will be reduced by 10% (Harries 2013). In Greece, similarly, 54% of the consolidation burden comes from expenditure fall (Lalountas 2014). On the other hand, austerity policies in the private sector result in wage reductions and indirect tax increases (VAT) that mostly affect lower-income households (Callan et al. 2012) and give rise to strong demand for essential public services such as health and welfare. IMF provides evidence suggesting that (a) fiscal consolidation has significant distributional effects by raising inequality, decreasing wage income, and increasing long-term unemployment (b) spending-based adjustments have had, on average, larger distributional effects than tax-based adjustments (Ball et al. 2013). Therefore, austerity based on linear spending cuts downgrades essential public services and leads to a vicious circle that reduces the well-being of large social groups.

Some thinkers and commentators (mostly from a pro-austerity stance) believe that austerity can function as a *window of opportunity* for the modernization of public services. The question is whether the 'spending pressure can be a catalyst for innovation and fresh thinking' (Harries 2013) or whether it merely reduces the operational capacity of public agencies and, therefore, deteriorates public policies' outputs, outcomes, and impact. UK evidence reveals that only policing services seem to improve under austerity, while education and the health system do not change (Harries 2013). Evidence from Mediterranean countries (Citroni et al. 2016; Magre Ferran and Pano Puey 2016; Tsekos and Triantafyllopoulou 2016) confirms that austerity is not an appropriate tool for policy and administrative innovation.

A similar tactic aimed at accommodating public services with austerity is to approach policies through outcomes and not inputs. From this point of view, success is defined 'by the health of the nation and the level of crime, not just the number of nurses and police officers [...] not by the money we spend but the difference we make' (Harries 2013). While policy evaluation based on outcomes and not on inputs and throughputs is essential for policy improvement, dissociating policy results from policy means is not an approach capable to stimulate efficiency and effectiveness. 'Doing more for less' is a fundamental NPM postulate. Still, valuating outputs but ignoring inputs is nothing more than a discursive strategy aiming at legitimizing austerity policies.

At the beginning of the recent crisis, Mediterranean public services were not particularly extensive and expensive. In 2010 public services in Mediterranean Europe (Italy, Spain, Greece, and Portugal) were clearly below the EU average as regards both employment and investment (Cambridge Econometrics 2013: 27–30). Even under these rather sound conditions, the inadequate performance and poor policy outcomes frequently observed in the Mediterranean administrations justified the adoption of reform programs targeting structural, functional, and outcome quality improvements. However, after 2009 increased public debts gave rise to quite different policies concentrated on immediate spending reduction, not on structural reforms permitting long-term cost-benefit optimization. Such programs were more or less effective in spending cuts.

At the local level, austerity has very asymmetrical social and political repercussions in time and place. Some cities have been fully exposed to 'urban austerity', while others continue to follow a more normal path of everyday life and development. Austerity policies have much greater impact in Greek and Spanish metropolitan areas such as Athens and Barcelona than in French cities like Nantes. Strategies to deal with the crisis's repercussions and to accommodate austerity policies differ as well. They do so according to path dependencies such as the local political traditions, the capacities, and the resources of local public institutions (Davies 2016).

The social consequences of austerity policies are important in Mediterranean Europe. Unemployment, job insecurity, income reduction, and poverty are among the most serious repercussions of the crisis at the socioeconomic level. As a result, a significant increase in the need for social and health services has occurred. In contrast, public expenditure reductions have caused significant shortcomings and deficiencies in the public health system. The discrepancy between supply and demand for public services in the social and health sector threatens to undermine social cohesion and can be considered a major failure of austerity policies.

Austerity measures in Portugal doubled unmet medical needs between 2010 and 2012 and increased co-payments at primary and hospital level. They thus generated a negative effect on the most vulnerable people and downgraded the quality of care. A similar effect has been registered in Greece (Ifanti et al. 2013). Measures are now needed to remedy the damage caused by the recession and austerity. The reasons for not seeking care include financial barriers, an inability to take time off work, or family responsibilities. Individual-level studies from Portugal also suggest co-payments, and health-care professionals have concerns about the impact of the recession and subsequent austerity measures on the quality of the care provided (Legido-Quigley et al. 2016).

The financial crisis in Spain provoked increases in malnutrition and mental health problems linked to income losses, unemployment, and cuts to social support services. Moreover, the austerity measures imposed on the country's health-care system have deteriorated the quality of its outcomes (Cervero-Liceras et al. 2015).

How Is Austerity Transferred to the Mediterranean Local Public Services?

Given the above-described situation, this book raises the questions of *how* austerity policies have affected the management of LPSs in Mediterranean Europe, and the extent to which measures and outcomes can really be credited to external influences or to domestic interests, opportunities, and dynamics. The background to this reasoning concerns the crucial role played by the financial crisis as an extraordinary opportunity for institutional change and readjustments in search of a paradigm shift (Peters 2011). Financial crises usually open windows for restructuring and re-allocating power, responsibilities, and duties. As demonstrated by Peters et al. (2011), governments are induced to launch reforms in times of crisis as a reaction to external shocks and to gain legitimacy. Consequently, a financial turmoil leading in one way or another to sovereign debt crises can influence the national and local pattern of governance, leaving room for downsizing and rescaling. This critical juncture is not taken for granted or predetermined, but it creates space for local dynamics. Hence, the national and local democracy can be variably influenced and adjusted according to these inputs.

LPSs are influenced by a stream of measures imported from external sources, like international agencies, the European Commission, and the ECB. But all these measures are adopted and managed at domestic level by the central governments and then implemented by the subnational authorities. So the book aims at dealing with an interesting multi-level transfer. Austerity measures can detrimentally affect the management and delivery of public services at local level. At the same time, local democracy and citizens' rights can be also damaged. But to understand this fact, one must directly observe *how* austerity measures have been issued, decided, and implemented in each context, also looking at the subsequent impacts on LPSs. The underlying assumption is that in each Mediterranean country austerity has triggered different processes according to that country's particular features: for instance, (i) the institutional design (and specific rules on bankruptcy), (ii) the political conditions and resources, as well as (iii) the political climate and (iv) the relationships between center and peripheries. On considering the differences among countries in the same geographical area and with a similar policy input (the austerity measures), we can generalize what the impact has been on the LPSs and its extent.

This point of view fits to the 'reorganization question' raised by the institutionalist paradigm (Kuhlmann and Wollmann 2014) and particularly focuses on the *institutionalization* matter well developed by the neo-institutionalist studies in terms of influences among institutions (i.e. the matter of isomorphism as a permanent hypothesis raised by DiMaggio and Powell (1983)). The institutionalism is polity-related (who, which institution is doing what?), because it primarily concerns a description of the institutional design. In the study of change it also calls for a policy-related neo-institutionalism, which in the social sciences has often been broadly categorized in the field of *policy transfer* (Dolowitz and Marsh 1996, 2012; Benson 2012; Stone 2012). According to both of these theoretical assumptions (polity-related and policy-related) the book focuses on the institutionalization of austerity as a policy transferred among different sets of institutions producing different types of institutionalization.

The underlying hypothesis is that austerity is transferred and assembled from a global discourse to a local practice (Christensen 2012). According to Dolowitz and Marsh (2000: 3), 'policy transfer is a process by which knowledge of policies, administrative arrangements, institutions and ideas in one political system (past or present) is used in the development of similar features in another'.

The basic idea pays attention to the systematic activity of relocating strategies and instruments from a given institutional arrangement or international model or theoretical pattern considered as a best practice to another context in which these solutions are deemed feasible and suitable (McCann and Ward 2013). The background of this book is the policy transfer and the subsequent local assemblage of austerity policies in Mediterranean Europe since 2010. The LPSs are suitable units of analysis for this purpose because of their importance in terms of citizenship and local democracy.

Accordingly, the study of austerity policies includes at the same time descriptions of institutions (who and what) and processes (when and how): the second one implies a *process tracing approach* (Collier 2011) of policy transfer from agenda-setting to decision-making and the implementation of austerity measures in LPS. A two-way movement can be observed. Firstly, it concerns the external/internal divide: how austerity has been promoted by supranational agencies and imposed on (or suggested to) the selected countries. Secondly, there is the domestic policy from the center to the periphery, that is, the austerity measures affecting the management and delivery of public services and implemented at local level, also including all the provisions that indirectly involve the LPS but are equally incisive, such as rescaling, recentralization, or national supervision of local autonomy. As a result, impacts in terms of outputs and outcomes are described in order to give the reader an idea of the degraded autonomy at the local level (including reactions as social protest).

Looking at this approach, the book is aimed at reconstructing the main factors that influenced how austerity policy affected the local management and delivery of Public Services. The goal is to look for *commonalities among the different trajectories* (Ongaro 2009; Kuhlmann and Bouckaert 2016) starting from many (but very similar) inputs (the austerity programs) to differentiated responses (output) and outcomes. A comparative design among 'most similar cases' supports this strategy. Comparison includes seven Mediterranean countries affected by austerity measures in the last seven years.

A geographic classification of the case studies was not the most appropriate to highlight the common characteristics and the particularities of the Mediterranean austerity policies. Although regional clusters, such as the Latin Mediterranean (Portugal, Spain, Italy), the Adriatic (Croatia and Albania), and the Greek eastern Mediterranean (Greece and Cyprus) countries, could be followed, this would not be a suitable option. Neither the national economies nor the types of crisis were internally homogeneous within these three geographical areas.

The selection of cases for comparison has, therefore, been based on the methodological criteria just described. As shown in Table 1.1, there are two types of Mediterranean countries covered by the book: Old Southern Four (first movers) and the other countries (newcomers). This is a matter not only of timing but also of relevance. A core set of countries is directly involved in the economic crisis and consequently more directly subject to supranational intervention. This is the case of the so-called Portugal, Italy, Greece and Spain (PIGS) countries, and dramatically so Greece, Portugal, Spain (and Cyprus) with detrimental effects on their democracies. Besides the first movers, there is Italy, which received an austerity recommendation from the ECB in summer 2011 and adopted a set of radical measures for five years.

Table 1.1 Observed countries and LPSs

What/ where	*Greece (2010)*	*Portugal (2010)*	*Spain (2012)*	*Italy (2012)*	*Cyprus (2013)*	*Croatia (2013)*	*Albania (2014)*
Health	X	X		X		X	
Social services	X	X	X	X	X		X
Water and waste	X	X		X	X	X	

The second cluster comprises countries that are only indirectly affected by the initial stream of reforms, but deeply touched by Europeanization. This is the case of Croatia, which followed the first movers as a new member of the EU and underwent fiscal consolidation as a EU candidate. Finally, it is also the case of Albania, which is still a candidate and has received strong fiscal recommendations from the International Monetary Fund (IMF) to limit its public spending.

Actually, three types of LPSs are discussed in this book: health, social services, and public utilities (water management and waste collection and disposal). These LPSs will be described according to the national profile and the types of public services that are the responsibility of local governments. Evidence deriving from public services sectors will be adopted as unit of analysis in each country to analyze the above described variables and processes.

The Structure of the Book

The theoretical approach to policy transfer and administrative reforms in Mediterranean Europe is debated in Chap. 2 by Andrea Lippi and Theodore N. Tsekos. The scope of this chapter is threefold. First, it surveys the literature on public sector reforms, with particular attention to public services and local government, as well as studies on the so-called Mediterranean or southern European style of public-sector reforms. As in the case of NPM so in that of austerity, prescriptions and models developed outside the Euro-Mediterranean area, are then transferred into it with contradictory outcomes. The chapter then reviews the main approaches, strategies, and tools of austerity policies according to the literature. This review is essential because there is a great deal of ambiguity in the debate about what austerity policies really are and what strategies can be categorized as 'strictly' or 'broadly' related to the concept. Finally, the policy transfer theoretical background behind the austerity programs is discussed in the section 'The Geography of Austerity: Why Does Mediterranean Europe Matter?', which deals with well-known concepts like lesson drawing, policy diffusion, assemblage, and translation. The empirical part of the study consists of seven separate country chapters arranged in a chronological sequence of gravity. According to the starting time for launching austerity measures drawn in the above section, the order is the following: Greece, Portugal, Spain, Italy, Cyprus, Croatia, and Albania.

Chapter 3 on Greece by Theodore N. Tsekos and Nikos K. Hlepas discusses the outbreak of the sovereign debt crisis; the austerity policies imposed by the lenders, through the three successive MoUs, as a prerequisite for the respective bailouts; the specific impact of these policies in areas such as health, social policy, and the water supply and drainage; and finally the main effects that have occurred in local communities.

Chapter 4 on Portugal by Patricia Silva and Filipe Teles gives an account of the Portuguese crisis and how the municipalities faced severe conditionality which weakened the local democratic government. Consequently, in order to cope with unprecedented budget reductions, municipalities were forced to accept an increase of central supervision and control tools over their activities, as a condition for receiving loans from the central government while the social demand for services was increasing.

Chapter 5 on Spain by Carmen Navarro and Esther focuses on the austerity agenda launched by the Spanish government in recent years, and it considers measures and impacts. The authors concentrate on the reaction by the local governments and the self-government capacity of Spanish local governments to respond to the economic restraints and the austerity measures. According to the framework of the book, the chapter assesses the implementation and discusses the outcomes in light of the reduced local autonomy.

Chapter 6 on Italy by Giulio Citroni, Andrea Lippi, and Stefania Profeti describes the mixture between external pressures and domestic opportunities to promote severe retrenchment of local governance and LPSs in a fragmented but highly detrimental way in the Italian case.

Chapter 7 on Cyprus by Andreas Kirlappos, Philippos Philippou and Kalliope Agapiou-Josephides analyzes the variety of austerity measures and their impact on Cyprus's LPSs through a mapping exercise of austerity measures and impacts. By doing so, the chapter reviews the issue of learning and development and it argues that the design and delivery of LPSs depends on historical continuities between central and local government that have not been influenced by the austerity.

Chapter 8 by Ivan Koprić, Mihovil Škarica and Romea Manojlović Tomań stresses the influence of the economic crises on local service delivery, especially in health care and water and waste sectors. The Croatian case is outstanding because the economic crisis happened parallel with the final stage of the Croatian European Union accession (2013), which has significantly added to the environmental complexity of local service delivery. As a result, looking at the Croatian case we can grasp the intertwining relation between two external pressures: Europeanization and the global Austerity cycle.

Chapter 9 on Albania by Vizar Dizdari, Arjeta Troshani and Elvisa Drishti assesses how austerity policies have influenced LPSs in Albania. The contribution deals with the question of the austerity measures' impact undertaken in the central level to the local level and shows a latecomer dilemma of a EU candidate. The authors describe how the fiscal consolidation adopted by the central government in 2014 according to the IMF's recommendation was coupled with a number of important structural reforms, including public financial management, pensions, local government reform, and in light of Albania's potential acceptance as a new member of the EU.

Finally, a comparison and an attempt for generalizing findings will be presented and discussed in Chap. 10 by the editors of the book, Andrea Lippi and Theodore N. Tsekos. Here beyond the description of detrimental impacts and emerging trends between external pressures and domestic opportunities to sustain or reshape austerity 'recipes' in each country, evidence about transfer, factors, and actors of the politics of fiscal retrenchment will be scrutinized looking at commonalities and variance. The following impacts in each system of LPS really display how different combinations equally depressed capabilities and social rights, but at the same time left room for side effects and domestic re-allocation of power despite the original and merely economic end of the austerity programs. As a consequence, the final remarks include some limited recommendations to restore the LPS system in Mediterranean Europe 'after the storm' and address policy makers to look forward when assessing the real effectiveness of such 'global recipe' faced to specificities and local needs.

References

Alesina, A., & Giavazzi, F. (2015). *The Effects of Austerity: Recent Research*, NBER Reporter 2015, No. 3.

Alesina, A., & Ardagna, S. (2010). Large Changes in Fiscal Policy: Taxes Versus Spending. In J. R. Brown (Ed.), *Tax Policy and the Economy* (pp. 35–68). Chicago: The University of Chicago Press.

Attinasi, M. G., & Metelli, L. (2016, February). *Is Fiscal Consolidation Self-Defeating? A Panel-VAR Analysis for the Euro Area Countries*, ECB Working Paper 1883.

Batini, N., Callegari, G., & Melin, G. (2012). *Successful Austerity in the United States, Europe and Japan*, IMF Working Paper, WP/12/190.

Ball, L., Furceri, D., Leigh, D., & Loungani, P. (2013). *The Distributional Effects of Fiscal Consolidation*, IMF Working Paper, WP/13/151.

Benson, D. (2012). Policy Transfer Research: Still Evolving, Not Yet Through? *Political Studies, 10*(3), 333–338.

Blyth, M. (2013). *Austerity: The History of a Dangerous Idea*. Oxford: Oxford University Press.

Bosco, A., & Verney, S. (2012). Electoral Epidemic: The Political Cost of Economic Crisis in Southern Europe, 2010–11. *South European Society and Politics, 17*(2), 129–154.

Callan, T., Keane, C., Savage, M., & Walsh, J. R. (2012). Distributional Impact of Tax, Welfare and Public Sector Pay Policies: 2009–2012. *Quarterly Economic Commentary, The Economic and Social Research Institute, 2012*(4), 46–56.

Cambridge Econometrics. (2013). *Mapping Evolutions in Public Services in Europe: Towards Increased Knowledge of Industrial Relations*. Covent Garden – Cambridge. The Cambridge Trust for New Thinking in Economics. www.neweconomicthinking.org

Cervero-Liceras, F., McKee, M., & Legido-Quigley, H. (2015). The Effects of the Financial Crisis and Austerity Measures on the Spanish Health Care System: A Qualitative Analysis of Health Professionals' Perceptions in the Region of Valencia. *Health Policy, 119*(1), 100–106.

Christensen, T. (2012). Global Ideas and Modern Public Sector Reforms: A Theoretical Elaboration and Empirical Discussion of a Neo-Institutional Theory. *American Review of Public Administration, 42*(6), 635–653.

Citroni, G., Lippi, A., & Profeti, S. (2016). Still Fragmentation. Local Public Service in Italy. In H. Wollmann, G. Marcou, & I. Kopric (Eds.), *Public and Social Services in Europe: From Public and Municipal to Private Sector Provision*. London: Palgrave.

Clarke, J., & Newman, J. (2012). The Alchemy of Austerity. *Critical Social Policy, 32*(3), 299–319.

Collier, D. (2011). Understanding Process Tracing. *Political Science & Politics, 44*(4), 823–830.

Davies, J. (2016). *How Is Austerity Governed in Cities? Our First Reflections on International Findings*. Brussels: Centre for Urban Research on Austerity.

Di Mascio, F., & Natalini, A. (2015). Fiscal Retrenchment in Southern Europe: Changing Patterns of Public Management in Greece, Italy, Portugal and Spain. *Public Management Review, 17*(1), 129–148.

DiMaggio, P. J., & Powell, W. W. (1983). The Iron Cage Revisited: Collective Rationality and Institutional Isomorphism in Organizational Fields. *American Sociological Review, 48*(2), 147–168.

Dolowitz, D. P., & Marsh, D. (1996). Who Learns What from Whom: A Review of the Policy Transfer Literature. *Political Studies, 44*(2), 343–357.

Dolowitz, D. P., & Marsh, D. (2000). Learning from Abroad: The Role of Policy Transfer in Contemporary Policy-Making. *Governance, 13*(1), 5–23.

Dolowitz, D. P., & Marsh, D. (2012). The Future of Policy Transfer Research. *Political Studies, 10*(3), 339–345.

Hall, S. (2011). The Neo-Liberal Revolution. *Cultural Studies, 25*(6), 705–728.

Harries, R. (2013, October 2). Austerity Government Means a New Approach to Public Services. *The Guardian.*

Hein, E., & Truger, A. (2013, September). *Fiscal Policy and Rebalancing in the Euro Area: A Critique of the German Debt Brake from a Post-Keynesian Perspective*, Levy Economics Institute, Working Paper No. 776.

Hlepas, N. K., & Getimis, P. (2010). Impacts of Local Government Reforms in Greece: An Interim Assessment. *Local Government Studies, 37*(5), 517–532.

Hood, C. (2010). *Reflections on Public Service Reform in a Cold Fiscal Climate.* London: 2020 Public Service Trust-ERSC.

Hood, C., & Himaz, R. (2017). *A Century pf Fiscal Squeeze Policy. 100 Years of Austerity, Politics and Bureaucracy in Britain.* Oxford: Oxford University Press.

Hopkin, J. (2012). A Slow Fuse: Italy and the EU Debt Crisis. *The International Spectator, 47*(4), 35–48.

Ifanti, A. A., Argyriou, A. A., Kalofonou, F. H., & Kalofonos, H. P. (2013). Financial Crisis and Austerity Measures in Greece: Their Impact on Health Promotion Policies and Public Health Care. *Health Policy, 113*(1), 8–12.

Kickert, W. (2007). Public Management Reforms in Countries with a Napoleonic State Model: France, Italy and Spain. In C. Pollitt, S. van Thiel, & V. Homburg (Eds.), *New Public Management in Europe: Adaptation and Alternatives* (pp. 26–51). London: Palgrave.

Kickert, W. (2011). Distinctiveness of Administrative Reform in Greece, Italy, Portugal and Spain, Common Characteristics of Context, Administrations and Reform. *Public Administration, 89*(3), 801–818.

Kickert, W., Randma-Liiv, T., & Savi, R. (2013). *Fiscal Consolidation in Europe: A Comparative Analysis* (COCOPS Report, Deliverable 7.2). Brussels: EU Commission.

Kitson, M., Martin, R., & Tyler, P. (2011). The Geographies of Austerity. *Cambridge Journal of Regions, Economy and Society, 4*(3), 289–302.

Krugman, P. (2015, April 29). The Austerity Delusion. *The Guardian.*

Kuhlmann, S., & Wollmann, H. (2014). *Introduction to Comparative Public Administration. Administrative System and Reforms in Europe.* London: Edward Elgar Press.

Kuhlmann, S., & Bouckaert, G. (Eds.). (2016). *Local Public Sector Reforms in Times of Crisis. National Trajectories and International Comparisons.* London: Palgrave.

Lalountas, D. A. (2014). *Fiscal Consolidation: The Greek Case, Directorate of Macroeconomic Policy & Forecasts*, Ministry of Finance. http://ec.europa.eu/economy_finance/events/2014/20140211-meeting/documents/sessioniii1lalountas_en.pdf

Legido-Quigley, H., Karanikolos, M., Hernandez-Plaza, S., de Freitas, C., Bernardo, L., Padilla, B., Sá Machado, R., Diaz-Ordaz, K., Stuckler, D., & McKee, M. (2016). Effects of the Financial Crisis and Troika Austerity Measures on Health and Health Care Access in Portugal. *Health Policy, 120*(7), 833–839.

Leigh, D., Devries, P., Freedman, C., Guajardo, J., Laxton, D., & Pescatori, A. (2010, October). Will It Hurt? Macroeconomic Effects of Fiscal Consolidation. In *World Economic Outlook: Recovery, Risk, and Rebalancing International Monetary Fund* (pp. 93–124). https://www.imf.org/external/pubs/ft/weo/2010/02/pdf/c3.pdf

Léon, M., Pavolini, E., & Guillén, A. M. (2015). Welfare Rescaling in Italy and Spain: Political Strategies to Deal with Harsh Austerity. *European Journal of Social Security, 17*(2), 182–201.

Lodge, M., & Hood, C. (2012). Into an Age of Multiple Austerity? Public Management and Public Service Bargains Across OECD Countries. *Governance, 25*(1), 79–101.

Magre Ferran, J., & Pano Puey, E. (2016). Delivery of Municipal Services in Spain: An Uncertain Picture. In H. Wollmann, I. Kopric, & G. Marcou (Eds.), *Public and Social Services in Europe. From Public and Municipal to Private Provision*. London: Palgrave.

Matsaganis, M., & Leventi, C. (2014). The Distributional Impact of Austerity and the Recession in Southern Europe. *South European Society and Politics, 19*(3), 393–412.

Mayer, N. (2013). From Jean-Marie to Marine Le Pen: Electoral Change on the Far Right. *Parliamentary Affairs, 66*(1), 160–178.

McCann, E., & Ward, D. (2013). A Multi-Disciplinary Approach to Policy Transfer Research: Geographies, Assemblages, Mobilities and Mutations. *Policy Studies, 34*(1), 2–18.

Miller, D. B., & Hokenstad, T. (2014). Rolling Downhill: Effects of Austerity on Local Government Social Services in the United States. *Journal of Sociology & Social Welfare, 16*(2), 93–108.

Monokroussos, P., & Thomakos, D. (2015). Greek Fiscal Multipliers Revisited: Government Spending Cuts vs. Tax Hikes and the Role of Public Investment Expenditure. In D. Thomakos, P. Monokroussos, & K. I. Nikolopoulos (Eds.), *A Financial Crisis Manual: Reflections and the Road Ahead*. London: Palgrave.

Morlino, L., & Quaranta, M. (2016). What Is the Impact of the Economic Crisis on Democracy? Evidence from Europe. *International Journal of Political Science Review, 37*(5), 618–633.

Morlino, L., & Raniolo, F. (2017). *The Impact of the Economic Crisis on South European Democracies*. London: Palgrave.

Moury, C., & Freire, A. (2013). Austerity Policies and Politics: The Case of Portugal. *Pole-Sud, 39*, 35–56.

Ongaro, E. (2008). Introduction: The Reform of Public Management in France, Greece, Italy, Portugal and Spain. *International Journal of Public Sector Management, 21*(2), 101–117.
Ongaro, E. (2009). *Public Management Reform and Modernization. Trajectories of Administrative Change in Italy, France, Greece, Portugal and Spain*. London: Edward Elgar.
Ongaro, E. (2010). The Napoleonic Administrative Tradition and Public Management Reform in France, Greece, Italy, Portugal and Spain. In M. Painter & B. G. Peters (Eds.), *Tradition and Public Administration*. London: Palgrave.
Ongaro, E. (2014). The Relationship Between the New European Governance Emerging from the Fiscal Crisis and Administrative Reforms: Qualitatively Different, Quantitatively Different, or Nothing New? A Plea for a Research Agenda. *Administrative Culture, 15*(1), 10–20.
Overmans, J. F. A., & Noordegraaf, M. (2014). Managing Austerity: Rhetorical and Real Responses to Fiscal Stress in Local Government. *Public Money and Management, 34*(2), 99–106.
Peters, B. G. (2011). Governance Responses to the Fiscal Crisis—Comparative Perspectives. *Public Money and Management, 31*(1), 75–80.
Peters, B. G., Pierre, J., & Randma-Liiv, T. (2011). Global Financial Crisis, Public Administration and Governance: Do New Problems Require New Solutions? *Public Organization Review, 11*(1), 13–27.
Pierson, P. (2001). Coping with Permanent Austerity: Welfare State Restructuring in Affluent Democracies. In P. Pierson (Ed.), *The New Politics of the Welfare State*. Oxford: Oxford University Press.
Pollitt, C. (2010). Cuts and Reforms—Public Service as We Move into a New Era. *Society and Economy, 32*(1), 17–31.
Posner, P., & Bloendal, J. (2012). Democracies and Deficits: Prospects for Fiscal Responsibility in Democratic Nations. *Governance, 25*(1), 11–34.
Reinhart, C. M., & Rogoff, K. S. (2009). *This Time Is Different*. Princeton: Princeton University Press.
Schaefer, C., & Streeck, W. (Eds.). (2013). *Politics in the Age of Austerity*. Cambridge: Polity Press.
Sen, A. (2015, June 4). The Economic Consequences of Austerity. *New Statesman*, 06.
Silva, C., & Bucek, J. (Eds.). (2014). *Fiscal Austerity and Innovation in Local Governance in Europe*. Farnham: Ashgate.
Sommers, J., Woolfson, C., & Juska, A. (2014). Austerity as a Global Prescription and Lessons from the Neoliberal Baltic Experiment. *Economic and Labour Relations Review, 25*(3), 397–416.
Sotiropoulos, D. A. (2004). South European Bureaucracies in Comparative Perspective. *West European Politics, 27*(3), 405–422.

Sotiropoulos, D. A. (2006). Old Problems and New Challenges: The Enduring and Challenging Functions of Southern European State Bureaucracies. In R. Gunther, P. N. Diamandouros, & D. A. Sotiropoulos (Eds.), *Democracy and the State in the New Southern Europe* (pp. 197–234). Oxford: Oxford University Press.

Stone, D. (2012). Transfer and Translation of Policy. *Policy Studies, 33*(6), 483–499.

Streeck, W. (2013). *The Politics of Public Debt* (MPifG, No.7). Koeln: Max-Plank Institute for the Studies on Societies Press.

Teperoglou, E., Freire, A., Andreadis, I., & Leite Viegas, J. M. (2014). Elites' and Voters' Attitudes Towards Austerity Policies and Their Consequences in Greece and Portugal. *South European Society and Politics, 19*(4), 457–476.

Tsekos, T. N., & Triantafyllopoulou, A. (2016). From Municipal Socialism to the Sovereign Debt Crisis: Local Services in Greece 1980–2015. In H. Wollmann, I. Kopric, & G. Marcou (Eds.), *Public and Social Services in Europe: From Public and Municipal to Private Sector Provision.* London: Palgrave.

Van Reenen, J. (2012). Fiscal Consolidation: Too Much of a Good Thing? In G. Corsetti (Ed.), *Austerity: Too Much of a Good Thing?* (pp. 55–64). CEPR-The Centre for Economic Policy Research. www.cepr.org

Verney, S. (2009). Flaky Fringe? Southern Europe Facing the Financial Crisis. *South European Society and Politics, 14*(1), 1–6.

Verney, S., & Bosco, A. (2013). Living Parallel Lives: Italy and Greece in an Age of Austerity. *South European Society and Politics, 18*(4), 397–426.

Whitfield, D. (2013). *Unmasking Austerity: Lessons for Australia.* Adelaide: Australian Workplace Innovation and Social Research Centre, The University of Adelaide Press.

Weiss, C. H. (1995). Nothing as Practical as Good Theory: Exploring Theory-Based Evaluation for Comprehensive Community Initiatives for Children and Families. In J. P. Connel et al. (Eds.), *New Approaches to Evaluating Community Initiatives: Concepts, Methods, and Contexts* (Vol. 1, pp. 65–92). Washington, DC: Aspen Institute.

Wollmann, H. (2014). Public Services in European Countries: Between Public/Municipal and Private Sector Provision—And Reverse? In C. Silva & J. Bucek (Eds.), *Fiscal Austerity and Innovation in Local Governance in Europe* (pp. 49–76). Farnham: Ashgate.

Wollmann, H. (2016). Local Government Reforms: Between Multifunction and Single Purpose Organisations. *Local Government Studies, 42*(3), 376–384.

Wollmann, H., Kopric, I., & Marcou, G. (Eds.). (2016). *Public and Social Services in Europe. From Public and Municipal to Private Provision.* London: Palgrave.

CHAPTER 2

Importing or Constructing Austerity? Global Reforms and Local Implementation as a Case of Policy Transfer

Andrea Lippi and Theodore N. Tsekos

Austerity as a Global Policy

The logic of public expenditure cutbacks, although predating the Second World War, assumed unprecedented importance thereafter in concomitance with the growth of public service delivery. In the 1960s and 1970s, the public deficit increasingly severely undermined the states' capacity to provide public services in the face of the reduced degree of fiscal recovery. In the 1980s, the neoliberal approach to reform adopted the logic of performance budgeting and cost saving through the introduction of private management guidelines into the public sector (Pollitt and Bouckaert 2011). The New Public Management (NPM) programmes triggered

A. Lippi (✉)
Department of Political and Social Sciences, University of Florence,
Firenze, Italy
e-mail: lippi@unifi.it

T. N. Tsekos
Department of Business and Public Administration, Technological Education
Institute of Peloponnese, Kalamata, Greece

A. Lippi, T. N. Tsekos (eds.), *Local Public Services in Times of Austerity across Mediterranean Europe*, Governance and Public Management, https://doi.org/10.1007/978-3-319-76225-8_2

reforms designed to improve performance rather than defend and broaden rights, and to enhance the capacity to supply services, rather than meet social needs. The core of these reforms was the idea of a global 'recipe' supposedly suited to different objectives and institutional arrangements, and capable of ensuring optimum cost-benefit trade-offs and of balancing expenditure and performance (Hood 1995; Aberbach and Christensen 2005; Pollitt and Bouckaert 2011). The local level of government, and especially the management and delivery of local public services (LPSs), was directly affected by these measures (Kuhlmann et al. 2008; Wollmann 2004). In some countries, like Italy, NPM was prominently implemented at local level in order to deal with local public deficits and rescue the public sector as a whole (Lippi 2003).

More recently, the idea of cost saving as justification for public action has been legitimized in general by the momentum of Europeanization and, in more specific terms, by certain provisions of the Treaty of Maastricht, which since 1993 have established a framework for reducing public debt and stabilizing budgetary policy (Balassone and Franco 2000; Buti and Giudice 2002). The Stability Pact and the subsequent fiscal restrictions, limited states' actions and created a cognitive framework for public measures, delimited by fiscal performance (Issing 2004). This approach substantially impacted multilevel governance within European States and made the management of public services conditional upon financial performance and break-even budgets. Europeanization also implied the involvement of local authorities in other policy fields, and the delegation of greater duties and responsibilities. As noted by Goldsmith (2011: 47), the European framework meant subsidies and opportunities, but also more rules and less cash. Local governments were caught up in a global trend, and they experienced supranational influences; however, at the same time they had to bear the setting of benchmarks and reductions in cash flow. These conditions foreran the period of austerity measures and the current policy framework oriented towards fiscal measures and the reorganization of public services, especially at local level.

As certain scholars have pointed out (Blyth 2013; Streeck 2013), austerity is now more than just a set of financial measures. It is a kind of policy style comprising strategies, design and instruments, and involving many sectors at the same time, as represents a specific, contingent 'regime of policy making'. Austerity policies need to be considered as a complex economic and social phenomenon, made up of a framework of ideas on economic efficiency, a collection of financial instruments, and most importantly, the real interests of social actors and a redistribution of power between the market and the public sphere (Corsetti 2012).

Scholars also agree on the unprecedented severe, global nature of the economic crisis since 2008 (Reinhart and Rogoff 2009; Frans et al. 2017). Pressures encouraging fiscal retrenchment are prominently the result of a global trend affecting states (and local governments) as a subsequent development, as it originates from broader, more problematic dynamics. While the fiscal restrictions ensuing from Europeanization and the advent of NPM were politically and institutionally driven, this package of reforms is economically driven. It reflects a global trend in the economic system that affects political and administrative institutions. Hence, austerity has ceased to be only a means, becoming an end in itself. Its economic nature is now accompanied by a more political one. Public agencies have been forced to limit their actions so as to leave the markets greater room for manoeuvre.

Austerity as an Ambiguous Semantic Umbrella

The concept of austerity has developed considerably, going well beyond its clear economic origins. Firstly, periods of austerity are long-lasting. In 2017, just as prior to 2008, the Europan Central Bank (ECB) and other supranational institutions were still calling for cutbacks and fiscal measures, despite the fact that the economic situation had changed to a certain degree. Secondly, austerity measures have been institutionalized, and now constitute a permanent way of establishing relations between member states and the EU, and at the same time as a way of governing multilevel relations within individual states (Pierson 2001). Austerity is a keyword to connecting problems with their solutions, and to intertwining different, fragmented public measures. As such, it covers a variety of meanings and interests, values and institutions, international and domestic coalitions. As regards NPM, austerity is an enduring programme 'for many seasons': a catchword that potentially plays the garbage can role.

This is to say that austerity is not only an historical, unique occurrence, but has become a political climate affecting the policy-making process. The so-called *politics of fiscal austerity* (Posner and Bloendal 2012: 27) can be considered as a permanent, institutionalized milieu affecting the political lives of states, sub-states, authorities and citizens. It means that the deterioration in public funding in the rich post-war democracies can influence (and undermine) their democratic nature, and affect their politics in terms of expectations, roles and the cognitive framework. According to the aforesaid assumption, the latest economic crisis is more incisive and pervasive. Schaefer and Streeck (2013: 16–18) have argued that the fiscal crisis can trigger specific dynamics deriving from fiscal retrenchment, and that these programmes rapidly involve all politics and all of democratic society. The external shock provokes domestic reactions within the political, institutional and social realms.

As a result, Schaefer and Streeck claim that the 'austerity state' encounters the contradiction between market logic and the logic of citizenship. Such logics are in conflict, and the impact of this conflict on democracy can be potentially detrimental. This scenario may be overstated, but there is no doubt about the expected, often indirect, effects on democracy brought about by austerity measures: 'this is because an economic crisis limits governments' capacity to spend and it involves a general decline in citizens' wealth' (Morlino and Quaranta 2016: 2).

More specifically, three main arguments may be examined here.

The first is that austerity policies are not voluntarily introduced by national governments but are the result of the external influence of outstanding, legitimated, preeminent supranational institutions and experts, think tanks and prestigious advisory agencies. This is because 'austerity' policy comprises a common set of beliefs, strategies and instruments, together with a shared cognitive framework. All these factors offer generic, almost homogeneous input, albeit one consisting of a range of policy mixes, depending on the specific economic conditions of each country, which drive the state's reaction to economic adversity. Central governments are directly or indirectly compelled to adopt such measures, but they are rarely proactive. Sometimes they launch anticipatory measures, but this is always in response to external pressures. After receiving an austerity input, each government puts together its own policy mix on the basis of the country's financial requirements, the political feasibility of such policy, electoral campaigning contingencies, party preferences and pressure from interest groups, institutional design and the financial framework, including the nation's bankruptcy provisions (Pollitt 2010). External inputs give rise to intense internal political dynamics.

The second argument is that austerity can mean several things at one and the same time, and implies a wide variety of sub-policies ranging from welfare to infrastructures, from urban policies, public utilities and transport to social services and healthcare. Austerity occurs because of the intersecting character of fiscal measures. However, it also depends on the intrinsic dynamics of the diverse policy fields affected by cutbacks. At the same time it possibly implies institutional rearrangements, reorganization, the relaunching of NPM and a number of other structural changes. Under the 'umbrella' of austerity, governments can relaunch aborted policies or ideologically driven restrictions on the welfare state or social rights. As a result, austerity also serves as a policy window for national decisions and an arena for political battles of purely national significance.

As Overmans and Noordegraaf (2014: 99–102) have pointed out, austerity implies four different types of policy aim, all pursued at the same time: decline, cutbacks, retrenchment and downsizing. There is no agreement among scholars on any unambiguous use of the concept, apart from of its representing an 'executive and managerial response aimed at restoring the fiscal balance, against the background of increasing demands for public services and political and public expectations of organizational performance' (id.: 102). Nevertheless, this formulation is extremely generic, and leads to the aforementioned variance. Decline, cutbacks, retrenchment and downsizing may be interpreted in various different ways, and combined to produce a mix of policies with a significant array of implications. This ambiguity is not a weakness, but rather a strength, since it gives stakeholders the opportunity to pursue various different aims.

Finally, austerity is not only a trait of politics and policies at national level, but it specifically involves local government, since the majority of policies are delivered at local level; moreover, the fiscal measures in question strongly impact the autonomy of local government.

Austerity as Multilevel Governance Policy

Because of their intersecting, multivariate nature, austerity policies offer countries the opportunity to reflect on local governments' destiny and to examine whether to deinvest or reinvest in local government (Ladner 2017: 8), that is, whether to strengthen or weaken the structures and activities of local government (Wollmann 2016). As a result, the opposition of 'effective service delivery for citizens and cost-cutting' (Schwab et al. 2017: 3) represents a threat to local government autonomy as a whole, and questions the role and future of local government as such. As regards the state, austerity constitutes an ambiguous, multifaced window 'raising a question on local autonomy when the states and subnational authorities are seeking greater savings from local governments than from their activities and thus they impose (sometimes induced from external factors, but often also pushed by national politics) spending restrictions and priorities for local levels. Hence, central pressures can also be interpreted as a resource for local governments to modernize their procedures, organizational settings and service delivery, as a window of opportunity, but at the same time it can also mean that central governments withdraw resources from the local level and at the same time give them more autonomy to act or more degree of freedom, without resources or with more conditionality' (id.).

As matter of fact, local governments saw austerity as an ambiguous window concerning their destiny within multilevel governance relations, where many stakeholders can benefit from its adoption in various different ways. As the Council of Europe has stated, an agenda of development and empowerment (including increased accountability), and not only a reduction in local autonomy, may result from these potential choices (Davey 2011). Thus there is room for variance among patterns of local government (Kuhlmann and Wollmann 2014; Kuhlmann and Bouckaert 2016: 10–12), together with different degrees of vulnerability. Northern and Central European models of local government appeared more resilient, due to more strictly controlled public finances, and also to the consolidated autonomy of local government and its flexible response to external pressures and its adaptability to innovation (Pollitt and Bouckaert 2011). On the contrary, the Southern/Eastern European patterns and the continental post-Napoleonic one revealed considerable vulnerability together with a strong degree of resistance to innovation, and consolidated degrees of clientelism, bureaucracy and political patronage (Sotiropoulos 2006). Attempts at budgetary balancing in the Mediterranean countries, for instance, seemed primarily based on frontloaded programmes offering immediate fiscal results, and this has had a significant negative impact on essential public services, which are indispensable if social cohesion is to be preserved at times of crisis. On the other hand, the structural reforms aimed at long-term cost-benefit optimization have been largely neglected. Equally, one significant problem has been the 'domestic inability' of Mediterranean governments to provide effective crisis management (Verney and Bosco 2013), and this has not been tackled.

In the case of Greece, while the austerity programme has complied with the need for fiscal adjustment, structural reforms have been very poorly implemented. This has led to an imbalanced policy mix of fiscal measures and structural reforms. Overall, fiscal measures display an impressive full implementation rate of 82–99%, and a partial implementation rate of 17%, whereas the rate of implementation of structural reforms remains below 30% (Iakovides et al. 2016).

Mediterranean countries, as a subset of southern-eastern and southern European countries, seem particularly exposed to austerity policies (Morlino and Raniolo 2017): evidence from Italy, Portugal, Spain and Greece shows that the financial crisis has negatively affected the transfers that municipalities receive from the state (Ladner 2017: 23) In these cases, among others, municipalities have been forced to pursue a similar, or an even greater, range of objectives and tasks (Moury and Freire 2013). As Ladner argues, only a limited number of European countries have experienced any reduction in local autonomy due directly to austerity measures. On the contrary, in the majority of European countries, reduced autonomy has been due to an indirect, complicated system of restrictions, and of the recentralization and delegation of tasks, in the absence of additional funding. Similarly, there is evidence that the combination of a more coercive system, and the aforesaid reduction in autonomy, has affected a significant number of countries. As Ladner points out: 'the perceived reduction in autonomy had more to with a reduced margin of manoeuvre due to a lack of resources than with institutional changes—explicitly—reducing their autonomy' (id).

These documented measures have tackled public service management and delivery at local level in a less visible, yet more incisive, way compared to central state level (Hlepas 2016). The threat to local autonomy arose when reforms were perceived solely as public spending cutbacks. This comprised dealing with the fiscal crisis by passing on the financial and social burden to local authorities, at first, and then to citizens (Schwab et al. 2017: 55).

Austerity as a Policy Window for Restructuring

There is no common way of reacting to crises. Accordingly, there is no common way of selecting or implementing austerity measures (Peters 2011). The way politicians adopt a campaign for fiscal retrenchment, and how national or local stakeholders formulate their choices and strategies, both vary (Posner and Bloendal 2012: 27). We know that governments tend to launch radical reforms at times of crisis as a reaction to external shocks and in order to achieve legitimacy and a paradigm shift (Peters et al. 2011). According to the Peters et al., times of crisis are productive for decision-making processes, and external shocks may trigger opportunities for promoting policy change (Kamkhaji and Radaelli 2017).

In the social sciences, this point had been examined in depth by several scholars. Crises have been interpreted (t'Hart and Boin 2001) as extraordinary windows for institutional change and readjustment in the pursuit of a paradigm shift and learning. Scholars have pointed to the different paths that crises take (cathartic, fast burning, long shadow and slow burning), which opens the way for differentiated policy change (id.: 32) and policy learning (Birkland 2009). Here, the most important issue is the distinction between changes that occur between, or during, crises. Intra-crisis change is more relevant and problematic, because of the limited span of time and the dramatic contingencies witnessed where it takes place. The fiscal crisis affecting Europe may be classified as an intra-crisis dynamic potentially leading to learning. For this reason, it seems more difficult and challenging because actors 'must engage in sense-making under limited time, dynamic conditions and intense pressures, evaluating the nature and scope of the crisis and searching for appropriate response' (Moynihan 2009: 191). The fiscal crisis may consequently be interpreted as a window for different meanings, values, interests and strategies. Hence, EU integration has been described and interpreted as a successive series of crisis leading to opportunities (Ioannou et al. 2015). Lefkofridi and Schmitter (2014) shed light on the intra-crisis implications of this reasoning in regard to the EU crisis. They point out that the fiscal trigger is exogenous, and that most responses are seemingly beyond the control of domestic (central and local) policy makers. The relevance of this discourse lies with the potential development of a global tendency within the EU domain, on the one hand, and in individual member states, on the other.

Consequently, financial turmoil can impact national and local patterns of governance, leaving room for downsizing and rescaling (Hlepas and Getimis 2010). This critical juncture is not taken for granted, nor is it predetermined, but it opens the way for local dynamics. Hence, democracy can be variably influenced and readjusted depending on these pressures. An external shock may 'shrink' democratic arrangements or modify the arrangement of services management and delivery. As stated by Posner and Bloendal (id.: 20) 'an exogenous event or "shock" bearing down on all actors of the system requires some kind of policy response. [It] helps us to control for endogeneity where political leaders already committed to proactive fiscal policy contrive crises to mobilize support for their pre-existing positions'.

In brief, exogenous dynamics trigger endogenous ones. Austerity policies are conceived as external shocks promoted by international or supranational agencies, but they are managed at the domestic level by central government and are implemented by subnational authorities. This leaves room for decisions to be taken at international, national and subnational loci: austerity policies 'travel' from an 'external' source and are then adopted to different degrees and in different ways, by the states that impose or transmit them to the subnational authorities. Importation leaves room for internal restructuring.

There are three implications of this reasoning. Firstly, austerity is not predetermined and does not include a given tool-kit. Secondly, it can vary substantially depending on multilevel governance within each national context. Thirdly, the 'journey' gives (national and local) policy makers room for revising, deconstructing or reconstructing their own concept of austerity.

Austerity's Interplay with NPM as Global Discourse and Local Practice

According to Christensen's claim (2012) regarding the 'global discourse', austerity may be labelled as a mainstream or 'political mantra' in agenda setting across countries, in terms of blame shifting perpetrated by international agencies, European institutions and other EU member states. In fact, global discourse consists of several sources promoting a similar input, which in turn triggers local practices. Both austerity and NPM represent a kind of global discourse which materialized in the form of local measures. NPM developed gradually during the 1980s and the '90s, starting with English-speaking countries such as the United Kingdom, the United States, Australia, Canada and New Zealand. These nations launched ground-breaking programmes of administrative reform inspired by market principles. Contrary to the dominant trend of the mid-60s to late-70s, NPM was based on a market-oriented philosophy. According to Pollitt and Bouckaert (2011: 9), the NPM umbrella covers a very wide range of reforms across an equally broad range of countries.

Scholars like Hood (1991: 10–16) and Osborne and Gaebler (1992) believed that NPM was a 'one-best-way' globally accepted and locally applied, promoted by influential think tanks and international organizations (the OECD, the World Bank). People from NPM anglophone countries occupied key positions in the major international agencies spreading the word about NPM. Such agencies influenced not only the English-speaking world where they were favourably received, but also less welcoming administrations such as that of France (Pollitt and Bouckaert 2011: 6–13).

Their reform formulae were fuelled by the belief that the public sector could be improved through the introduction of business-based concepts and techniques. These include: rendering senior executives 'free to manage'; the disaggregation of monolithic organizational units; performance management based on output controls and measurements; the introduction of competition within the public sector; contracts instead of a hierarchical employment structure; the idea of citizens as customers with a choice of alternative providers; and greater parsimony in the use of resources.

Despite the purported convergence towards NPM at the international level, evidence suggests that diversity and lack of homogeneity are the main characteristics of local NPM implementation: 'the term NPM was coined because some generic label seemed to be needed for a general, though certainly not universal, shift in public management styles. The term was intended to cut across the particular language of individual projects or countries' (Hood 1995: 95). Ferlie and Geraghty (2005) claim the existence of two main forms of NPM at the international level: on the one hand, the hard Anglo-American model, and on the other, the soft version of both the *Rechtstaat* model (Germany and France) and the Nordic model based on decentralization, corporatism and consensus.

Most scholars agree that the NPM model exhibits specific cultural and political features which do not suit certain countries such as France, Germany or the Mediterranean states. Countries with strong 'Napoleonic-state' traditions have only adopted NPM solutions on a limited, selective basis. In Germany and Italy, certain NPM-type reforms were implemented at the subnational level, whereas the nation state has never implemented NPM on a large scale. In the Mediterranean countries in particular, certain aspects of NPM have been introduced, but they have not represented the main instrument of reform.

In contrast to the original concept of *mimétisme administratif* mainly developed in France in the 1970s (Bugnicourt 1973; Langrod 1973), which perceived 'administrative imitation' as 'a mechanical reproduction of attitudes', the experience of the international diffusion of NPM shows that the transposition of administrative standards and practices to different contexts is not done mechanically but is actually filtered through institutional traditions and existing administrative and socio-political interrelations. There is a kind of path dependence in the 'acceptance' and adoption of international reform trends within/to national contexts.

Austerity as a Set of Strategies and Instruments

Austerity consists of a wide set of strategies, designs and instruments recommended by diverse think tanks and international institutions to central governments, which then impact local administrations. Different attempts have been made to classify the phenomenon, but a final taxonomy based on clear criteria has yet to appear. Different criteria—mainly of a political, organizational, financial or accounting nature, have been used. We list some of these criteria below.

Austerity strategies have been variously classified. A preliminary distinction has produced the following two broad categories: austerity *by inspection or prescription* (*hard austerity*, as seen in Greece and Portugal, for example); and austerity *by recommendation* (*soft austerity*, as seen in Italy). Hard austerity is direct and compulsory, while soft austerity is indirect. Accordingly, Hood (2010: 5–9) has portrayed three recurrent scenarios for this new 'cold fiscal climate': to do 'more with less', to do 'the same with less', and to do 'less with less'. The 'less with less' strategy implies renouncement, as Hood suggests, in the form of the 'withdrawal [of] state provision from some existing domains of public services altogether so that the diminished resources can be concentrated more effectively' (id.: 8). Differently, 'the same with less' scenario implies improved productivity through reorganization and the better use of tools. Finally, 'more with less' implies an innovative approach to policy objectives, and the restructuring of organizational arrangements in order to improve results.

Another classification that falls within the strategic approach is that provided by Kickert et al. (2013: 10). They grouped together the available strategies into two categories: the rational-comprehensive strategy, and the incremental-compromise strategy: efficiency (goal-oriented problem solving) versus consensus (political muddling through). The first strategy includes political priority setting, rational core-task analysis and long-term decision making, while the incremental-compromise approach favours pragmatic, short-term compromise solutions.

Furthermore, as regards strategies, Pollitt also suggests (2010: 27) that account should be taken of NPM's strategies of privatization and increasing certain measures to save money. Consequently, it paves the way for reshaping the LPS' mission, the allocation of resources and spending standards (Lodge and Hood 2012).

The economic rationale stresses the fact that austerity may be pursued by means of different policy designs: increasing taxes or spending cuts (Alesina et al. 2015; Jimenez 2012: 928). *Cutbacks include* targeted cuts, reducing the travel budget, eliminating or reducing services, reducing salaries, postponing capital expenditure, reviewing employment contracts, freezing salaries, leaving vacant positions as such; while *tax increase measures* comprise increased sales taxes, increased property taxes, the introduction of new fees, or amending old fees, for service delivery, and applications for grants.

In translating strategies into instruments, Di Mascio and Natalini (2014) classified the above-mentioned strategies into three main categories of instrument: 'across the board' cutbacks; 'efficiency gains' and 'centralize priority' setting.

The *across-the-board* (cheese-slicing) category is 'egalitarian': it 'refers to cuts affecting all the policy areas in equal amounts independently from their differentiated impact on strategic priorities' (Di Mascio and Natalini 2015: 182). It does not alter the fundamentals of the administrative system, and it is less risky than other approaches. It represents a prudent, delaying approach or a slow downturn ('doing less with less'). Pollitt claims the advantage consists in the fact that policy makers can avoid choosing which services must immediately suffer (*blame avoidance*). Accordingly, decisions are delegated to experts who make provision for cutbacks from a technical standpoint, although they may equally take unpopular decisions.

Efficiency gains is a middle-range set of instruments. It often appears to be the most desirable way to make savings from the political and organizational viewpoints ('doing more with less' or 'doing the same with less'). It calls for maintenance ('gain without pain') and stands for a general restructuring of the public sector (reforms) to preserve the preceding delivery. As a consequence, it involves technological and organizational innovation and new regulations. New Public Management can consequently be relaunched, and territorial rescaling implemented.

Finally, *prioritized cutbacks* represent a complete fiscal instrument that paves the way for policy responsiveness, enabling governments to protect the most effective programmes to the detriment of the remaining ones. This is selective retrenchment and concerns the question of effectiveness.

A more detailed toolkit is provided by Kickert et al. (2013). They distinguish between *Operational expenditure, Programme expenditure* and *Investments expenditure*:

Operational expenditure cutbacks include reduced overtime or working hours, the slowing down of promotion and early retirement, wage freezes, reductions in the rate of salary increases, filling posts with less qualified, lower-paid resources, reducing the salary levels of vacant positions, salary cuts, the reshuffling of staff, the use of the furlough, hiring freezes, layoffs, spending limits and bans in regard to utilities, supplies, equipment, travel and communications.

Programme expenditure cutbacks refers to reduced service provision, shortened reception time or limits to service hours, the reduced frequency of service provision or a smaller number of service outlets, limited quality requirements for service provision, the generalized termination of programmes, the engagement of voluntary, part-time and third-party service providers, reduced transfers, shift in part of the entitlement cost to the private sector or to citizens.

Finally, *Investments/capital expenditure cutbacks* specifically refer to the capital spending freeze on new or nonessential projects, or the more strategic transfer of cost to the private sector, postponing procurement, deferring maintenance operations, and the book keeping expenditure of cuts on investments.

While these two classifications are based on different criteria (strategy and instruments), a more effective approach would be a crosscutting strategy based on selected criteria, designed for the analysis of empirical cases.

Austerity Seen as a Policy Transfer

The key observation in the above sections is that austerity is a policy that has moved from one country to another in the light of an expected learning process. Despite the absence of any commonly agreed meaning of austerity, we know there are several processes whereby it 'travelled' from one or more 'sources' to certain 'recipients'. This is the core of austerity policy making; it concerns the divulgation of an agenda across different settings and levels of government, producing heterogeneous (and sometimes unexpected) outcomes. Here we wish to closely examine the analytical toolkit, in order to better understand this 'repositioning' process.

A couple of preliminary concepts key to this analysis are provided by lesson drawing (Rose 1991) and policy diffusion (Berry and Berry 1999). Lesson drawing concerns the transmission of a programme deemed successful in a given setting, and then 'taught to learners'. It regards intergovernmental institutions and learning about institutional arrangements or policy content, design and implementation practices. Lesson drawing involves the prestige of the source (the drawer) and the learning capacity of the recipients. It includes copying, emulation, adoption with adjustments, hybridization, the combination of elements from several different sources, and inspiration. The concept has been criticized due to the overly rational perspective involved. In the real world, lesson drawing is not neutral or automatic: sources may not be 'good drawers', and learning may be biased as a result of contextual factors (James and Lodge 2003: 183).

On the other hand, policy diffusion describes the successive, sequential adoption of practices or policy programmes. It assumes a 'biological' perspective (osmosis): something that is 'contagious' rather than chosen. It involves the spreading or dispersion of practices. This 'bio-mechanical' perspective emphasizes cross-level interactions between 'contagious' and 'infected'. The concept neglects the domestic dynamics of the states concerned and takes for granted the innovation's adoption regardless of the internal factors favouring or resisting policy change, such as culture, interests and institutional design, which will lead to either success or mismatching (Stone 2004: 546).

The concept of policy transfer has taken over from the aforementioned mechanical and linear perspectives and seems to fit the case in question well (Benson and Jordan 2011; Benson 2012; Dussauge-Laguna 2012). According to Dolowitz and Marsh's definition (2000: 3) 'policy transfer is a process by which knowledge of policies, administrative arrangements, institutions and ideas in one political system (past or present) is used in the development of similar features in another'. According to Wolman and Page (2002: 480), policy transfer can encompass the transfer of policy goals, concepts, instruments, design, techniques in a broad, inspired way. The transfer can pertain to ideas as well as to structures and concerns the institutionalization of both in the recipient countries at different level of government. In a broader sense, policy transfer refers to generic inspiration and vague orientation in terms of *policy labels*, namely *symbolical umbrellas* applied to a range of policies reflecting ambiguous, loosely bundled ideas (i.e. privatization) (Mossberger and Wolman 2003). The subject to be transferred can be very wide-reaching and difficult to define (e.g. smart cities, etc.) and variously detailed.

Dolowitz and Marsh pointed out that the initial condition is the unsatisfactory internal status quo, which consequently leads policy makers to look abroad for improvements. The internal/external divide matters. Hence, policy transfer mainly concerns relations among states (one to one or one to many) or international think tanks (Stone 2000).

At the subnational level, it affects federal arrangements and cross-level interaction between central government and local authorities.

In any case, policy transfer concerns expected homogenization. This is where the purported convergence comes into play. Bennett (1991) pointed out four patterns: (i) emulation (best practices to be imported), (ii) harmonization (the endogenous adaptation to external heterogeneous innovations), (iii) transnational communities networking (shared knowledge and brokering by policy entrepreneurs) and (iv) penetration (the passive, mandatory acceptance of practices from outside). It means that an isomorphic input does not automatically imply a similar outcome: failures, readjustments, betrayal as well as unsuccessful implementation can occur at different stages. According to Dolowitz and Marsh (2012: 346), a policy cycle can entail promotion of change or resistance to the same. For instance, penetration may be expected at the issue-making stage, while harmonization or resistance may occur during implementation.

Thus Dolowitz and Marsh (1996: 346–348) classify policy transfers into three types: (i) voluntary, (ii) direct coercive and (iii) indirect coercive. A voluntary transfer occurs whenever policy makers are in search of further legitimacy or pursue a mimetic isomorphism (DiMaggio and Powell 1983). Mimetic transfer is a specific quest for legitimacy by the national (or subnational) political system, since it is entitled to copy according to democratic rules and procedures (Radaelli 2000: 27–29), –for example, the case of Europeanization.

A direct coercive transfer occurs whenever one government forces another to comply. According to DiMaggio and Powell, this is a case of coercive isomorphism: a supranational institution or a leader state is able to influence the national policy agenda of one or more other states pursuing compliance (again, the case of EU directives is a case in point).

Finally, indirect coercive policy making concerns non-governmental agents (McCann and Ward 2013: 7), such as foundations, think tanks, academics, interest groups and advisory bodies. There is a loose connection here with DiMaggio and Powell's concept of normative isomorphism. As Stone (2000) points out, the policy transfer in such cases is frequently induced and indirectly promoted by non-governmental actors, who do so in a more incisive, successful way than national institutions.

This sheds some light on the distinction between hard and soft transfers (Stone 2012: 270; Benson and Jordan 2011: 371). A hard transfer is the strict, intentional, declared transmission through an institutionalized channel (act, claim, declaration, directive) requiring compliance and detailing what goals are to be pursued and which instruments have to be adopted. A soft transfer concerns a more generic, loosely coupled form of transmission by certain sources to certain recipients, performed in a more inductive, appealing manner by way of imitation or reinterpretation, local adaptation and reshaping. It is more appealing because of its legitimacy and because it involves local reformulation and the bottom-up influence of the recipients (Stone 2001).

Political assemblage is the concept used to describe this local adaptation (Benson 2012). It is taken from geographical studies, and concerns the rearranging, organizing and putting together of a policy mix consisting of preexisting elements and new ones, thus generating hybridization. Policies are not 'local constructions, neither are they entirely extra local impositions on a locality. Rather, policies and governance practices are gatherings, or relational assemblages of elements and resources—fixed and mobile pieces of expertise, regulation, institutional capacities—from close by and faraway' (McCann and Ward 2013: 8). As a consequence, 'rules are always selected, interpreted and adapted. Agency is nullified by the institutional structure' and policy transfer goes beyond mere mechanical dissemination, in the direction of a processual phenomenon (Radaelli 2000: 39).

In other words, policy transfer may be successful (or unsuccessful), but it does not consist of the convergence/divergence alternative (Stone 2000: 49, 2004: 548). It probably lies somewhere between top-down and bottom-up adaptations (Stone 2012: 485). As a consequence, policy transfer implies 'indigenization' (Freeman 2009; Stone 2012: 487) and *allomorphism* (instead of *isomorphism*), that is, a global discourse intentionally aimed at homogeneity, but then practically generating local reshaping and heterogeneity (Lippi 2000).

Importing and/or Constructing Austerity?

The preceding analysis highlights certain basic facts regarding the ways in which austerity policies have been developed and divulged internationally. The main conclusion of this analysis is that austerity policies have been gradually constructed at the international level.

The interaction of ideological and economic factors, synthesized in, and shared by, academic research centres, international organizations and politically engaged think tanks, has resulted in the formulation of guidelines and policy tools, which have subsequently been transferred to states through key networks.

This transfer has come about through several different means, such as ideological and political influence, institutional obligations, conformity with financing procedures through the European Structural Funds—especially for the EU member states—but also through the conditional nature of loan facility agreements for indebted countries.

However, this transfer has been neither mandatory nor mechanical, nor indeed of a uniform nature in all member countries. The specific conditions of each member state—its institutional history, the political orientation and strategies of its governments during the reform period—have acted as filters determining the specific nature of the mix of austerity measures finally adopted. Likewise, local drivers such as the kind of promoters involved, together with political contingencies and institutional profiles, may contribute to the political assemblage performed at the local level through adjustments and adaptation to the domestic context.

The same may also be said of the further downward diffusion of austerity towards the local level. Here too there has been no single, unique way of doing things. The policy mix has depended on relations between central, intermediate and local levels of government, and on how they have adapted policies so as to maximize benefits. In some cases, the effects have even been transferred directly from international to local level, mainly through the conditional nature of loan agreements.

Studies have pointed to the existence of two distinct phases in the diffusion of austerity. During the first phase, prior to the advent of the 2008 global economic crisis, the dynamics of the diffusion of austerity were of a political nature.

The first wave of reforms involving public spending cuts was instigated by the dominance of neo-liberal ideas regarding the state and its functioning, which first emerged with the rise to power of Margaret Thatcher in the United Kingdom and of Ronald Reagan in the United States, in the early 1980s.

These ideas, which were summarized in the framework theory of NPM, laid the foundation for restrictive fiscal policies, on assumptions such as 'doing more for less'. The use of planning techniques, cost-benefit analyses, outsourcing and privatization were all used as means to reduce the cost of public action.

NPM has combined reduced public spending with organizational and institutional changes that have strengthened the freedom of public managers from political interference, and the delegation of executive functions to semi-autonomous organizations.

The significant coordination problems encountered during implementation of the principles of New Public Management, together with the downgrading of the Central State's strategic capacity, has led to a global waning of NPM ideas, and the gradual abandonment of its methods, since the early 2000s.

The current crisis that began in 2008 and has continued to this day seems to have offered new impetus to NPM. Although the principal rationale for the new wave of austerity is now financial, the standard public spending cuts approach seems to respond equally efficiently to both ideological and economic stimuli. However, present-day crisis-driven attempts to reintroduce New Public Management methods, have been largely restricted to fiscal targets, allowing scholars like Dunleavy to call this phenomenon 'zombie NPM' (Dunleavy 2010).

Overall, we could thus argue that the diffusion of austerity has taken place in two stages: the first is that of the introduction of a general model developed at international level; the second has involved the construction of the specific versions of that model, based on national and local particularities. Both concern three idea-typical tradeoff.

The first tradeoff is between *external push and internal reception* (that is, opportunities for, and threats to, local actors) and concerns the extent to which austerity is an importation or an internal (re)shaping.

The second tradeoff is that between measures introduced *before* the economic crisis and those adopted *thereafter* (are austerity measures different?).

The third division concerns multilevel governance and the following tradeoff between *decentralization* and *recentralization* (is austerity a trigger for the redistribution of power? for example, recentralization, downsizing and downgrading of local autonomy).

All three tradeoffs lead to an analysis of the imported or constructed nature of austerity in each context. One has to look at a specific context in order to gather the evidence required to test the above-mentioned hypotheses.

Consequently, the key questions posed in this book arise from the belief that austerity is at one and the same time a global, and a local, phenomenon, and that the creation of an austerity policy limiting local government and the management and delivery of public services, is partly related to contingent internal factors. As a result, the approach to understanding the austerity phenomenon in the LPS as a whole may encompass fourth analytical dimensions used to observe individual cases studies (Wollmann et al. 2016).

The first of these analytical dimensions concerns external shocks. The forces shaping the conditions for the transfer of austerity to a country are of vital importance. One has to consider the type of reasons underlying the importation of an austerity agenda and those actors promoting this transfer process.

A second dimension concerns the policy mix of austerity measures, that is, the designs, strategies and instruments that have been employed by policy makers, including the strategies and arrangements of institutional players.

Indeed, a third analytical dimension driving austerity concerns the institutional paths leading to the austerity policy mix at central government, regional government and local government levels.

Fourthly, there is the question of the effects of austerity. One key question concerns the expected changes, and the state of public expenditure, before and after austerity 'therapy'. It also concerns the different stages of austerity policy implementation and the significant differences between such stages: the first stage of austerity extended from the early 1990s to 2008, while the second stage began in 2008 and has continued up to the present. It also concerns the effects on LPSs of the downgrading of local government in general, and the decline in LPS consequent to the bypassing of social rights.

References

Aberbach, J. D., & Christensen, T. (2005). Citizens and Consumers: An NPM Dilemma. *Public Management Review, 7*(2), 225–246.

Alesina, A., Barbiero, O., Favero, C., Giavazzi, F., & Paradisi, M. (2015). *Austerity in 2009–13 Economic Policy*, CEPR, CESifo & Science Po, UK.

Balassone, F., & Franco, D. (2000). Public Investment, the Stability Pact and the 'Golden Rule'. *Fiscal Studies, 21*(2), 207–229.

Bennett, C. J. (1991). Review Article: What Is Policy Convergence and What Causes It? *British Journal of Political Science, 21*(2), 215–235.

Benson, D. (2012). Policy Transfer Research: Still Evolving, Not Yet Through? *Political Studies, 10*(3), 333–338.

Benson, D., & Jordan, A. (2011). What Have We Learned from Policy Transfer Research? Dolowitz and Marsh Revisited. *Political Studies, 9*(3), 366–378.

Berry, F. S., & Berry, W. D. (1999). Innovation and Diffusion in Policy Research. In P. A. Sabatier (Ed.), *Theories of Policy Process*. Boulder: Westview Press.

Birkland, T. A. (2009). Disasters, Lessons Learned, and Fantasy Documents. *Journal of Contingencies and Crisis Management, 17*(3), 147–156.

Blyth, M. (2013). *Austerity: The History of a Dangerous Idea*. Oxford: Oxford University Press.
Bugnicourt, J. (1973). Le mimétisme administratif en Afrique: obstacle majeur au développement. *Revue française de science politique, 23*(6), 1239–1267.
Buti, M., & Giudice, G. (2002). Maastricht's Fiscal Rules at Ten: An Assessment. *Journal of Common Market Studies, 40*(5), 823–848.
Christensen, T. (2012). Global Ideas and Modern Public Sector Reforms: A Theoretical Elaboration and Empirical Discussion of a Neo-Institutional Theory. *American Review of Public Administration, 42*(6), 635–653.
Corsetti, G. (2012). Introduction. In G. Corsetti (Ed.), *Austerity: Too Much of a Good Thing?* (pp. 1–10). CEPR-The Centre for Economic Policy Research. www.cepr.org
Davey, K. (Ed.). (2011). *Local Government in Critical Times. Policies for Crises, Recovery and a Sustainable Future*. Strasbourg: Council of Europe.
Di Mascio, F., & Natalini, A. (2014). Reform Processes: Performance Management Within Italian Local Government. *International Public Management Journal, 16*(1), 141–166.
Di Mascio, F., & Natalini, A. (2015). Fiscal Retrenchment in Southern Europe: Changing Patterns of Public Management in Greece, Italy, Portugal and Spain. *Public Management Review, 17*(1), 129–148.
DiMaggio, P., & Powell, W. W. (1983). The Iron Cage Revisited. Institutional Isomorphism and Collective Rationality in Organizational Fields. *American Sociological Review, 48*(2), 147–160.
Dolowitz, D. P., & Marsh, D. (1996). Who Learns What from Whom: A Review of the Policy Transfer Literature. *Political Studies, 44*(2), 343–357.
Dolowitz, D. P., & Marsh, D. (2000). Learning from Abroad: The Role of Policy Transfer in Contemporary Policy-Making. *Governance, 13*(1), 5–23.
Dolowitz, D. P., & Marsh, D. (2012). The Future of Policy Transfer Research. *Political Studies, 10*(3), 339–345.
Dunleavy, P. (2010). What Is the Cameron-Clegg Governance Strategy? Zombie 'New Public Management' Cannot Work in the Face of Massive Public Expenditure Cutbacks. *blogs.lse.ac.uk*. http://blogs.lse.ac.uk/politicsandpolicy/2010/10/07/what-is-the-cameron-clegg-governance-strategy. Accessed 12 June 2017.
Dussauge-Laguna, M. (2012). On the Past and Future of Policy Transfer Research: Benson and Jordan Revisited. *Political Studies, 10*(3), 313–324.
Ferlie, E., & Geraghty, K. J. (2005). Professionals in Public Service Organizations: Implications for Public Sector "Reforming". In E. Ferlie, L. E. Lynn Jr., & C. Pollitt (Eds.), *The Oxford Handbook of Public Management* (pp. 434–436). Oxford: Oxford University Press.
Frans, K. M., van Nispen, M., & de Jong, M. (2017). Evidence-Based Budgetary Policy: Speaking Truth to Power? In M. Brans, I. Geva-May, & M. Howlett (Eds.), *Routledge Handbook of Comparative Policy Analysis*. London: Taylor & Francis.

Freeman, R. (2009). What Is Translation? *Evidence & Policy, A Journal of Research, Debate and Practice, 5*(4), 429–427.

Goldsmith, M. (2011). Twenty Years On: The Europeanization of Local Government. In E. Van Bever, H. Reynaert, & K. Steyvers (Eds.), *The Road to Europe. Main Street or Backward Alley for Local Governments in Europe?* Brugge: Vanden Broele.

Hlepas, N. K. (2016). Le crépuscule de la décentralisation? Tester les limites des réformes fonctionnelles à l'époque de l'austérité. *Revue Internationale des Sciences Administratives, 82*(2), 287–308.

Hlepas, N. K., & Getimis, P. (2010). Impacts of Local Government Reforms in Greece: An Interim Assessment. *Local Government Studies, 37*(5), 517–532.

Hood, C. (1991). A Public Management for All Seasons? *Public Administration, 69*(1), 3–19.

Hood, C. (1995). The "New Public Management" in the 1980s: Variations on a Theme. *Accounting, Organizations and Society, 20*(2/3), 93–109.

Hood, C. (2010). *Reflections on Public Service Reform in a Cold Fiscal Climate.* London: 2020 Public Service Trust-ERSC.

Iakovides, M., Stamatis, M., Katsimardos, P., Stefopoulou, E., & Bouas, K. (2016). *Seven Years of Greek Crisis: Highlighting the Need for an Independent Monitoring Body of the Memoranda.* Athens: Greek Liberties Monitor.

Ioannou, D., Leblond, P., & Niemann, A. (2015). European Integration and the Crisis: Practice and Theory. *Journal of European Public Policy, 22*(2), 155–176.

Issing, O. (2004). The Stability and Growth Pact: The Appropriate Fiscal Framework for EMU. *International Economics and Economic Policy, 1*(1), 9–13.

James, O., & Lodge, M. (2003). The Limitations of 'Policy Transfer' and 'Lesson Drawing' for Public Policy Research. *Political Studies Review, 1*(2), 179–193.

Jimenez, B. S. (2012). Raises Taxes, Cut Services or Lay Off Staff: Citizens in the Fiscal Retrenchment Process. *Journal of Public Administration Research, 24*(1), 923–953.

Kamkhaji, J. C., & Radaelli, C. M. (2017). Crisis, Learning and Policy Change in the European Union. *Journal of European Public Policy, 24*(5), 714–734.

Kickert, W., Randma-Liiv, T., & Savi, R. (2013). *Fiscal Consolidation in Europe: A Comparative analysis.* COCOPS Report, Deliverable 7.2. Brussels: EU Commission.

Kuhlmann, S., & Bouckaert, G. (Eds.). (2016). *Local Public Sector Reforms in Times of Crisis. National Trajectories and International Comparisons.* London: Palgrave Macmillan.

Kuhlmann, S., & Wollmann, H. (2014). *Introduction to Comparative Public Administration. Administrative System and Reforms in Europe.* London: Edward Elgar Press.

Kuhlmann, S., Bogumil, J., & Grohs, S. (2008). Evaluating Administrative Modernization in German Local Governments: Success or Failure of the "New Steering Model". *Public Administration Review, 68*(5), 851–863.

Ladner, A. (2017). Autonomy and Austerity: Re-investing in Local Government. In C. Schwab, G. Bouckaert, & S. Kuhlmann (Eds.), *The Future of Local Government in Europe. Lessons from Research and Practice in 31 Countries.* Berlin: Nomos.

Langrod, G. (1973). Genèse et conséquences du mimétisme administratif en Afrique. *International Review of Administrative Sciences, 39*(2), 119–132.

Lefkofridi, Z., & Schmitter, P. C. (2014). A Good or a Bad Crisis for European Union? In M. J. Rodrigues & E. Xiarchogiannipoulou (Eds.), *The Eurozone Crisis and the Transformation of EU Governance. Internal and External Implications* (pp. 11–28). Farnham: Ashgate.

Lippi, A. (2000). One Theory, Many Practices. Institutional Allomorphism in the Managerialist Reorganization of Italian Local Governments. *Scandinavian Journal of Management, 16*(4), 455–477.

Lippi, A. (2003). As a Voluntary Choice or as a Legal Obligation? Assessing New Public Management Policy in Italy. In H. Wollmann (Ed.), *Evaluation in Public-Sector Reform: Concepts and Practice in International Perspective.* Cheltenham: Edward Elgar Press.

Lodge, M., & Hood, C. (2012). Into an Age of Multiple Austerity? Public Management and Public Service Bargains Across OECD Countries. *Governance, 25*(1), 79–101.

McCann, E., & Ward, D. (2013). A Multi-Disciplinary Approach to Policy Transfer Research: Geographies, Assemblages, Mobilities and Mutations. *Policy Studies, 34*(1), 2–18.

Morlino, L., & Quaranta, M. (2016). What Is the Impact of the Economic Crisis on Democracy? Evidence from Europe. *International Journal of Political Science Review, 37*(5), 618–633.

Morlino, L., & Raniolo, F. (2017). *The Impact of the Economic Crisis on the Southern European Democracies.* London: Palgrave.

Mossberger, K., & Wolman, H. (2003). Policy Transfer as a Form of Prospective Policy Evaluation: Challenges and Recommendations. *Public Administration Review, 63*(4), 428–440.

Moury, C., & Freire, A. (2013). Austerity Policies and Politics: The Case of Portugal. *Pole-Sud, 39,* 35–56.

Moynihan, D. P. (2009). From Inter-Crisis to Intra-Crisis Learning. *Journal of Contingencies and Crisis Management, 17*(3), 189–198.

Osborne, D., & Gaebler, T. (1992). *Reinventing Government: How the Entrepreneurial Spirit Is Transforming the Public Sector.* Reading: Addison-Wesley.

Overmans, J. F. A., & Noordegraaf, M. (2014). Managing Austerity: Rhetorical and Real Responses to Fiscal Stress in Local Government. *Public Money and Management, 34*(2), 99–106.

Peters, B. G. (2011). Governance Responses to the Fiscal Crisis—Comparative Perspectives. *Public Money and Management, 31*(1), 75–80.

Peters, B. G., Pierre, J., & Randma-Liiv, T. (2011). Global Financial Crisis, Public Administration and Governance: Do New Problems Require New Solutions? *Public Organization Review, 11*(1), 13–27.

Pierson, P. (2001). Coping with Permanent Austerity: Welfare State Restructuring in Affluent Democracies. In P. Pierson (Ed.), *The New Politics of the Welfare State*. Oxford: Oxford University Press.

Pollitt, C. (2010). Cuts and Reforms—Public Service as We Move into a New Era. *Society and Economy, 32*(1), 17–31.

Pollitt, C., & Bouckaert, G. (2011). *Public Management Reform. A Comparative Analysis New Public Management Governance and the New Weberian State*. Oxford: Oxford University Press.

Posner, P., & Bloendal, J. (2012). Democracies and Deficits: Prospects for Fiscal Responsibility in Democratic Nations. *Governance, 25*(1), 11–34.

Radaelli, C. M. (2000). Policy Transfer in the European Union: Institutional Isomorphism as a Source of Legitimacy. *Governance, 13*(1), 25–43.

Reinhart, C. M., & Rogoff, K. S. (2009). *This Time Is Different*. Princeton: Princeton University Press.

Rose, R. (1991). What Is Lesson-Drawing? *Journal of Public Policy, 11*(1), 3–30.

Schaefer, C., & Streeck, W. (Eds.). (2013). *Politics in the Age of Austerity*. Cambridge: Polity Press.

Schwab, C., Bouckaert, G., & Kuhlmann, S. (2017). *The Future of Local Government in Europe Lessons from Research and Practice in 31 Countries*. Berlin: Nomos.

Sotiropoulos, D. A. (2006). Old Problems and New Challenges: The Enduring and Challenging Functions of Southern European State Bureaucracies. In R. Gunther, P. N. Diamandouros, & D. A. Sotiropoulos (Eds.), *Democracy and the State in the New Southern Europe* (pp. 197–234). Oxford: Oxford University Press.

Stone, D. (2000). Non-Governmental Policy Transfer: The Strategies of the Independent Policy Institutes. *Governance, 13*(1), 45–62.

Stone, D. (2001). *Learning Lessons, Policy Transfer and the International Diffusion of Policy Ideas*. CSGR Working Paper, No.69. Warwick: Warwick University Press, CSGR.

Stone, D. (2004). Transfer Agents and Global Networks in the 'Transnationalization' of Policy. *Journal of European Public Policy, 11*(3), 545–566.

Stone, D. (2012). Transfer and Translation of Policy. *Policy Studies, 33*(6), 483–499.

Streeck, W. (2013). *The Politics of Public Debt*. MPifG, No.7. Koeln: Max-Plank Institute for the Studies on Societies.

t'Hart, P., & Boin, R. A. (2001). Between Crisis and Normalcy: The Long Shadow of Post Crisis Politics. In U. Rosenthal, A. R. Boin, & L. K. Comfort (Eds.),

Managing Crises: Threats, Dilemmas, Opportunities (pp. 28–46). Springfield: Charles C Thomas.

Verney, S., & Bosco, A. (2013). Living Parallel Lives: Italy and Greece in an Age of Austerity. *South European Society and Politics, 18*(4), 397–426.

Wollmann, H. (2004). Local Government Reforms in Great Britain, Sweden, Germany and France: Between Multi-Function and Single-Purpose Organisations. *Local Government Studies, 30*(4), 639–665.

Wollmann, H. (2016). Local Government Reforms: Between Multifunction and Single Purpose Organisations. *Local Government Studies, 42*(3), 376–384.

Wollmann, H., Marcou, G., & Kopric, I. (Eds.). (2016). *Public and Social Services in Europe: From Public and Municipal to Private Sector Provision*. London: Palgrave Macmillan.

Wolman, H., & Page, E. (2002). Policy Transfer Among Local Governments: An Information-Theory Approach. *Governance, 15*(4), 447–501.

CHAPTER 3

Greek Municipalities Before and During the Austerity Era: Imposed Policies, Local Resistance and Unsuccessful Reforms

Theodore N. Tsekos and Nikos K. Hlepas

Introduction

Greece is a typical South-European example of the Napoleonic state launched at the very beginning of the nation state-building era (Sotiropoulos 2004). Until the last quarter of the twentieth century, centralism had traditionally been perceived as necessary in order to sustain Greece's national unity and (re-)distributive capacities, in the face of political instability, weak economic development and regional divergence (Hlepas and Getimis 2011). This centralism, however, could not depend on a strong, independent bureaucracy. The Greek state bears some traits

T. N. Tsekos (✉)
Department of Business and Public Administration, Technological Education Institute of Peloponnese, Kalamata, Greece

N. K. Hlepas
Department of Political Science and Public Administration at the National and Capodistrian, University of Athens, Athens, Greece

A. Lippi, T. N. Tsekos (eds.), *Local Public Services in Times of Austerity across Mediterranean Europe*, Governance and Public Management, https://doi.org/10.1007/978-3-319-76225-8_3

of the legal-rational bureaucratic model, mixed with certain aspects of the patrimonial bureaucracy. However, the Greek state's administration, including its senior civil service, was subordinate to political leadership, and the country lacked a stable bureaucratic elite in most areas of the state apparatus. Therefore, Greece's senior bureaucrats were not trusted as bearers of managerial knowledge and expertise. Quite often, reformist governments would invite "non-partisan" foreign experts to give advice on policy. However, strong resistance throughout Greek society, located in the market and civil society as well as in the political system and state and local administrations, systematically undermined implementation of those reforms proposed by said foreign experts and the technical assistance they offered (Makridimitris and Michalopoulos 2000).

Thus, for lengthy periods, the weakness and instability of national bureaucracy was accompanied by a lack of technocratic influence on the political decision-making process. Populism, verbalism, symbolism and personalization all characterize Greek political culture. Rationalist choices were therefore not easy to defend in public debate and virtually impossible to implement in practice. Strong, ambitious leaders thus preferred to promote such choices by adopting strategies of surprise, non-transparent bargaining and authoritarian enforcement. Weak social capital (especially the lack of trust in public institutions and in rules in general) rendered changes and reforms even more difficult, while governing under conditions of mistrust was like walking on a tight rope, especially for governments dependent on volatile parliamentary majorities.

While centralism remained a fundamental characteristic of politics and administration, at the same time a peculiar kind of "behind the scenes" localism characterized Greek politics and complemented the country's majoritarian, polarized, strictly representative political system. Civil society is rather weak, and its demands are filtered through a complex system of political patronage. Interest group systems are characterized by their extreme fragmentation, segregated sectoralization, uneven access to, and influence over, policy- and decision-making, ad hoc mobilization, and a lack of open pluralism (Hlepas and Getimis 2011). The legally strong, unitary institutions of the paternalistic Jacobin state do not make up for overall, multi-level, multi-sector, multi-actor fragmentation and weak coordination, resulting in the asymmetric nature of policy implementation (Featherstone and Papadimitriou 2013).

One major problem of the Greek political-administrative system is its incapacity to effectively program and evaluate public action at both central and local levels. This is the result of the clientelistic nature of the Greek state.

The clientelistic management of the public service leads to informal procedures prevailing over formal ones. Thus, personal and interpersonal relations weigh more than rules and regulations, with the latter easily bypassed to the benefit of the political patron.

What emerges is a political-administrative system similar in appearance to the Weberian ideal-type, but not functioning in the same way and not producing the same results. Such a state, with Weberian features but not functioning in the ideo-typical way, has been qualified as a *"non-Weberian bureaucracy"* (Tsekos 2013).

In view of this context, it is surprising to discover that successive Greek governments have managed to implement successive decentralization reforms, from the beginning of the 1980s up to the outbreak of the large-scale financial crisis in 2010. During the '80s, however, centralism was perceived as a core attribute of post-war authoritarian state practices, and decentralization was a purported tool of democratization, bringing the decision-making arena closer to the citizen and enhancing government's accountability. During the 1990s, the establishment of second-tier local governments (1994), the devolution of certain state tasks, followed by the first wave of amalgamation measures through the "Kapodistrias" Plan (1998), offered new career opportunities to ambitious party politicians while enhancing party politicization also at lower levels of public administration, which in turn strengthened party influence and structures (Hlepas 2010). Another, even more important driver of reform was the process of Europeanization that strongly encouraged decentralization through funds, regulations, policy design and institutional isomorphism (Spanou 2008).

The Situation Before Austerity

The Expansion of Municipal Competencies in Greece

The '80s and the 1990s were a long period of successive decentralization reforms and the transfer of many additional responsibilities in several fields (small business' licensing and controls, environmental protection, sport, culture, education and training, employment social services etc.) to the local level. New roles have been assigned to local government and municipalities were earmarked to promote local development through innovative institutional tools such as inter-municipal "Developmental Associations", and "Programmatic Agreements" between municipal and other agencies in the public and the social economic sector.

Apart from the traditionally clientelistic nature of the country's political-administrative system, one of the main causes of the spectacular increases in numbers of municipal enterprises (Tsekos and Triantafyllopoulou 2016) was that from 1994 onwards, municipal corporations, mainly in the health and social services sector, were increasingly eligible for European funding, while "in-house" activities were not. Very few of such corporations were actually self-sustaining, while others functioned as policy-making instruments subsidized by local government or in receipt of EU funding.

So it is easy to see how the flexibility arising from corporatization is used less for operational development and performance improvement, than for strictly clientelistic purposes.

Turning in the Opposite Direction? Retrenchment of LG Powers and Flexibility

From the mid-1990s onwards, methodical efforts in the opposite direction have been made to curb municipal powers and operational flexibility. There are two main reasons for this tendency. First of all, there are the European policies of an open market and free competition, and the ensuing compulsory institutional compliance. Secondly, there is the clientelistic conflict between central and local political elites, which gives the former to seek ways of curbing the increasing political influence of the latter. European pressure to abolish shady, selective, preferential terms and practices has led to the generalized use of mandatory public bidding for contracts between municipalities and municipal corporations, and for the provision of goods and services by such corporations. The central political elites (members of parliament and of government) aim to reduce the capacity of local politicians (mayors, counselors) to directly appoint staff, thus depriving them of a powerful instrument of political patronage.

In 1994, the construction of public works through municipal companies came under the special law on public procurement requiring public tenders for such works. In 1997, tax exemptions were abolished for municipal companies other than those providing water supply, sewage and waste management. The same year, the hiring of blue-collar and secretarial staff was placed under the law on public recruitment. By 2002, all staff, with the exception of senior management, became the subject of selection procedures controlled by the independent High Commission for Public Personnel Selection (ASEP).

In 2006, the possibility of establishing municipal companies was restricted. Municipalities were thus deprived of their main means of expansion, and this led to the first serious slowdown of municipal initiatives and flexibility.

Austerity Policies Resulting from the Current Sovereign Debt Crisis, and Their Impact on Local Government

The sovereign debt crisis that affected Greece in early 2010 had a serious impact on the country's local governments. The three Financial Assistance Agreements (2010, 2012 and 2015) and the accompanying Adjustment Programs and technical MoUs, contain numerous conditions governing local administrations (Tsekos and Triantafyllopoulou 2016).

The 2010 program foresaw extending the spending cuts introduced by the local administration reform, by replacing only 20% of retiring employees and by consolidating municipalities and local councils, with the aim of reducing operating costs and wage bills (European Commission 2010). The second agreement dating from March 2012 aimed at a more thorough restructuring of government operations, the closing and downsizing government units, outsourcing functions, identifying redundancy opportunities, restructuring both central and local public administrations, as well as reducing the number of fixed-term contracts and the entity of local government operating costs (European Commission 2012).

The "Kallikrates" reform of the local governance system (Law 3852/2010), that became part of the structural reforms of the Greek Adjustment Program was politically conceived and debated prior to the crisis, but only finalized and implemented thereafter, was accepted as an adequate policy option by both Greek and supranational decision makers. Later on, stabilization and austerity policies also led to the extensive centralization of fiscal policy and control mechanisms.

The economic crisis appeared to be a critical juncture in facilitating reforms (Ladi 2014). New historical institutionalism was to highlight persistent institutional arrangements and path dependencies that predetermine further developments (Pierson 2000). Major change (or policy paradigm change) would be more likely to take place at such "critical junctures", and therefore the timing of reforms is extremely important (Pierson 2000).

However, even during the introduction of these reforms, carried out as prerequisites of the bailout agreements, policy makers have failed to resolve the aforementioned problems (Tsekos 2015). The European Court of Auditors published a report entitled "More attention to results needed to improve the delivery of technical assistance to Greece" (European Court of Auditors 2015). This report emphasizes the fact that the recent reforms have not improved the Greek administrative machinery. The report states that the reforms are poorly designed, without adequate use of planning techniques such as problem definition, options analysis and *ex-ante* evaluation.

The Political Framework of Austerity Policies

In 2004, the newly elected center-right government reported an upward review of the 2003 budget deficit figure to 3.2% of GDP. Subsequently, an excessive deficit procedure was initiated by the European Commission (EC), which indicated that the quality of public data was "not satisfactory", stating that Eurostat had not certified data provided by the National Statistical Service of Greece since 2000. According to the subsequent review of figures made between 2004 and 2007, Greece's public deficit had exceeded the 3% of GDP limit every year since 2000, with this figure topping out at 7.9% in 2004. The EU closed the excessive deficit procedure in 2007 (the year of parliamentary elections in Greece), with the Commission declaring that it was satisfied that the Greek government had taken sufficient measures. Some of these measures referred to public enterprises (e.g. through Act 3429/20005) and tended to streamline policies and impose extensive reporting obligations that seemed to include municipal enterprises, whose legal framework was rationalized in 2006 (Act 3463/2006).

In 2008, a law on the "transparency of the state budget and control over public spending" (Act 3697/2008) covering "general government entities", including municipalities and second-tier local governments, introduced certain additional obligations for such entities. More specifically, first- and second-tier local governments had to submit "operational plans" including budgets for several years, and had to submit accurate data on the implementation of their budgets to an "Inter-Ministerial Committee of General Government Entities" composed exclusively of ministerial representatives. This Inter-Ministerial Committee could define concrete "organizational, operational and administrative measures" to be adopted by each entity of general government within a given schedule. In the event of non-compliance, the Committee could fine local governments up to 15% of the annual General State Grant, which generally constitutes no less than 60% of municipal revenue and 90% of second-tier revenue (Hlepas 2012).

During the following months, however, this centralist system of fiscal supervision, which could even include obligatory fiscal measures, was not implemented. There were vehement protests by local government associations, who denounced violation of constitutional safeguards by the actual provisions of Act 3697/2008 designed to abolish local government's fiscal and budgetary autonomy. On the other hand, the authority of the center-right government was undermined by a series of scandals and bad publicity.

Faced with the 2008 Global Financial Crisis, Premier Karamanlis initially reassured people that the Greek economy would be "armoured", since the Greek banking sector would not be exposed to so-called toxic assets (Pagoulatos and Triantopoulos 2009). Pretty soon, however, the Premier was forced by the clear recession to revise his make-believe-rhetoric, and he invited the opposition to "act responsibly" and join "national efforts" aimed at fiscal stabilization.

Opposition leader Papandreou refused to offer a helping hand, probably because his party was eager to return to power, while many leading socialist politicians were still angry about the vehement opposition style that Karamanlis himself had adopted when former socialist leader Simitis was still in power. In 2009, while the country's public deficit was out of control, no one seemed to have any clear idea of the entity of the problem, since the hiding of deficits by various methods was common practice in many public authorities (hospitals, municipalities, social or/and health security bodies etc.). Public institutions that were supposed to be technocratic and to offer accurate and reliable information, such as the "National Statistics Service", were also party-politicized and played a crucial role in a major governmental operation designed to deceive Greek public opinion as well as several decision makers abroad. Even the independent Bank of Greece, which in the summer of 2009 had expressed "serious concern" was later criticized for not strongly warning "everyone" about the dramatic situation of state finances early enough. Later on, there were several reports that not only in Greece, but also in the European Union as a whole, in several international institutions and elsewhere there was considerable awareness of the reality of the Greek deficit problem, but political considerations prevailed over technocratic concerns. Nevertheless, Greece was going to have an early parliamentary election in October 2009, and a new government enjoying a "fresh mandate" from the people would be in a better position to face some uncomfortable truths.

Papandreou achieved an impressive victory in the early parliamentary election held in October 2009. He had promised "green growth" and had claimed that austerity measures would not be necessary, since "money exists" in the country, and what was missing were proper tax authorities and a redistribution of income. His impressive reform agenda included, inter alia, the systematic reform of local government and peripheral forms of governmental administration, as well as a comprehensive policy of transparency and accountability.

In the meantime, the public deficit estimates of the previous government, and even the statistical data provided by the National Statistical Service, were questioned. The previous estimate of the government's budget deficit for 2009 was revised upwards, to nearly twice the previous figure, from 6.7% to 12.7% of GDP. Investor confidence fell, and a series of downgrades of Greek bonds by major credit-rating agencies followed (Roscini et al. 2011). Within a few weeks, no less than one-fifth of all cash deposits had been taken out of the country.

This economic turbulence, however, did not seem to slow down or downsize the local government reform process. As originally planned, and based on proposals of local government associations and their scientific institutions, the government unfolded its "Kallikrates" reform. The advent of the crisis, however, overshadowed this reform plan; moreover, it had visible repercussions on certain aspects of the reform, particularly that of the fiscal management of municipalities. The "Kallikrates Law" introduced the mandatory ex-ante control of spending orders and municipal contracting (the latter in cases of contracts worth more than 100,000 euros) by the Court of Auditors. Moreover, most municipal enterprises were placed, for the first time, under the spending and contracting control of said court. The double-entry accounting system became mandatory for all local governments, while new loans were only allowed for investment purposes, or for the refinancing of old loans. The law introduced the following additional provisions: (a) total annual payments of interest and principal could not exceed 20% of a municipality's ordinary annual revenue; (b) total debt could not exceed 60% of total annual revenue. In this way, the law introduced the so-called debt brake and new borrowing was made impossible for a minority of municipalities with problems of over-indebtedness, whereas some of them were big and important municipalities, such as the City of Piraeus.

The "Kallikrates" law established that Greece's municipalities would be part of a "Special Economic Recovery Program" if faced with fiscal problems as defined by law. Such problems comprised: (a) the inability to draft a balanced budget, due to insufficient revenue compared with existing liabilities; (b) annual payments of loan instalments exceeding 20% of annual municipal revenue; (c) total debt exceeding a predefined proportion of annual revenue. Adhering to this "Recovery Program" would provide access to special funding; however, at the same time this would be combined with a freeze on recruitment, predefined budgeting options and other fiscal measures, concrete implementation schedules and monitoring by a Central Audit Committee at the Ministry of the Interior.

The decision to adhere to the "Recovery Program" was a voluntary one taken by the Municipal Council in question. For those municipalities without access to the credit market due to the new restrictions imposed by the Kallikrates Law (see above), and/or to the strict borrowing requirements that gradually prevailed in the banking sector after the outbreak of the crisis, this "Recovery Program" could in theory be a bitter, but necessary, pill to take.

The law also provided for the compulsory implementation of the aforesaid "Recovery Program" in the case of over-indebted municipalities. The Minister of the Interior could launch the thorough scrutiny of the financial situation of a municipality, by independent accountants. Finally, based on their report, the Central Audit Committee could decide that the scrutinized municipality had to adopt and implement a "Recovery Program". The latter, obligatory version of such a "Recovery Program" in particular was once again met by the protests of local government associations.

In the meantime, in May 2010, following the Memorandum of Understanding between the Greek government and the "Troika" (IMF, EU and ECB), a rescue package was offered to Greece designed to deal with its public debt crisis. Cuts in salaries and pensions, together with a sudden, unprecedented increase in taxation, led to Papandreou's popularity plummeting. Nevertheless, he managed to survive after declaring local government elections, due to be held in November 2010, to be a kind of "referendum" that would test the public acceptance and democratic legitimacy of his government. If the socialist candidates were defeated, he would resign and new parliamentary elections would be held. Faced with the uncertainties of an unprecedented crisis, people were reluctant to bring down their government under such circumstances, and Papandreou's gamble seemed to pay off. Popular anger was expressed through the extremely low turnout (46%), but many socialist candidates won. The opposition proved incapable of taking advantage of the situation, even though not only left-wing parties, but even, conservatives, had adopted a populist rhetoric against the existing government and the "Troika". Indeed, many conservatives even refused to take responsibility for the dramatic public deficit, claiming that this had been "exaggerated" on purpose by the government and by "foreign interests" wishing to see the Greek economy under their control.

Despite furious opposition, a series of reforms were introduced by the socialist government, not only in the field of economic policy, but also in other sectors such as pensions, labor relations, higher education and public administration. New impetus was given to the reforms after Greece and the EU agreed on a second rescue package in July 2011. Many observers were hopeful that this external stimulus to reform, together with international pressure demanding radical changes to the Greek economy, would finally bring about those structural and policy changes that had many times been announced and legislated for since Greece's transition to democracy (1974), but which had never actually been implemented. Initial optimism that the country would overcome the crisis and rejoin the financial markets by 2012 soon faded. The stabilization program did not work (or/and was not properly implemented), and many socialist MPs withdrew their support for the party's policies, or even left the party. The whole political system seemed to be disintegrating, while paralyzing strikes, violent demonstrations and protest actions became part of daily life.

Restrictions on Local Financial Management

For a long period, municipal fiscal management did not seem to result in any major risks, since most municipalities were small, dealt with insignificant sums, and their borrowing was subject to severe restrictions, while the state-owned "Loans and Deposits Fund" was the exclusive creditor. This situation changed radically after the amalgamations of 1998 (Hlepas 2010), when the average size of municipalities sextupled; moreover, local authorities were offered access to the private credit market. Soon, the ex-ante spending control exercised by the Court of Auditors (for each payment order, excepting wages, other operating expenses etc.) was introduced for certain larger municipalities, following a request from certain mayors wanting to safeguard the correctness of spending procedures, and to prevent future charges of mismanagement. Later on, this ex-ante spending control became accessible to all municipalities over 5000 inhabitants, which meant that 85% of the municipalities had their spending orders controlled by the local auditor. However, this did not prevent municipalities from increasing spending, especially after the Karamanlis government gave tenure to several thousands of contract workers and employees in 2005. Municipal spending, as a percentage of the country's GDP, had grown remarkably (from 1.98% of GDP in 1995 to 3.09% in 2009), due to additional responsibilities, personnel growth and, last but not least, EU funds. However, it remained one of the lowest figures in Europe (Dexia 2008).

Local government associations strongly opposed austerity policies affecting their municipalities. They pointed out the fact that municipal debt constituted just a very small percentage of total public debt in Greece (less than 1%, DEXIA 2011). The state should therefore first "put its own house in order", before trying to dictate local fiscal policy, and even to define actual budgeting in those municipalities enjoying constitutional safeguards and possessing their own, directly elected, democratically accountable political leaders and representatives. After all, mean debt per capita in municipalities was only 157 euros in the "crisis year" 2010 while the mean debt per capita of Greece's government reached 31,818 euros (Stolzenberg et al. 2016: 50).

The fact that total municipal debt was just a very small percentage of total public debt, was just a half truth. There were some certain large cities with severe problems of over-indebtedness. Moreover, quite a few municipalities were simply not meeting their financial obligations to private suppliers and contractors, thus causing severe problems of liquidity to a large number of (mostly small- and medium-sized) enterprises that were already under pressure, through the crisis. This illegal practice of "borrowing through overdue payments or non-payments" to suppliers, was quite common among the majority of Greece's public entities (Hlepas 2016).

Following specific agreements with the Troika (EU, ECB and IMF), fiscal policy in 2012, included a total sum of nearly 6 billion euros that would be offered to public entities in order to pay off suppliers and contractors and to meet their outstanding liabilities. Over the course of the following months, 197 municipalities (out of a total of 325) applied for this special funding, while central government approved 690 million euros to be transferred to these municipalities. In this way, central government also covered part of the unprecedented losses caused by the reduction in general grants (a 60% reduction in 2013 compared to 2009) that used to make up no less than 70% of total municipal revenue (ADEDY 2014). There was one main prerequisite to be met in order to receive this special funding. Each municipality had to submit a commitment to the Ministry of the Interior, and sign an agreement, whereby the municipality's financial obligations would, from now on, be met immediately, with the consequence that no overdue liabilities would be created in the future (Hlepas 2016).

In 2012, the new mid-term framework for fiscal strategy ("MTFS"—Ministry of Finance 2012), required the creation of an Observatory for Local Government's fiscal management (the official title was "Observatory of financial autonomy of Local Authorities"). This observatory was to be established in order to coordinate the Ministry of the Interior's supervision of local governments, to agree on targets, and to ensure the implementation of budgets accordingly. Furthermore, a new budgetary process was designed to integrate local governments within the framework of the MTFS: local government budgets were to become the subject of a process of review by the observatory; they were to be assessed and adjusted before their adoption, in order to be realistic and to be in keeping with MTFS projections. The observatory was launched by Act 4111/2013 (Section 4): it comprises a committee supported by the Financial Directorate of the Ministry of the Interior, and consists of tax judges and senior civil servants, as well as representatives of local government associations (from the first and second tiers, respectively). The observatory assists with the implementation of balanced budgets by local government authorities; furthermore, it regularly monitors budget implementation and formulates instructions and mandatory opinions in order to safeguard the fiscal consolidation and overall economic viability of local governments. Budget implementation is reviewed on a monthly basis, while the "Consolidated Action Framework", comprising monthly and quarterly targets, actions and deadlines established by local governments themselves, is also monitored. Should there be a negative variation of more than 10% from the aforesaid quarterly budgetary targets, the observatory can step in and provide further instructions and opinions to local government authorities. If budget variance persists for a further two quarters, and specific measures have not been effectively implemented, the local authority may be subjected to a mandatory Special Consolidation Program (Hlepas 2016).

Up until now, however, no such case has ever been recorded. Even in cases of persistent budget variance, the observatory tends to apply "soft" methods of persuasion. The mandatory opinions of the observatory on several matters and occasions have been submitted to all entities (893 in total), sometimes even containing instructions for draft budgets in 2014. Corrective mechanisms designed to control budget implementation in terms of annual targets had already been introduced in 2012; however, such mechanisms cannot be adopted to their full extent if ceilings are not used in the budgetary process over the course of time. In 2013, local authorities' budgets were not fully consistent with the projections of the MTFS for the local government sector as a whole. The consistency of local governments' budgets with MTFS projections improved in 2014 as a result of cooperation between the observatory and local governments (European Commission 2014).

The institutionalization of such an "Observatory" and other central fiscal control mechanisms, including obligatory measures, was once again met by vehement opposition from local government associations and from trade unions representing local government employees. Its opponents claimed that fiscal autonomy, budgeting and fiscal management had become the subject of "unprecedented centralization", of increased decision-making powers at central government level, abolishing local authorities' power over their own budgets. It was claimed that these new centralized institutions and mechanisms would destroy local government. The National Associations of Local Governments appealed in the High Administrative Court ("Council of State") against the observatory's actions. They claimed the observatory violated constitutional safeguards, and in particular the provisions governing the operational and economic autonomy of local government authorities (Art. 102 par. 2 of the Greek Constitution). Finally, the court (with decisions 1716 and 1717/2014) ruled that legal provisions concerning the observatory did not violate the financial autonomy of local government. The new institution operated according to guidelines and instructions, while municipal and regional councils still had sufficient discretionary powers. Furthermore, the court ruled that the fiscal targets imposed by the international agreements stipulated by the Greek government, the "Troika" and Greece's European partners, were binding on all general government entities.

Apart from financial consolidation as such, the observatory also aims to reduce fiscal performance disparities among different local governments, by imposing unitary standards of budgeting and reporting, and even predefining fiscal policy and fiscal measures within local government. The observatory appears to be the end product of a long process of gradual uniformization of fiscal management in local government. The Maastricht criteria obviously triggered this process several years ago, when municipal spending was submitted to the ex-ante control of the Court of Auditors, and the double-entry accounting system gradually became mandatory. Later on, the "Kallikrates" reform expanded fiscal controls (to municipal enterprises and municipal contracting), and it created new control mechanisms, and even the possibility of special consolidation status for municipalities burdened by severe problems of over-indebtedness. However, strong opposition from local government associations and local political leaders, against a background of governmental weakness and political instability from 2011 through till the summer of 2012, led to the shelving of special Stabilization Programs for over-indebted municipalities. Finally, the problem of old debts and, more importantly, of amounts owed to private suppliers, businessmen and freelancers, was resolved, to a significant extent, by the special subsidy covering overdue liabilities in 2013. However, the problem of disparities among fiscal policies and the management of different municipalities persisted; indeed, there were even certain municipalities facing financial problems that in 2013 opted not to receive the aforementioned subsidy, so as to avoid any consequential commitments. Such disparities were not only a problem that affected state efforts at fiscal consolidation: different municipal business policies and fiscal practices had clearly been problematic for various business communities and potential investors for several years, frustrated as they often were by the uncertain environment that certain local politicians tended to create.

There were increasing protests against the "systematic practice of many municipalities" not to meet their financial obligations to private concerns, or to delay payments to them. The call for "public intervention" that would protect businesses and freelancers against unreliable and insolvent local governments understandably got louder during the crisis. Therefore, the standardized, centrally monitored fiscal management of local government was not short of influential supporters, and even the wider public became increasingly critical toward local governments, as the sharp fall in public confidence toward municipalities and regions shows (ADEDY 2014, referring to Eurobarometer).

It is therefore no surprise that with a view to establishing governmental stability, and under strong pressure from the "Troika",[1] an institution like the "Observatory" finally came into action in 2013, despite the vehement

[1] Following the bailout agreements, a tripartite (EU, European Central Bank, International Monetary Fund) Troika is scrutinizing implementation of bailout agreements and assessing stabilization performance step by step, prior to each installment ("conditionality principle").

opposition to its deployment. After all, the consolidation of local government finances as a result of previous measures was already visible in 2011, and increasingly so in 2012. For this reason, at first sight it could be said that there were certain “positive outcomes” of the national austerity policies (debt break, balanced budgets etc.) imposed on local governments. Therefore, due to the rather successful performance of local governments, compared to the central level, the new bailout plan signed in August 2015 did not introduce any additional requirements regarding the oversight of local governments (Cohen and Hlepas 2017).

Following the third Adjustment Program in 2015, as set out in the Multiyear Plan and the Medium-Term Program 2018–21, Greece’s local governments remain nevertheless subject to austerity measures. Provision has been made for a further reduction in transferred resources, and for the freezing of recruitment for two years (2018–2019), while a high surplus is forecast to persist until 2021.

The provisions of the Medium-Term Program 2018–21 regarding transfers from the state coffers to Greece’s local authorities (Section 38 of Law 3986/2011) have been amended, and from 1 January 2018 the total amount of the General Grant, the so-called Central Autonomous Funds (CAF), exceed 3.4 billion euros per year. The previous nominal limit was 5.2 billion euros, so the threshold has been reduced by about 3.5%.

Thus the Central Autonomous Resources transferred by the Central Government to local self-Administrations amounted to 2930 million euros in 2015 and to 3226 million euros in 2016; the entity of such resources to be allocated in 2017 amounts to 3035 million euros and to 3319 million in 2018; municipalities and regional governments are to be allocated the amount of 3469 million euros in both 2020 and 2021. In fact, the 60% cut in pre-crisis transfers to municipalities and regional governments is not seen as an exception but has been legitimated and made permanent.

Furthermore, the Medium-Term Financial Strategy Framework 2018–2021 foresees that the primary surplus of local government will persist from 2018 to 2021 and will be shaped as follows: 469 million euros in 2018, 443 million euros in 2019, 355 million euros in 2020, and 520 million euros in 2021.

The Impact on Municipal Structures and Local Public Services

Reducing Services and Staff

The Kallikrates reform abolished thousands of municipal legal entities, while the new parent municipalities would only be able to maintain a very limited number of public law legal entities and private corporations, following concrete organizational types introduced by law. The following austerity policies have also had a negative impact on local government staffing. In January 2011, 89,111 employees worked for the Greek local government (including the core services and the local agencies operating under public law).[2] After five years of austerity policies, in March 2017 there were 82,702 employees of municipal and regional administrations[3], representing a staff reduction of 7.8%.

The third adjustment program provides for further reductions in local government personnel. The "Medium-Term Financial Strategy Framework 2018–2021" (Article 163 and "Annex"—Chapter A 'Macroeconomic developments')—reveals that a total of 10,221 will be leaving their employment with municipal and regional government during the period 2016–2021, while total recruitment will amount to 6087. This means that the labor force of Greece's local authorities will be further reduced by 4144 people (that is, by approximately 5%).

Pressures in Favor of Privatization

Pressure for the privatization of the two major state-owned public water suppliers and sewerage and wastewater treatment system operators—The Athens Water Supply and Sewerage Company (EYDAP S.A.) and the Thessaloniki Water Supply & Sewerage Company (EYATH S.A.)—but not for that of the smaller water and sewage municipal companies in other Greek cities increased.

Since April 2012, all remaining state-owned shares in EYATH and EYDAP have been transferred to the Hellenic Republic Asset Development Fund (HRADF/TAIPED), the Greek government's privatization fund. The municipalities' association for the Thessaloniki area proposed the establishment of an inter-municipal company to manage water supply and sewage services in the region, while "Initiative 136", a local activist network, campaigned for the acquisition of the company by a Union of Non-Profit Water Cooperatives of the Thessaloniki area, under the name "Citizens' Union for Water", through a fund created by contributions of 136 euros per user-stakeholder. The union submitted an offer that was rejected by HRADF/TAIPED. In 2013, the Economic and Social Council of Greece issued an opinion challenging the privatization of water supply

[2] Data provided by the Central Union of Municipalities and Communes In.gr 26/6/2012 -http://news.in.gr/economy/article/?Aid=1231202207, accessed 30/5/2017.

[3] Data from the Hellenic Republic Human Resources Registry, http://apografi.yap.gov.gr/apografi/2017/View2017, accessed 30/5/2017.

corporations. The January 2015 elections temporarily stalled such developments. The SYRIZA (Coalition of Radical Left) government undertook "[...] to support private investment that can play a key role in the productive reconstruction of the country [but] not to sell off networks and infrastructure that are the country's national capital". However, the financial and economic dependence of the country on institutional loan contracts leaves little room for non-compliance with the conditions imposed by lenders. As the SYRIZA government has had to adapt to reality, HRADF/TAIPED is currently preparing the further privatization of both public companies by selling those EYDAP and EYATH shares it holds.

Concerning waste management, the "Kallikrates" reform plan requires the establishment of a single Solid Waste Management Agency (FODSA) per region, as an inter-municipal public law association replacing all existing district agencies. Besides the creation of these inter-municipal bodies, the central government has promoted the involvement of private funds in integrated waste management through the institution of 25-year Public/Private Partnership (PPP) contracts. The shortage of funding for the implementation of such complicated and expensive projects encouraged certain local governments to get involved in PPPs. Four regional governments and six municipalities participate. Originally opposing these schemes, SYRIZA made a U-turn after coming into power. and now SYRIZA's appointed Minister declares that "ideological obstacles should be removed in order to proceed with PPPs".[4]

Increased Needs and Scarce Resources for Local Social Policy

The sovereign debt crisis pushing unemployment up to 23.5%[5] and driving 250,000 small and medium-sized businesses into bankruptcy,[6] has provoked a humanitarian emergency situation. In order to deal with this crisis, local governments have had to organize a wide range of services targeting those social groups affected. Social grocery stores, public dispensaries and pharmacies, free supportive classes for low-income students, and so on are on the increase nationwide, while about 20% of the staff involved, such as doctors, teachers, pharmacists and administrative personnel, are volunteers.

[4] Tharros Daily Kalamata, https://goo.gl/nTBFOL, accessed 5/6/2107.

[5] According to Eurostat data, CNN.gr, 2/5/2017 http://www.cnn.gr/oikonomia/story/78998/statheri-i-anergia-stin-ellada-ton-ianoyario-toy-2017, accessed 30/5/17.

[6] According to data released by the Hellenic Confederation of Professionals, Craftsmen & Merchants (GSEVEE), Newmoney.gr 31/5/2016 http://www.newmoney.gr/palmos-oikonomias/286432-gsebee-%C2%ABlouketo%C2%BB-se-250-000-mikromesaies-epixeiriseis-logo-krisis, accessed 30/5/17.

In endeavoring to bridge the significant gaps in the public funding of municipal activities, and to counter substantial staff reductions, local governments have resorted to social economy tools and substantial European funding. Whereas the social economy sector has always been very weak in Greece, an innovative legal framework was introduced in 2011, and subsequently modified in 2016, designed to boost social entrepreneurship and align the country with European best practices in the field. Even though municipalities and municipal corporations are not allowed to participate in social enterprises, they can nevertheless support them by subsidizing their activities, by granting them the use of premises and other assets, and by stipulating programmatic agreements with them for the direct purchase of goods or services without the constraints of the rules governing competitive tendering procedures. Consequently, a significant number of municipalities have lent their support to the creation of social enterprises within their constituencies and have assigned the delivery of a wide range of services to them, through programmatic agreements. About 10% of the over 500 social enterprises established following the introduction of the new legal framework (European Commission 2014) are closely related to local government activities. More than 1000 social enterprises are currently operating in Greece. This expansive tendency of local government toward social entrepreneurship has been met by a strong negative reaction from both political and institutional actors who consider it to be either an instrument of indirect privatization or a means of consolidating clientelistic practices. Left-wing parties consider the involvement of social enterprises in local policy-making as the "Trojan Horse" of privatization. Municipal employees' unions see it as a means of cutting staff numbers within local government. In fact, the main reason why local governments are outsourcing services to social enterprises is the drastic staff cutbacks made in the municipal core services as a result of austerity measures. On the other hand, the Court of Auditors has not authorized contract payments to social enterprises, judging that the delegation of core municipal competencies such as waste and social services exceeds the legal limits. The General Inspector of Greece's Public Administration has similarly adopted a restrictive interpretation of the right of municipalities to conclude programmatic agreements with social enterprises (Tsekos and Triantafyllopoulou 2016).

Conclusions

Although Greek local government is part of a strongly centralized political-administrative system, it has gradually acquired greater autonomy, as well as operational capacity and flexibility, especially under the Socialist governments in power from the 1980s onwards.

This trend was evident in the broadening of municipalities' responsibilities, their amalgamation for greater operational capacity through the Kapodistrias Program, and their ability to create legal entities (quasi-independent agencies) in order to provide local services in a more flexible manner.

From the mid-1990s onwards, under the influence of European policies aiming at strengthening the market and competitive principles and rules, this trend began to be reversed. European policies imposed the gradual opening of local services to the market. One instrument employed for this purpose was the conversion of municipal legal entities into SAs (public limited companies). The reaction of the Greek political-administrative system to these external pressures was to establish SAs in which the majority of shares remained under public control. In this way, while New Public Management principles were formally applied following the requirements of the European Union, their adaptation to Greece's administrative reality was used by central and local players to strengthen their own hand in the political game.

In this case, ideas apparently play a crucial role, albeit concealing collective actors and their ploys and strategies. The dominant ideas defining rational policy-making and efficient design and implementation methods represent the main instruments guiding reforms. EU policies promoting markets and competition were institutionally imposed on Greece by the EC; such policies had become a dominant feature of the EC in the 1980s and '90s. Insofar as such reforms were affecting the interests of national and local elites, as well as a broad range of social benefits, habits and practices, strategies were formulated to neutralize their negative impact. A key method for the implementation of these strategies was that of their formal adaptation and substantive divergence: in other words, the expected mechanisms and procedures were put in place, but they were used in a distorted manner in order to promote specific interests, rather than controlling and curbing them.

The sovereign debt crisis, which first emerged in 2010, has fundamentally changed the rules of the game. External players, that is, lenders and the "Troika" (the EC, ECB and IMF, recently joined by the ESM to form a "quartet"), have now a clearer plan for implementation of the agreements that goes beyond the general promotion of competitive rules, and they no longer see the modernization of central and local administrations as a means with which to downsize the public sector and boost the market. The goal now is to immediately reduce public spending and create the necessary conditions to keep it at a lower level in the future, so as not to see Greece's public debt rise once again.

From the lenders' perspective, local government was another area of increased public spending. Austerity policies, in addition to reducing those state grants and imposing restrictive financial management measures, also included staff reductions and a privatization program. On the eve of the bailout agreement domestic political system has already launched a new wave of amalgamations through the Kallikrates program. Lenders adopted this program and linked it with specific quantitative targets regarding savings of public resources.

Although Greece's local governments' debts were not particularly high, certain large municipalities were in fact over-indebted, and this permitted the creation of a series of financial mechanisms for the management of existing debt and for the avoidance of future debt.

Local governments, under pressure from the crisis, had to deliver a multitude of social services with reduced resources and staff. To achieve this, they had to take advantage of new legislation on the social economy and volunteer programs. However, while on the one hand these are not key instruments for efficient public policy-making, on the other hand accusations were made that these means were being used by mayors for their own clientelistic purposes. At the same time, local government workers unions opposed these policies, arguing that they are indirect ways of pushing through privatization.

Faced with this situation, local actors adopted a series of strategies to cope with the pressure of austerity on their specific interests. So, one main assumption is that under such circumstances, unitary, top-down austerity policies in Greece (and other countries with similar backgrounds) are unsustainable in the long run, since they disregard local contexts and locally prevailing perceptions, actor groupings and power games.

In view of the long-term trends and recent developments, we have reached the following conclusions.

Under the specific conditions of the sovereign debt crisis, the transfer of austerity policies and the reforms that complement them, takes place within a specific context, insofar as national and local resistance is weakened by the country's dependence on foreign funding. Contrary to policy transfers observed under "normal" (non-crisis) conditions, when the core instruments are to be found in the field of dominant ideas (e.g. the transfer of New Public Management models in the 1990s), during a bailout period financial pressures become the main instrument of policy transfer. The mechanism is a simple one: the funding of the indebted country is accompanied by the demand for structural reforms (conditionalities) (Spanou 2016), the implementation of which is managed as a large-scale project. Evaluation mechanisms and procedures are put in place, and implementation milestones are introduced, including the specific content of laws and deadlines for their parliamentary approval, the establishment of new agencies and control procedures, and so on. Such details are part of the lending agreement, in the form of MoUs. Payment of financial aid instalments strictly depends on the lenders' positive evaluation of the progress of reforms. The indebted country thus has to proceed with reforms while constantly threatened by a lack of funds necessary for payment of amortization and other urgent expenses.

In some cases, such as the general management of public finances, reforms are chiefly engineered at the international level and imposed directly on the policy field, while the national government sees its substantive decision-making powers curtailed. In other cases, only quantified targets for cutbacks are agreed, meaning that the national government is free to decide which forms of spending it will try to curtail. This latter category has been gradually limited, and the options of local elites restricted, insofar as the solutions they have proposed have proven largely unsuccessful from a financial perspective.

Consequently, the criteria used to establish the areas of cuts and to guide reforms, vary significantly. Several such criteria derive directly from the urgent need for a substantial, immediate, sustainable reduction in public spending. Other criteria derive from the ideological positions and priorities of lenders. Finally, a few of them are established through national and local bargaining processes: such processes involve powerful individual and group interests, which pressure the government or even try to find ways of communicating with the representatives of the lenders, so as to promote their chosen solutions, meaning those solutions that limit their own losses.

What ultimately result from austerity are reform policies of varying shapes and sizes, which are thus of restricted consistency and, consequently, of limited effectiveness.

References

ADEDY – Confederation of Public Servants. (2014). *Survey on the Impacts of the Crisis on Financial Situation, Human Resources and Public Goods in Local Government* [in Greek]. Athens: Koinoniko Polykentro.

Cohen, S., & Hlepas, N. (2017). Financial Resilience of Greek Local Governments. In I. Steccolini, M. Jones, & I. Saliterer (Eds.), *Governmental Financial Resilience* (pp. 135–152). Bingley: Emerald Publishing Limited. Published Online: 31 May 2017.

DEXIA. (2008). *Sub-National Governments in the European Union. Organisation, Responsibilities and Finance*. La Defence: Dexia Editions.

DEXIA. (2011). *Sub-National Public Finance in the European Union*. La Defence: Dexia Editions.

European Commission. (2014). *European Economy. The Fourth Economic Adjustment Program for Greece*. Fourth Review Occasional Papers 192. Luxembourg: Publications Office of the European Union.

European Commission, Directorate-General for Economic and Financial Affairs. (2010). *The Economic Adjustment Programme for Greece*, European Economy Occasional Papers, No. 61. http://ec.europa.eu/economy_finance/publications/occasional_paper/2010/op61_en.htm. Accessed 4 June 2017.

European Commission, Directorate-General for Economic and Financial Affairs. (2012). *The Second Economic Adjustment Programme for Greece*, Occasional Papers, No. 94. http://ec.europa.eu/economy_finance/publications/occasional_paper/2012/op94_en.htm. Accessed 4 June 2017.

European Court of Auditors. (2015). *Special Report. More attention to results needed to improve the delivery of technical assistance to Greece*. Publications Office of the European Union, 19, p. 60.

Featherstone, K., & Papadimitriou, D. (2013). The Emperor Has No Clothes! Power and Resources within the Greek Core Executive. *Governance, 26*(3), 523–545.

Hlepas, N. (2010). Incomplete Greek Territorial Consolidation: From the First (1998) to the Second (2008–09) Wave of Reforms. *Local Government Studies, 36*(2), 223–249.

Hlepas, N. (2012). Local Government in Greece. In A.-M. Moreno (Ed.), *Local Government in the Member States of the European Union: A Comparative Legal Perspective* (pp. 257–281). Madrid: Instituto Nacional de Administracion Publica.

Hlepas, N. (2016). Is It the Twilight of Decentralization? Testing the Limits of Functional Reforms in the Era of Austerity. *International Review of Administrative Science, 82*, 273–290.

Hlepas, N., & Getimis, P. (2011). Greece: A Case of Fragmented Centralism and 'Behind the Scenes' Localism. In J. Loughlin, F. Hendriks, & A. Lidstrom

(Eds.), *The Oxford Handbook of Local and Regional Democracy in Europe* (pp. 410–432). Oxford: Oxford University Press.

Ladi, S. (2014). Austerity Politics and Administrative Reform: The Eurozone Crisis and Its Impact Upon Greek Public Administration. *Comparative European Politics, 12*, 184–208.

Makridimitris, A., & Michalopoulos, N. (Eds.). (2000). *Experts' Reports on Public Administration – 1950–1998*. Athens: Papazisis. (in Greek).

Ministry of Finance. (2012). *Mid-term Framework for Fiscal Strategy 2013–2016*. Athens: National Printing House. (in Greek).

Pagoulatos, G., & Triantopoulos, C. (2009). The Return of the Greek Patient: Greece and the 2008 Global Financial Crisis. *South European Society and Politics, 14*(1), 35–54.

Pierson, P. (2000). Increasing Returns, Path Dependence, and the Study of Politics. *The American Political Science Review, 94*(2), 251–267.

Roscini, D., Shlefer, J., & Dimitriou, K. (2011). *The Greek Crisis: Tragedy or Opportunity?* (pp. 1–36). Boston: Harvard Business School.

Sotiropoulos, D. (2004). Southern European Public Bureaucracies in Comparative Perspective. *West European Politics, 27*(3), 405–422.

Spanou, C. (2008). State Reform in Greece: Responding to Old and New Challenges. *International Journal of Public Sector Management, 21*(2), 150–173.

Spanou, C. (2016). Policy Conditionality, Structural Adjustment and the Domestic Policy System. Conceptual Framework and Research Agenda. *Robert Schuman Centre for Advanced Studies, RSCAS 2016/60*.

Stolzenberg, P., Terizakis, G., Hlepas, N., & Getimis, P. (2016). *Cities in Times of Crisis. Fiscal Consolidation in Germany and Greece*. Baden-Baden: Nomos Verlagsgesellschaft.

Tsekos, T. N. (2013). Structural, Functional and Cultural Aspects of the Greek Public Administration and Their Effects on Public Employees' Collective Action. *Comparative Labor Law & Policy Journal, 34*(2), 457–477.

Tsekos, T. (2015). Structural Changes and Administrative Reform. In N. Georgarakis & N. Demertzis (Eds.), *The Political Portrait of Greece. Crisis and the Deconstruction of the Political* (pp. 359–377). Athens: Gutenberg Publications, National Center of Social Research (in Greek).

Tsekos, T. N., & Triantafyllopoulou, A. (2016). From Municipal Socialism to the Sovereign Debt Crisis: Local Services in Greece 1980–2015. In H. Wollmann, I. Koprić, & G. Marcou (Eds.), *Public and Social Services in Europe* (pp. 135–149). Basingstoke: Palgrave Macmillan.

CHAPTER 4

The Biggest Loser? Local Public Services Under Austerity Measures in Portugal

Patrícia Silva and Filipe Teles

Introduction

The problems of national debt and the Eurozone crisis plunged several nations into recessions. The financial crisis of 2007 and the subsequent sovereign debt crises put Portugal at the centre of a borrowing cost upward spiral. Given the ever-increasing borrowing costs and the plea to the European Union (EU), the European Central Bank, and the International Monetary Fund (IMF) for financial support meant that Portugal would embark on a narrative of austerity, implementing wide-ranging fiscal consolidation measures to reduce public spending.

This drift towards increasingly restrictive adjustment programmes hit particularly hard the Portuguese local government, where the economic downturn has acted as a catalyst for (long-awaited) structural reforms (Teles 2014). Because the debt among Portuguese municipalities grew steadily through European financial crisis, Portuguese municipalities faced severe conditionalities that tested a fragile and relatively new system of

P. Silva (✉) • F. Teles
Research Unit in Governance, Competitiveness and Public Policies (GOVCOPP), University of Aveiro, Aveiro, Portugal
e-mail: patriciasilva@ua.pt; filipe.teles@ua.pt

A. Lippi, T. N. Tsekos (eds.), *Local Public Services in Times of Austerity across Mediterranean Europe*, Governance and Public Management, https://doi.org/10.1007/978-3-319-76225-8_4

local democratic government. In order to face unprecedented budget reductions, municipalities were forced to accept an increase of the central supervision and control tools over their activities, as a condition for receiving loans from central government. In a sense, then, Portugal was pressured by European institutions to adopt measures of reform, which severely undermined local governments' achievements of previous decades.

Notwithstanding, it can hardly be posited that austerity measures imposed on Portuguese local governments were designed and demanded by supranational institutions. Indeed, while induced by external agents, Portuguese government had some room of manoeuvre and was able to adjust the reforms. This adjustment did not necessarily translate into more compromises with local government.

In parallel, the economic downturn amplified the demand for local public services in the face of high unemployment. These distinct features seem to depict the Portuguese local public services as the biggest loser of the austerity narrative. However, the precise extent of austerity measures on local public services is yet to be fully assessed.

Within this backdrop, this chapter seeks to identify the specific measures implemented and to test the impact of austerity measures on local public services in Portugal. It does so by empirically analysing the scale, nature and distribution of the cuts and the extent to which it has ensured the provision of local public services. The chapter draws on data from municipal budgets before and after the financial crisis, across different policy areas to assess how different local public services were affected by the politics of fiscal consolidation.

This chapter is structured as follows. The first section seeks to present the Portuguese scenario, by describing the macroeconomic situation before the bailout. It also presents the main traits of the Portuguese local government. The second section seeks to present the main policy options regarding the reforms of local government and to assess the actors supporting or opposing such reforms. Three main threads of reform are presented: the financial retrenchment, the organization of the territory and the reduction of local government enterprises. This section also seeks to discuss the impacts of these strands of reform.

Overall, the Portuguese case illustrates how local government reforms were enforced under the shadow of the European financial crises. As the major political parties in central government are the most electorally vulnerable to austerity measures, they presented the reforms as the "only game in town", and where national governments would have limited control over agenda-setting. This enabled the enactment of long-awaited structural reforms that would narrow the financial and managerial autonomy of local governments. While the provision of local public services was not unaffected, the tight schedule for the implementation of reforms reduced the possibility of engaging with citizens and local representatives, reducing an important source of legitimacy of local government.

The Scenario: Defying Local Government

Portugal was one of the EU countries most severely affected by the economic and financial crisis. Indeed, its highly fragile structural position and the unsustainability of public finances can be traced back to long before the Euro area crises, when it was already running a high fiscal deficit of 3 percent of gross domestic product (GDP) and with a deficit that reached over 11 percent of GDP in 2010. The economy was shrinking steadily since 2008, with GDP growth rates of 0.2 percent in 2008 and of −3.0 percent in 2009, reaching a fall to −4.0 in 2012 (Eurostat 2017). This downturn slowed down in 2013, although not sufficiently to generate yearly growth.

With this scenario, Portuguese government reached out for assistance in the form of strengthened cooperation between the IMF, the European Commission and the European Central Bank, dubbed the "Troika" in 2011. The bailout package was formally requested in April 2011, following the resignation of the prime minister after failing to win parliamentary confidence vote for the fourth and most severe package of austerity measures put forward by the minority government in less than a year. The Memorandum of Understanding (MoU) was signed on 17 May 2011 and its actual implementation only began in earnest after the 5 June 2011 legislative elections. The centre-right Social Democrats (PSD) led by Pedro Passos Coelho obtained 40.3 percent of the valid vote and sought the support from its usual ally, the Conservative Centrist Democrats-Popular Party (CDS-PP), in order to form a cabinet enjoying majority support in parliament. This coalition government envisaged the bailout agreement as an opportunity to achieve major reforms.

Overall, the MoU envisaged two types of measures: those targeted at fiscal consolidation and those aimed at structural reforms. Fiscal consolidation measures aimed at reducing the deficit to meet the Maastricht criteria of 3 percent of GDP, through hiring and salary freezing, fiscal cutbacks and reduction of expenditures both at central and subnational levels of government. Concerning structural reforms, the memorandum presented a set of far-reaching reforms ranging from the need to increase transparency in public financial management, to modernize tax administration, increase the efficiency of the judiciary and reduce unemployment insurance benefits. Portugal was also expected to "reorganize local government" administration (Governo de Portugal 2011b, p. 2), reducing "management positions and administrative units by at least 15%" (Governo de Portugal 2011b, p. 2).

These hit Portuguese local government particularly hard. Under the aegis of European officials, Portuguese government put into motion a core of reforms for long recognized but always delayed. Indeed, it was the opportunity to deal with the country's degree of centralization and its scale problems (Teles 2014). We proceed with a description of these two traits of Portuguese local government.

Portugal is characterized by a considerable organizational fragmentation. Its stable administrative and territorial organization is composed of a multitude of organizations that manage and control different arenas of public life, operating at different scales and overlapping territories of operation. Since 1976, Portuguese Constitution established three types of local authorities—4.259 civil parishes, 308 municipalities and administrative regions. Administrative regions remain, however, as a mere constitutional feature, since only two levels of governance—central and local government (parishes and municipalities)—exist in the mainland. The administrative regions of Azores and Madeira are the exceptions.

This does not mean that this is not a salient (political) issue. Regionalization has been delayed because the main political parties could not agree on it. In 1995, the Socialist Party advocated in its electoral manifesto the introduction of administrative regions, which would be subject to a referendum. However, while main left-wing parties—socialists and communists—were enthusiastic of regionalization, the right-centre parties—Social Democratic party and the Popular Party—were against the regionalization. Advocates of regionalization envisaged an opportunity to decentralize decision-making processes and increase the efficiency of policy implementation. Parties that opposed regionalization argued that the size of the country would render regions irrelevant, creating instead a new layer of bureaucracy. The regionalization project proposed by António Guterres in the 1998 referendum faced a sound defeat: nearly two-thirds of voters (63.5 percent) rejected it (Baum and Freire 2003, p. 33).

Despite the organizational fragmentation, it should be highlighted that the size of municipalities (in terms of population) is considerably higher than the scenario found across OECD countries (OECD 2008, p. 108). However, the size of municipality contrasts with the very narrow functions performed by Portuguese municipalities, which is reflected in the amount of municipal spending (Swianiewicz 2010, p. 186).

Indeed, concentration and centralization of powers make local government relatively fragile in Portugal—at least compared with most of its European counterparts (De Ceuninck et al. 2010, p. 807; Le Galès 2003). Although local government competences have increased gradually over the past 40 years, their financial means are not extensive, as depicted in Table 4.1. Overall, Portuguese local government revenues represent approximately 6 percent of GDP, which remains considerably below the EU average and Euro area.

The subnational public sector expenditure was also considerably lower in Portugal (7 percent of GDP in 2011) vis-à-vis the average subnational public sector expenditure in the EU (11.8 of the GDP) (Eurostat 2015). The centralization of powers is also reflected in local government debt as percent of the GDP. In 2007, local government debt as percent of the GDP was about 4.2, a percentage that consistently increased until 2011, when the overall debt of municipalities and municipal companies was about 7 percent of Portugal's GDP (Council of Europe 2011). Even though Portuguese public debt problems do not seem to be due to subnational authorities' indebtedness (Council of Europe 2011), the MoU encompassed major territorial and institutional reforms that would reshape the territory, finances and functions of local government. Ultimately, as will be demonstrated in the following sections, reforms ended up in the recentralization of power.

Table 4.1 Local government revenue (% of GDP)

	2004	*2005*	*2006*	*2007*	*2008*	*2009*	*2010*	*2011*	*2012*	*2013*	*2014*	*2015*
EU (28 countries)	10.9	10.8	10.9	10.9	11.1	11.7	11.6	11.4	11.5	11.4	11.3	11.2
Euro area (19 countries)	9.6	9.5	9.6	9.7	9.8	10.5	10.2	10	10.2	10.1	10.1	10
Portugal	6.1	6.1	6.4	6.4	6.5	6.7	6.6	6.7	6.7	6.8	6.4	6.3

Source: Eurostat (2016)

The Biggest Loser: More Functions, Less Money

Portugal's dire economic outlook forced central government to straight-jacket local governments by devising two—apparently contradictory—mechanisms. On the one hand, local governments experienced a significant expansion and diversification of municipal functions, and power has been devolved to intermediate governance arrangements, through intermunicipal associations. On the other hand, local authorities' activities were kept tightly under the radar of central government. As such, the political discourse favouring the decentralization and reinforcement of local autonomy was detached from the concrete outcomes of the multiple reforms made in the local government system.

This section seeks to take forward the story about how local government has tackled austerity. It does so by providing up-to-date national picture of the scale, nature and distribution of the local government's budget cuts currently available.

Triggered by the MoU, the Portuguese Council of Ministers assumed local government reforms as a priority, while "valuing proximity and the efficiency of local government management".[1] As a result, four streams of reforms can be identified with regard to local government, which can be found on the *Green Paper* published in October 2011 (Governo de Portugal 2011a): the reshaping of the administrative map of local government; the reduction of central government grants to municipalities and reduction of local government debt; reduction of the municipality staff by 2 percent in 2012 and 2013 and the implementation of stricter rules regarding the local corporate public sector.

While many of these policy options have been in the political discourse of the two main political parties, these were reinforced by the political compromise taken by the Portuguese government in the context of the economic adjustment programme. Indeed, in the programme of the XIX government there is a clear reference to the impact of the Troika, signalling that the main driver of the proposed local government reform was the need to reduce costs and increase efficiency in public service provision. As will be further detailed below, this might emerge as a rather simplistic picture of the drivers of the reform. In fact, while the financial requirements of the adjustment programmes played an important role, national government had some room of manoeuvre.

[1] See the Resolution of the Council of Ministers 40/2011, 22 September.

Financial Retrenchment

Local government's functions have not ceased to increase. While the legal rules defined in 1977[2] circumscribed local governments' activities into five main areas, subsequent legislation has gradually increased their functions. In 1999, municipalities were charged with responsibilities in the areas of rural and urban equipment; energy; transports; education; culture; sports; health; social action; housing; civil protection; environment, consumer protection; development, spatial planning; municipal policy and external cooperation.[3] More than a decade later, in 2011, municipalities were also charged with the responsibilities previously dealt with by civil governments[4]—that were extinguished as a consequence of the adjustment programme.[5]

Despite this scenario, the economic adjustment programme sought to achieve a considerable annual expenditure reduction through the decline of transfers to local and regional authorities, as depicted in Fig. 4.1. Since 2009, transfers from central government have steadily declined, reaching the lowest point in 2011, when transfers from central government were reduced 5.6 percent when compared to 2010. Overall, transfers were reduced 2.8 percent in 2015 when compared to the amount of transfers in 2008. Although the amount has slightly increased in 2015, it remains well below the amounts transferred in 2008 and 2009.

The analysis of the percentage of variation of government transfers also displays an interesting pattern. Despite the economic downturn, central government transfers tend to increase in the year of local elections (2009

[2] Law number 79/1977, 25 October 1977.

[3] See article 13, Law 159/99, 14 September 1999.

[4] See the Resolution of the Council of Ministers 13/2011, 27 June 2011.

[5] Occasionally, the debate over the competences of local government becomes salient. Over this year of 2017, it is currently being analysed the possibility of transferring more competences to local government. The decentralization of these functions may not emerge as problematic—with all political parties and the municipalities associations (ANMP) and Parishes associations (ANAFRE)—in favour. However, it is being contested the possibility that more competences will not be coupled with more financing. The Prime Minister, António Costa has, nonetheless, posited that government aims to allow municipalities to manage 19 percent of general state revenues (an increase to the 14 percent managed up to now) and an increase of 2.9 percent in terms of transfers to local government. (See "Descentralização. Deputados ouvem cem entidades até julho", In *Jornal de Notícias*, 17 April 2017 [available at http://www.dn.pt/portugal/interior/descentralizacao-deputados-ouvem-cem-entidades-ate-julho-6224416.html].)

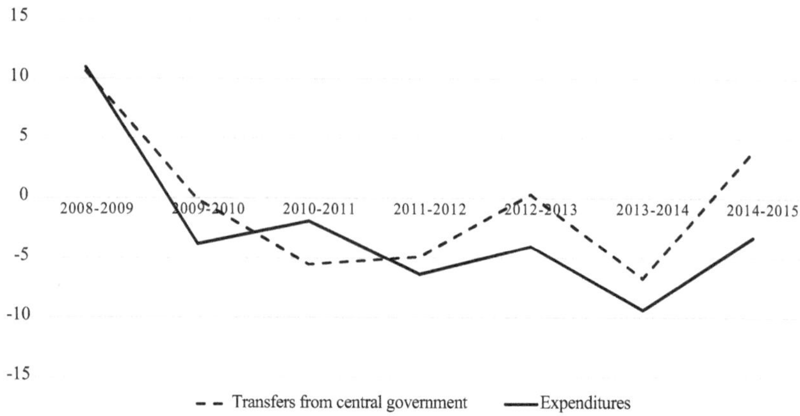

Fig. 4.1 Central government transfers and local government expenditures (% of variation). (Note: Percentage of variation of expenditures excludes expenses yet to be reimbursed. Source: Carvalho et al. 2015)

and 2013), potentially signalling the enduring usage of the electoral cycles to ensure re-election, a pattern already confirmed by others (Magone 2011; Veiga and Veiga 2007).

At the same time, the reimbursed expenses decreased dramatically since 2008, until 2015, in a sharp contrast with the upwards trend to devolve more functions to the local level. The reduction of transfers, coupled with a growing amount of functions and a generalized lack of capabilities and resources, created a constellation of political institutions with really narrow margins of real manoeuvre.

Another sign of recentralization emerges when we analyse the percentage of local revenues from taxes, as it provides an indicator of the degree of subnational control over resources. The protocol agreement under the surveillance of the Troika imposed that Portugal would enact reforms to optimize the revenues of local property taxes (IMI), especially by abolishing the temporary exemptions for owner-occupied dwellings and by changing the valuation methods. Despite these fiscal endeavours, revenues from taxes (including property transactions and the local surtax on companies [*derrama*]) continued to fall steadily until 2014. As Fig. 4.2 demonstrates, transfers compose the major component of local government revenues. Indeed, local government revenues were mainly dependent on transfers, which had a growing importance as a percentage of municipalities' revenues during the adjustment period.

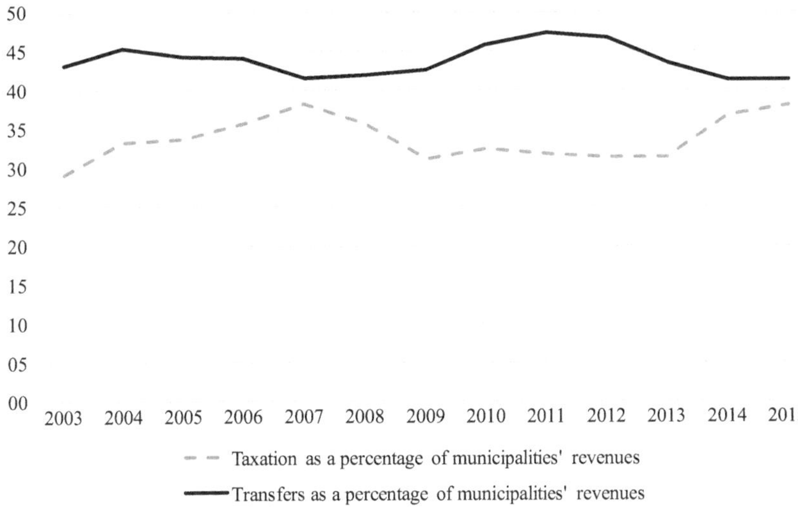

Fig. 4.2 Local government revenues: taxation and transfers (2003–2015). (Source: Authors' compilation, based on municipal budgets available at DGAL [http://www.portalautarquico.pt/pt-PT/dgal/])

As a consequence, municipalities' capacity to deliver public services was constrained. However, not all economic functions were equally affected, as demonstrated in Table 4.2.

As demonstrated, Portuguese local government increased the percentages of expenditures in the areas of education and social protection, signalling the buffering effect of local government. While local government in Europe also acted as a shock absorber in the area of social protection, expenses in the area of education reduced 0.8 percent, contrarily to the pattern in Portugal, where it registered an increase of 3.3 percent. The demand for local public services in the face of the drastic reforms implemented in employment protection and unemployment benefits is evident in the significant increase of expenditures in the area of social protection and, to a smaller extent, in health. While social-related economic functions registered an increase in expenditures, all other arenas experienced substantial cutbacks, at a higher pace than the average scenario in the EU.

Despite these cuts, pressure on local governments to deliver public services impelled local governments to seek other sources of revenues, resorting to loans, often beyond their financial capacities. However,

Table 4.2 Subnational government expenditure by economic function (as % of expenditure)

		Portugal	*% variation 2012–2007*	*EU-27*	*% variation 2012–2007*
Education	2007	8.3	3.3	20.8	−0.8
	2009	9.7		20.8	
	2012	11.6		20.0	
Social protection	2007	2.6	4.4	19.0	1.2
	2009	6.4		19.5	
	2012	7.0		20.2	
General services	2007	35.0	−2.9	15.7	1.4
	2009	31.7		15.9	
	2012	32.1		17.1	
Health	2007	5.5	0.4	12.9	0
	2009	5.3		13.1	
	2012	5.9		12.9	
Economic affairs	2007	19.2	−2.3	12.0	−0.7
	2009	19.0		11.8	
	2012	16.9		11.3	
Other	2007	29.3	−2.8	19.6	−1.2
	2009	28.0		18.8	
	2012	26.5		18.4	

Sources: Data for 2007 (CCRE-CEMR/Dexia 2010); data for 2009 (CCRE-CEMR/Dexia 2012); data for 2012 (OECD 2015)

Table 4.3 Subnational debt

	% of GDP		*% public debt*	
	Portugal	*EU-28*	*Portugal*	*EU-28*
2007	3.8	10.1	5.7	16.4
2009	5.6	12.2	6.0	15.2
2012	8.3	15.9	5.9	15.9

Sources: Data for 2007 (CCRE-CEMR/Dexia 2010); data for 2009 (CCRE-CEMR/Dexia 2012); data for 2012 (OECD 2015)

despite the decreasing tendencies in terms of transfers and the increases in the aforementioned areas, local governments were able to sustain subnational debt (see Table 4.3). This is, at least partially, the result of the Local Economy Support Programme to reduce local governments' debts to suppliers.

In order to maintain the fiscal discipline and economic stability, decision makers decided to implement legal rules to limit the possibility of indebtedness, with the approval of the Local Finances Law and Regional Finances Law (both approved in 2013). The laws also strengthened net debt ceilings and borrowing constraints for municipalities. Adjustment or restructuring plans for over-indebted municipalities were also created to provide assistance to distressed municipalities. In 2012, government approved the Local Economy Support Programme (PAEL).[6] This Programme consisted of a credit line to help municipalities reduce their debts. These initiatives were a success, since they restrained the rise in municipalities' indebtedness. Indeed, in 2013, subnational government debt was lower than the EU-28 average (15.9 percent of GDP and 15.9 percent of public debt).

It should not, however, be disregarded the fact that these measures reduced municipalities' autonomy (Ladner 2017, p. 51). The 112 municipalities assisted under the PAEL programme were forced to increase to the maximum all municipal fees and taxes limiting their financial autonomy (Silva and Buček 2016, p. 17).

Portuguese central government might have had significant room of manoeuvre in defining these initiatives to help municipalities. Indeed, in 2015, the former Deputy Minister and Minister for Parliamentary Affairs, Miguel Relvas, revealed that the Toika wanted indebted municipalities to declare bankruptcy, a solution also favoured by certain members of government (Relvas and Júlio 2015). However, such a solution would potentially negatively impact on the overall financial system,[7] pushing central government towards a different approach.

It should be highlighted that measures of centralization analysed up to this point can only provide a limited picture of the impact of reforms in local government autonomy. Actually, a relatively wide set of governmental decisions contributed to the concentration drift in central–local relationship. For example, municipalities were not involved in the definition of policy measures that would have an impact at the local level presented in the MoU (as the redefinition of the judiciary map, and the "definition of the new EU funding framework ('Portugal 2020') without appropriate negotiation with the municipalities" [Silva and Buček 2016, p. 18]).

[6] Law 43/2012, 28 August.

[7] See "Situação da banca condicionou políticas para as autarquias, revela Poiares Maduro", *In Eco-Economia Online*, 10 April 2017 (available at https://eco.pt/entrevista/situacao-da-banca-condicionou-politicas-para-as-autarquias-revela-poiares-maduro/).

Table 4.4 Transfers to non-profit organizations, as % of local government expenditures (2010–2015)

Year	*% of transfers*
2010	3.0
2011	2.9
2012	2.7
2013	2.8
2014	2.9
2015	3.1

Source: Authors' compilation, based on municipal budgets available at DGAL (http://www.portalautarquico.pt/pt-PT/dgal/)

This necessarily impacted on local governments' capacity to deliver public services. It is yet to be fully assessed the extent to which Portuguese local governments turned to newly emerging forms of social welfare delivery (Lowndes and McCaughie 2013), namely, through the involvement of third sector organizations. In fact, policy makers across Europe have increasingly turned to organizations between the market and the state in seeking to identify, manage or solve a range of economic, social and political problems (Kendall 2009; Somerville and Haines 2008).

Local government transfers to non-profit organizations can be assumed as an indicator of the extent to which municipalities relied on forms of organization and interactions to address societal needs in the area of welfare. Data regarding transfers to non-profit organizations as a percentage of the overall local government expenditures are only available from 2010 onwards, as depicted in Table 4.4.

Results suggest a U-shaped pattern of transfers, with transfers declining in the immediate aftermath of the bailout and throughout the years when local government reforms were enacted (2010 until 2013). In the latter years, this percentage has been rising. In 2015, 3.1 percent of local government total expenditures were transferred to non-profit organizations.

The Organization of the Territory

The sub-municipal landscape has changed radically since the 2008 financial crisis. The MoU recommended that Portuguese government should implement a local government reform as a strategy to "enhance service delivery, improve efficiency, and reduce costs" (Relvas and Júlio 2015;

Tavares and Rodrigues 2015; Teles 2014). The excessive fragmentation of Portuguese local government was considered to undermine efficiency and preclude scale economies (Tavares and Rodrigues 2015). Although the MoU assumed the need to reduce the fragmentation at the local level, it did not specify which institutions should be reorganized/reduced. Troika's demands to reorganize local government administration were translated into a programme aimed at the fusion and extinction of civil parishes (the lowest level of local government).[8] These are highly dependent on central government transfers, which are based on a fixed formula. However, municipal grants to parishes can be more flexible and the result of discretionary power by municipal governments (Tavares and Rodrigues 2015).

The European momentum was the window of opportunity to accomplish a long-awaited structural reform. Indeed, in 2006, the Socialist Government, headed by José Sócrates, prepared a Framework Law for the Creation of Local Authorities (Lei-Quadro de Criação de Autarquias Locais), and the issue of merging civil parishes was already present.[9] Moreover, all major political parties—PS and PSD—presented the need to promote this structural reform in their 2009 electoral manifestos.[10]

This territorial reform was highly contested. Indeed, the plan to reduce 1.165 parishes, out of the existing 4.259, was the responsibility of the PSD/CDS government, which set the criteria for the closure/elimination of parish councils. Despite the several attempts to initiate dialogue with ANAFRE (National Association of Parish Councils) and ANMP (National Association of Municipalities), a consensus was never reached.[11] Whereas

[8] See Law 22/2012, 30 May, which approves the Legal Framework of Administrative Territorial Reorganization, and the Law 11-A/2013, 28 January, that fulfils the obligation of the administrative reorganization of parishes, contained in Law 22/2012.

[9] See "Governo pretende reorganizar freguesias sem mexer nos concelhos", in *Público*, 11 February 2006 (available at https://www.publico.pt/2006/02/11/politica/noticia/governo-pretende-reorganizar-freguesias-sem-mexer-nos-concelhos-1247568).

[10] The Socialist Party defended the territorial reorganization of parishes, promoting the association of parishes, especially in urban areas and low-density regions, and suggested the need to create a new legal regime pertaining the creation, fusion and extinction of local authorities, given the new scales of local intervention (Partido Socialista 2009, p. 92). The Social Democratic Party stressed the need to reinforce network collaboration between parishes (Partido Social Democrata 2009, p. 31).

[11] ANAFRE organized a major rally against the aggregation of parishes in April 2012 (see "Milhares de autarcas e populares contra fusão de freguesias", in *Jornal de Notícias*, 30 March 2012 [available at http://www.jn.pt/sociedade/interior/milhares-de-autarcas-e-populares-contra-fusao-de-freguesias-2395289.html]), and the Platform Against the Extinction of Parishes

government was focused on establishing the criteria for the elimination of parishes, these associations stressed the need to ensure local deliberation among the various municipalities. While the 2011 Green Paper reform suggested the need to ensure significant consultation with local authorities, the tight schedule defined for this reform hampered such an approach. The inability was regarded as a top-down imposed reform that would undermine the subsidiarity principle and promote identity conflicts between amalgamated civil parishes (Teles 2014, p. 9). This perception would reinforce disengagement and protest that could further undermine the success of the reform process, as it tends to occur with top-down reforms (Copus 2010; De Ceuninck et al. 2010); all opposition parties voted against the law 11-A/2013.[12] Local government and civil society also urged against this reform and boycotted local elections in 2013—the first elections after the reform.[13]

In order to overcome resistances, government asked municipalities to propose the aggregation of their sub-municipal units, offering as a reward a 15 percent increase in transfers to the parish created by aggregation.[14] If they did not comply with the criteria defined in the legislation, these aggregations would be legally imposed. Of the 308 municipalities, 151 did not suggest any aggregation (Gato 2015). Occasionally, even when municipalities suggested an aggregation plan, aggregation was enforced.[15]

Despite the general discontent, the reform was enacted, always framed as an obligation under the MoU. This was not uncontested, though. The President of ANAFRE posited, after a meeting with the Troika, that the group never demanded such a reform (Silva 2014a), raising increasing concerns as to the extent to which government would be using the MoU to avoid blame for this reform—a pattern that is not uncommon when governments want to avoid the electoral consequences of unpopular mea-

also organized several manifestations (see "Extinção de freguesias discutida no Parlamento sob protesto" in *Público*, 6 December 2012 [available at https://www.publico.pt/2012/12/06/portugal/noticia/extincao-de-freguesias-discutida-no-parlamento-sob-protesto-1576322]).

[12] https://www.parlamento.pt/ActividadeParlamentar/Paginas/DetalheIniciativa.aspx?BID=37360

[13] There were two boycotts in aggregated parishes in 2013.

[14] See article 10° of Law 22/2012, 30 May.

[15] During the consultation period, municipalities were given the opportunity to suggest the aggregation of corresponding parishes. For example, Tavira's municipal assembly ruled in favour of keeping all of its parish councils. However, the Technical Unit for the Reorganization of Local Administration (UTRAT) decided for three mergers, bringing the number of parish councils in Tavira from 12 to 6.

sures. On the opposite spectrum, Miguel Relvas admitted in parliament that the reduction of parishes was subject to intense negotiations with the Troika, since it was Troika's intention to "extinguish half of municipalities and two thirds of civil parishes".[16]

The results, however, are yet to be fully assessed. It has been estimated that 80 percent of civil parishes that were aggregated did not manage to reduce their expenses. Only 20 percent posited that expenses were reduced,[17] resulting in annual savings of €6.5 millions,[18] a saving the opposition describes as "insignificant". Therefore, targeting parish councils is unlikely to have solved the government's public deficit and expenditure problems.

Although the aim of reducing the number of elected local representatives was achieved, the financial impact of such a reduction may be limited. Indeed, representatives are payed according to the number of citizens and the merger of civil parishes certainly increased those estimates.[19] Before this reform, less than 500 local representatives would be reimbursed. Aggregating parishes would, then, require professional politicians necessarily generating a more expensive local-level administration.

Intermunicipal Management

Besides eliminating some of the parishes, the reform sought to strengthen the competencies and financial resources of the 23 "intermunicipal communities" and two metropolitan areas of *Lisbon* and *Porto*.

These were not newly created institutions. Indeed, the associations of municipalities were first established by António Guterres in 1999.[20] When Durão Barroso headed a PSD/CDS coalition government, stronger and

[16] See "Redução de freguesias entre as mais contestadas reformas exigidas pela 'troika'", in *Sol*, 2 May 2014 (available at https://sol.sapo.pt/artigo/104701/reducao-de-freguesias-entre-as-mais-contestadas-reformas-exigidas-pela-troika).

[17] See "Fusão de freguesias fez crescer despesa", in *Jornal de Notícias*, 28 February 2017 (available at http://www.jn.pt/nacional/interior/fusao-de-freguesias-fez-crescer-despesa-5694809.html).

[18] See "Extinção de freguesias 'só' gera poupança de 6,5 milhões de euros", in *Expresso*, 15 June 2012 (available at http://expresso.sapo.pt/economia/extincao-de-freguesias-so-gera-poupanca-de-65-milhoes-de-euros=f733038).

[19] According to the law, parishes with more than 10,000 voters or parishes with more than 7000 voters and 100 kms have to be fully payed.

[20] See Law 172/99, 21 September 1999.

wider structures were created, namely, the Great metropolitan areas,[21] which aimed at achieving greater cooperation in larger cities. In the same year, intermunicipal communities were established[22] as a strategy to "overcome the isolationism and individualistic tendencies of Portuguese local authorities" (Magone 2011, p. 404). These voluntary intermunicipal associations could be set up at flexible geographical scales. However, their initial functioning revealed several flaws, as these were considered to be incoherent with the existing administrative, political and territorial organization (Nico 2013). Moreover, the lack of financial and institutional incentives undermined these intermunicipal associative experiments (OECD 2008, p. 20). In 2008, government sought to overcome these limitations and established several incentives to promote intermunicipal cooperation. Municipalities that associated at the Nomenclature of Territorial Units for Statistics (NUTS III) level were given the possibility to collect property taxes, instead of having central government collecting them and re-channelling them (OECD 2008, p. 115). Beyond higher fiscal autonomy, the Portuguese government decided that municipalities that prepared a territorial development plan at the NUTS III level would be given the possibility of managing a global grant from Regional Operational Programmes of the National Strategic Reference Framework (NSRF) following other European counterparts (OECD 2008; Silva et al. 2016). Within this backdrop, although municipalities were free to join these general purpose intermunicipal associations, not doing so would limit their access to the EU funding and restrict their capacity to influence the management of supra-municipal interests (Lopes 2009). As a consequence, all of the 308 Portuguese municipalities are currently engaged in one of the 25 intermunicipal associations.

Portuguese intermunicipal cooperation was, thus, defined within an unfavourable scenario, characterized by Portuguese low stocks of social capital (Teles 2012) and a lack of cooperative experience. Moreover, government enforced a predefined map, instead of promoting flexible boundaries that could enhance the potential synergies already existing. Notwithstanding, recent research has posited that although emerging from a purely instrumental involvement, intermunicipal arrangements have proven to be capable of accomplishing the aims they were initially set to realize. Moreover, results suggest that municipalities tend to be committed to the overall aims of intermunicipal associations and are willing to

[21] Law 10/2003, 10 May 2003.
[22] Law 11/2003, 13 May 2003.

use the partnership outside the scope of the intermunicipal associations. However, results also suggest that intermunicipal associations need to entail considerable efforts to improve the involvement of other local stakeholders, especially, citizens. Indeed, if citizens have a parochial focus, that is, are concerned only with their municipality, they will be potentially more reluctant to understand and accept matters that involve several municipalities. Ultimately, this may undermine their legitimacy (Silva et al. 2018).

Local Government Enterprises

Portuguese local government was not immune to administrative reforms, largely influenced by New Public Management (Rocha and Araújo 2007). The provision of local public services ceased to be circumscribed to local governments. Instead, it was gradually assumed by a highly fragmented public sector, especially by local government enterprises.

These new plethora of institutions attracted much attention from mayors, given the greater flexibility of these new forms of local governance. On the one hand, central government only had a scarce limited number of instruments to monitor the creation of these enterprises. On the other hand, they provided the prospect of avoiding a heavy and burdensome legal procedure that characterizes public administration in Portugal (Tavares and Camões 2010).

As a consequence, the last decades were characterized by a sustained growth of local government enterprise. Teles (2012, p. 689) estimates that “approximately 85 percent of the municipalities invested in public and private corporations” and Tavares and Camões (2010, p. 588) also contend an accelerated growth of the local corporate public sector, from 34 municipal corporations in 1999 to 114 in 2001. It is estimated that from 2000 to 2006, 218 new municipal corporations were created, reaching a local corporate public sector composed of 392 companies in 2009 (Martins et al. 2011).

Yet, significant budget deficits prompted the adoption of severe measures agreed with the IMF/EU. In 2010, the amount of debt of the local corporate public sector was around €1787 millions (Silva 2014a, b). As a consequence, the MoU required an evaluation of the municipal enterprises, the application of more restricted limits on the debt of municipal enterprises and the need to redefine the legal framework regarding the creation and functioning of these enterprises. Stronger control powers by

Table 4.5 Local public enterprise sector (2011–2016)

	Regional enterprises	*Local enterprises*
2011	30	200
2012	30	198
2013	28	183
2014	28	170
2015	26	152
2016	26	133

Source: See PORDATA, the Database of Contemporary Portugal, available at https://www.pordata.pt/en/Portugal/Enterprises+in+the+corporate+public+sector-2994

the central government were also encouraged as well as the suspension of the creation of these organizations.

As a consequence, the 2011 Green Paper reform established the need to rationalize local government enterprises by merging or extinguishing local corporations, especially the ones that presented negative economic results. Also, in 2011, legal rules suspended the creation of public companies.[23]

The consequence was a decline in the number of local companies due to an effort to rationalize expenses and infrastructures, as depicted in Table 4.5. Recent data estimate that local public sector enterprises are composed of 156 enterprises, which has limited the managerial autonomy to provide local public services.

Concluding Remarks

Portuguese local governments had to adjust to dramatic requirements and budget cuts. While assuming more responsibilities, local governments were not only deprived of financial transfers from the central government, but their fiscal and managerial autonomy was also curtailed. These reforms straightjacketed local governments that were obliged to react to budget cuts while struggling to find new ways of guaranteeing citizens' well-being in a context of a high demand of local public services. To some extent, it is safe to say that limited autonomy restrained the potential—and expected countercyclical—role of local government in welfare provision.

[23] See Law 55/2011, 15 November.

Local government reform was a highly salient political issue. Even though Portuguese public debt problems were not primarily driven by subnational authorities' indebtedness, political discourse often stressed that municipalities' debt was unmanageable, as a strategy to enhance public and political acceptance of the severe measures.

At the same time, the lines of accountability have been blurred. It is an unquestionable fact that the European financial crises provided the momentum required to implement strict measures. However, the external inputs left room for internal political dynamics—as was demonstrated by the room of manoeuvre of Portuguese government with regard to the design of measures to assist municipalities in worst financial situations and regarding the territorial reforms. Yet, political parties used discursive strategies of blame avoidance, arguing that certain local government policies were externally imposed as a potential attempt to be hold less accountable for unpopular measures.

These two trends generated protests against the reforms affecting the trust of the people in the political system and in public services in particular. Indeed, the discourse over the excessive debt of Portuguese local government was reflected in the levels of citizens' trust in these institutions. While subnational governments tend to present the greatest and most stable trust across the EU, it was in Portugal (along with Greece and Spain) that the lowest levels of trust in subnational authorities could be found in 2013. Average confidence in local-level authorities for Portugal fell by more than 10 percent between 2008 and 2013 to reach a level of just 32 percent.[24]

Portuguese local government can, thus, be regarded as the biggest loser of the austerity narrative. The provision of local public services was certainly affected by the stringent conditions under which local governments had to operate. Local governments' capacity to rely on co-governance to ensure local public service provision was also limited. Involvement of non-profit organizations was restricted given the need to restrict expenditures; and the changes in the organization of municipal enterprises, with the forced closure of some of them—despite their important social objectives—also limited resorting to new forms of governance.

But the image of local government as the biggest loser of the austerity narrative goes well beyond the stringent financial and managerial aspects

[24] Source: Eurobarometer 79.3, QA12: "Please tell me if you tend to trust it or tend not to trust Regional or local public authorities".

and the associated issues of local public service delivery. It also encompasses questions of legitimacy. Local government is not just concerned with the provision of public services. As the level of government closest to citizens, local governments are crucial to ensure the legitimacy. As Stoker (1998 p. 20) highlights, a "legitimation deficit undermines public support and commitment to programmes of change and ultimately undermines the ability of power-holders to mobilize resources". As we sought to demonstrate, the major reforms were designed and implemented without citizens' involvement or are occurring without citizens' interest. And this is vital for a healthy local government democracy.

References

Baum, M., & Freire, A. (2003). Parties and Territory in Portuguese Politics. In J. J. Bukowski, S. Piattoni, & M. E. Smyrl (Eds.), *Between Europeanization and Local Societies: The Space for Territorial Governance* (pp. 21–46). Lanham: Rowman & Littlefield.

Carvalho, J., Fernandes, M., Camões, P., & Jorge, S. (2015). *Anuário Financeiro dos Municípios Portugueses*. Lisbon: OTOC.

CCRE-CEMR/Dexia. (2010). *EU Sub-national Governments: 2008 Key Figures*. Brussels: Research Unit of Dexia Crédit Local/ Council of European Municipalities and Regions.

CCRE-CEMR/Dexia. (2012). *EU Subnational Governments: 2010 Key Figures*. Brussels. Research Unit of Dexia Crédit Local/ Council of European Municipalities and Regions.

Copus, C. (2010). English Local Government: Neither Local Nor government. In P. Swianiewicz (Ed.), *Territorial Consolidation Reforms in Europe* (pp. 95–128). Budapest: OSI/LGI.

Council of Europe. (2011). *Local Government in Critical Times; Policies for Crisis, Recovery and a Sustainable Future*. Strasbourg: Council of Europe.

De Ceuninck, K., Reynaert, H., Steyvers, K., & Valcke, T. (2010). Municipal Amalgamations in the Low Countries: Same Problems, Different Solutions. *Local Government Studies, 36*(6), 803–822.

Eurostat. (2015). *Government Revenue, Expenditure and Main Aggregates*. Luxembourg: Eurostat.

Eurostat. (2017). *Real GDP Growth Rate – Percentage Change on Previous Year*. Retrieved from http://ec.europa.eu/eurostat/tgm/table.do?tab=table&init=1&plugin=1&language=en&pcode=tec00115

Gato, J. P. (2015). A Reorganização Administrativa do Território no Programa de Assistência Económica e Financeira. In M. de L. Rodrigues & P. A. e Silva (Eds.), *Governar com a Troika: Políticas Públicas em Tempo de Austeridade* (pp. 299–316). Lisbon: Edições Almedina, S.A.

Governo de Portugal. (2011a). Documento Verde da Reforma da Administração Local. Uma Reforma de Gestão, uma Reforma de Território e uma Reforma Política. Gabinete do Ministro-adjunto e dos Assuntos Parlamentares. Available at http://www.portugal.gov.pt/media/132774/doc_verde_ref_adm_local.pdf

Governo de Portugal. (2011b). *Portugal—Memorandum of Understanding on Specific Economic Policy Conditionality*. Available at https://www.imf.org/external/np/loi/2011/prt/051711.pdf

Kendall, J. (2009). Terra Incognita: Third Sectors and European Policy Process. In J. Kendall (Ed.), *Handbook of Third Sector Policy in Europe* (pp. 3–20). Cheltenham: Edward Elgar Publishing.

Ladner, A. (2017). Chapter 1: Autonomy and Austerity: Re-investing in Local Government. In C. Schwab, G. Bouckaert, & S. Kuhlmann (Eds.), *The Future of Local Government in Europe: Lessons from Research and Practice in 31 Countries* (1st ed., pp. 23–52). Baden-Baden: Nomos Verlagsgesellschaft mbH & Co. KG.

Le Galès, P. (2003). The Changing European State: Pressures from Within. In J. Hayward & A. Menon (Eds.), *Governing Europe* (pp. 380–394). Oxford: Oxford University Press.

Lopes, L. (2009). O Regime das Comunidades Intermunicipais: mais um caso exemplar de degradaçao da autonomia municipal. *Revista de Direito Público E Regulaçao, 2*, 9–18.

Lowndes, V., & McCaughie, K. (2013). Weathering the Perfect Storm? Austerity and Institutional Resilience in Local Government. *Policy & Politics, 41*(4), 533–549.

Magone, J. (2011). Portugal: Local Democracy in a Small Centralized Republic. In J. Loughlin, F. Hendriks, & A. Lidström (Eds.), *The Oxford Handbook of Local and Regional Democracy in Europe* (pp. 384–409). Oxford: Oxford University Press.

Martins, M., Silva, A., Alves, A., Ferrão, J., Costa, J., Schmidt, L., Nazaré, M., & Gonçalves, P. (2011). *Livro Branco do Sector Empresarial local.* Lisbon: Instituto Superior de Economia e Gestão – Universidade Técnica de Lisboa. Available at http://mediaserver.rr.pt/NEWRR/LIVRO_BRANCO1006342e.PDF

Nico, R. (2013). *O papel das Comunidades Intermunicipais na descentralização administrativa – O caso da Comunidade Intermunicipal do Médio Tejo.* Lisbon: Instituto Superior de Ciências Sociais e Políticas – Universidade Técnica de Lisboa.

OECD. (2008). *OECD Territorial Reviews OECD Territorial Reviews: Portugal 2008.* Paris: OECD Publishing.

OECD. (2015). *Subnational Governments in OECD Countries: Key Data (Brochure)*. Paris: OECD Publishing.

Partido Social Democrata. (2009). PSD: Compromisso de verdade. Available at http://www.psd.pt/ficheiros/programas_eleitorais/programa-eleitoral-2009.pdf

Partido Socialista. (2009). *Programa de Governo do Partido Socialista: Avançar Portugal 2009–2013.* Lisbon. Available at http://phplist.ps.pt:8080/GabinetedeEstudos/SITE_GEPS/Programas_Eleitorais_PS/2009.27.set_Programa.de.Governo.do.Partido.Socialista_Avancar.Portugal.2009.2013.pdf

Relvas, M., & Júlio, P. (2015). *O Outro Lado da Governação*. Lisboa: Porto Editora.

Rocha, J. O., & Araújo, J. (2007). Administrative Reform in Portugal: Problems and Prospects. *International Review of Administrative Sciences, 73*(4), 583–596.

Silva, M. (2014a). Geografia do controle político-territorial: economia de recursos, agregação de freguesias e reordenamento do território em Portugal. In*XIII Coloquio Internacional de Geocrítica*. Barcelona: Universitat de Barcelona.

Silva, C. (2014b). The Economic Adjustment Programme Impact on Local Government Reform in Portugal. In C. N. Silva & J. Bucek (Eds.), *Fiscal Austerity and Innovation in Local Governance in Europe* (pp. 31–47). London: Routledge.

Silva, C. N., & Buček, J. (2016). Political and Administrative Decentralization in Portugal: Four Decades of Democratic Local Government. In C. N. Silva & J. Buček (Eds.), *Local Government and Urban Governance in Europe* (pp. 9–32). Cham: Springer International Publishing.

Silva, P., Teles, F., & Pires, A. R. (2016). Paving the (Hard) Way for Regional Partnerships: Evidence from Portugal. *Regional & Federal Studies, 26*(4), 449–474.

Silva, P., Ferreira, J., & Teles, F. (2018). Intermunicipal Cooperation in Portugal: The Quest for Governance Capacity? *International Review of Administrative Sciences*. https://doi.org/10.1177/0020852317740411.

Somerville, P., & Haines, N. (2008). Prospects for Local Co-governance. *Local Government Studies, 34*(1), 61–79.

Stoker, G. (1998). Governance as Theory: Five Propositions. *International Social Science Journal, 50*(155), 17–28.

Swianiewicz, P. (2010). If Territorial Fragmentation Is a Problem, Is Amalgamation a Solution? An East European Perspective. *Local Government Studies, 36*(2), 183–203.

Tavares, A., & Camões, P. (2010). New Forms of Local Governance: A Theoretical and Empirical Analysis of Municipal Corporations in Portugal. *Public Management Review, 12*(5), 587–608.

Tavares, A. F., & Rodrigues, M. (2015). The Economic and Political Impacts of Top- Down Territorial Reforms: The Case of Sub-City Governments. *Local Government Studies, 41*(6), 956–976.

Teles, F. (2012). Beyond Paternalism Towards Social Capital: Local Governance Reform in Portugal. *International Journal of Public Administration, 35*(13), 864–872.

Teles, F. (2014). Local Government and the Bailout: Reform Singularities in Portugal. *European Urban and Regional Studies, 23*(3), 455–467.

Veiga, L. G., & Veiga, F. J. (2007). Political Business Cycles at the Municipal Level. *Public Choice, 131*(1–2), 45–64.

CHAPTER 5

Spanish Local Government and the Austerity Plan: In the Eye of the Perfect Storm

Carmen Navarro and Esther Pano

Introduction

The process of decentralisation that took place in Spain between the early 1980s and the beginning of this century saw local governments take on the role of key players in the map of public service providers. The growth in the number of tasks for which they now have responsibility, the increase in local public expenditure and the favourable assessment afforded by citizens of their performance are just some indicators of the positive nature of this process (Navarro and Velasco 2016). However, Spain, in common with many of its neighbours in the Mediterranean and Southern Europe, was to suffer the effects of a severe economic crisis that has impacted these earlier achievements. This crisis—or rather crises, including as it did an economic crisis, a banking crisis, a fiscal crisis, a debt crisis and a real estate

C. Navarro (✉)
Department of Political Sciences and International Relations, Autonomous University of Madrid, Madrid, Spain
e-mail: c.navarro@uam.es

E. Pano
University of Barcelona, Barcelona, Spain

A. Lippi, T. N. Tsekos (eds.), *Local Public Services in Times of Austerity across Mediterranean Europe*, Governance and Public Management, https://doi.org/10.1007/978-3-319-76225-8_5

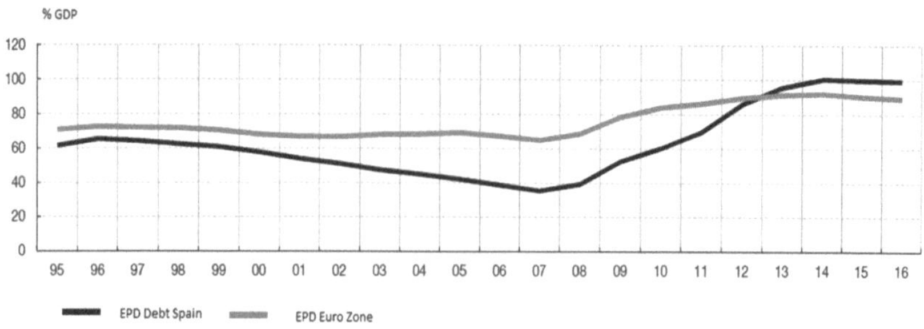

Fig. 5.1 Evolution of excessive deficit procedures (EDP) in Spain and Eurozone (% GDP) (1995–2016). (Source: Delgado et al. 2017. https://www.bde.es/f/webbde/SES/Secciones/Publicaciones/InformesBoletinesRevistas/NotasEconomicas/T2/fich/bene1702-nec6.pdf)

crisis—struck at the very heart of state and public administrations. Yet, in more general terms, most of the attention in this period focused on the evolution of the debt situation. Indeed, for decades the Spanish authorities had managed to keep the indebtedness indicators under control; however, the changes experienced in these few years were to prove dramatic. Figure 5.1 highlights the sharp upturn in excessive deficit procedures (EDP) recorded halfway through 2007 and how this rate had overtaken the Eurozone average by mid-2012.

The measures deemed necessary to respond to the economic problems changed over the years of crisis. The political narrative promoted during the initial phase was to undergo a radical shift in 2010: specifically, the country's local government system, at first considered part of the solution, was subsequently seen to constitute part of the problem. At the outset, the tone and content of the measures launched by President Rodríguez Zapatero's government in 2009 were clearly Keynesian in spirit and included the municipalities as key agents in the implementation of its economic stimulation policies. Indeed, the central government's expenditure programmes took a clearly territorial approach with considerable importance being attached to the municipal level. However, the events of the 2010 debt crisis saw government policy take a U-turn and, progressively, local governments came to be seen as a constituent factor of the crisis. Thus, in this second phase, strict debt controls were introduced as the political discourse underwent a reorientation. The government's new strategy was encapsulated in the local government reforms enacted in 2013. Spain's overcrowded system of local government—with more than

8000 municipalities in addition to provincial governments and submunicipal entities—was considered a source of inadequate fiscal control and of administrative duplicities and redundancies. Although the data show that the municipalities had never been a major source of debt—Fig. 5.2 shows that local debt remained largely stable across the decade—the new discourse proved persuasive and local governments were targeted by the central government and measures were implemented to ensure, supposedly, their efficient operation. Some of these actions were imposed directly while others were designed as adaptive strategies to be formulated and implemented by local government itself.

This chapter examines these actions and seeks to compare the theory underpinning approaches to crisis and the austerity measures with the reality of their implementation.

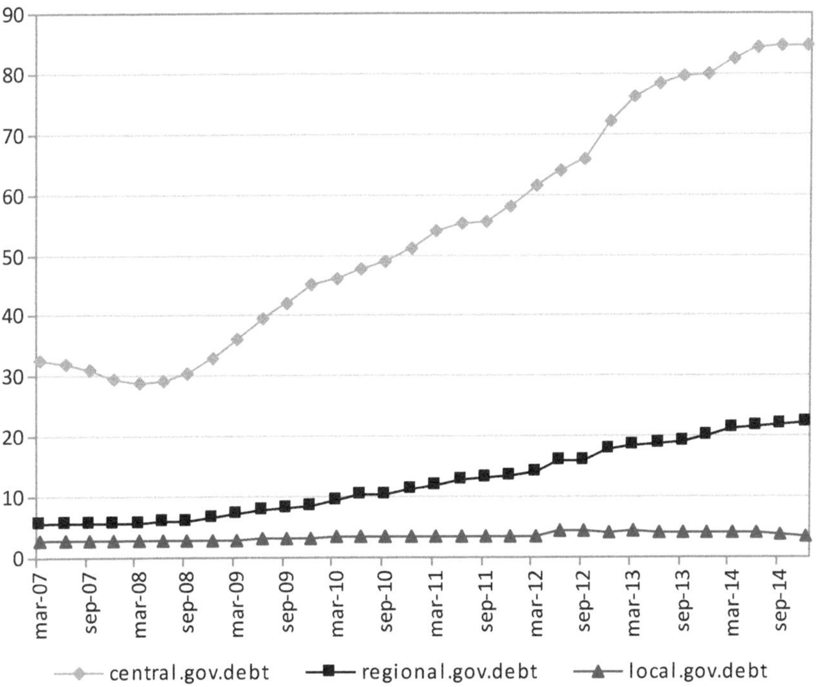

Fig. 5.2 Evolution of public debt by subsector of public administration. (Source: Based on data from the *Banco de España*)

The section that follows examines the positions taken up by the literature in relation to austerity strategies and describes their reported effects. It also presents the main features of the Spanish crisis and of its austerity programmes. The third section in this chapter analyses events at the local tier of government level and the particular profile of actions at the municipal level. In the fourth section, we examine various empirical reports of the impact of austerity measures on the municipalities and their response to them. Finally, we discuss the consequences of this overall process in terms of its impact on local autonomy.

The Austerity Agenda in Spain: From Theory to Practice

Over the last decade, the crisis and the implementation of austerity measures have characterised the agenda of many public institutions, with the corresponding strategies being analysed from a wide range of theoretical approaches. Here, to begin with, it should prove useful to explore what underpinned the crisis and its implications in terms of institutional change. There is no consensus regarding the definition of the term crisis and, indeed, more than one author has considered the concept to be one of the most "underdeveloped" terms in social and political theory (Hay 1999; Orr 2009). Hay (1999, 2013) conceptualises "crisis" as a moment (or a continuity of moments) of decisive intervention in order to redress organisational dysfunctionalities. In the framework of structural transformation and institutional change, Hay (1999) draws a distinction between two ideals of social, political and economic organisation: on the one hand, dynamic and pro-active systems that evolve through reflexive, strategic transformation; and, on the other, inertial and reactive systems that tend to evolve through unreflexive adaptation. Thus, responses to a crisis can be classified specifically according to the mode adopted in confronting the event (Hay 1999):

1. Responses to resolve the failures totally.
2. Responses to solve selective contradictions.
3. Responses that address the crisis as discursively constituted and build a narrative without necessarily resolving the failures.
4. Purely discursive responses.

The four options are associated with different degrees of pressure and, thus, diverse institutional effects. Accordingly, the strategies applied by different levels of government might be different and, in fact, the impacts and reactions may also vary. In the current framework of financial and economic restraints, coping with measures of austerity has become a major issue for governments and managers. The role played by government should be seen from a dual perspective: it has to deal with fiscal stress but it also has to provide solutions, which may include expansionist as well as restrictive policies (Overmans and Noordegraaf 2014).

Many studies highlight the ability of local government to adapt to changing environments, stressing their great resilience (Shaw 2012; Lowndes and McCaughie 2013). According to Overmans and Noordegraaf (2014: 101) responses to austerity are aimed at restoring the balance between income and expenditure. Specifically, they speak of "executive and managerial responses, aimed at restoring the fiscal balance, against the background of increasing demands for [public] services and [political and public] expectations of organisational performance".

Among the various austerity measures, those related to budgeting are especially relevant. The process of public budgeting is, after all, a competitive strategy among different programmes, although it has generally been accepted that there is a tendency to accept the previous year's distribution with just some minor incremental readjustments: "the budgetary process itself appears to push toward incrementalist outcomes, even in economic environments that appear to call for 'rational decrementalism'" (Peters 2010). The sequential and repetitive nature of the process and the technical content of this field affect policy makers by making them conservative and cautious. Any actor wishing to make any significant change from existing patterns has strong incentives to introduce adjustments slowly, an approach that is far more probable than the introduction of sudden shifts (Peters 2010).

As well as these specific responses to the crisis, other authors report that governments tend to centralise their decision-making when faced with a crisis (Peters 2011). They argue that this contributes to creating greater coherence in their responses and helps establish priorities, especially when the policy area falls within the domain of the central executive, as is the case of the economy. Similarly, when faced with a global priority for the public sector, such as guaranteeing trust in sovereign debt, centralisation increases as it is deemed necessary in order to achieve this policy priority.

Therefore, during crisis management, we would expect to see a centralisation of decision-making at the expense of local autonomy.

The experiences of the countries of the Mediterranean and Southern Europe over the last decade provide an interesting context in which to examine these theoretical expectations concerning responses to crisis situations and the introduction of austerity measures. Indeed, the case of Spain is especially interesting given the marked contrast between its initial strategies for facing the economic crisis and its subsequent response based more squarely on European economic policy guidelines. Between 2008 and 2011, few calls were made to restrict the budgetary process (Zapico 2012). On the contrary, the initial reaction of the Spanish government—in 2009—was to draw up an expansionist programme of 25,000 million euros. The programme, known as "Plan E", involved funding projects that were to be carried out by local governments, including small to medium investments in infrastructure and other specific policies such as technological development. Plan E, which was designed to stimulate the economy, was implemented by almost all the municipalities that requested funding. This Keynesian approach, however, came to an end in 2010 due to a set of factors that led to the deterioration of the economic situation. Its curtailment also meant the end of an era of contra-cyclical policies, which opened the door to the tightening of fiscal restrictions and the adoption of a strict discipline aimed at reducing debt. In this shift of approach, the role played by the European institutions was crucial.

In May 2010, the central government adopted a strict economic stability package in close adherence with the criteria laid down by the European economic authorities. This programme sought to cut public debt from 9.2 % of GDP in 2010 to just 3 % by 2013 and incorporated a wide range of measures including, among others, a 5 % reduction in the salaries of civil servants, a pension freeze, general cutbacks in the funding of public administration and the suspension of various projects and investments. Local governments were hit especially hard in this process. In May 2010, it was rumoured that local governments would be prevented from accessing credit and would no longer be allowed to get into debt. After a brief period of confusion—during which many local authorities took steps to overcome an eventual ban—the government finally clarified its position and announced that the measure would come into force on 1 January 2011.

This political U-turn was embodied in the "express" reform of the Spanish Constitution undertaken in the summer of 2011. According to the signatories of this initiative, taken against the backdrop of a severe and prolonged economic crisis, the effects of economic and financial globalisation had become increasingly evident and budgetary stability had acquired a strategic value, conditioning the capacity of the state to act. At the same time, the rules of the Eurozone's Stability and Growth Pact sought to prevent states from running up budget deficits. The reform of Article 135 of the Constitution was therefore an attempt at guaranteeing the principle of budgetary stability by committing all the public sector to a strict rule of no indebtedness. The article, which had originally comprised two sections authorising the government to issue public debt and committing it to include these credits in the public budget, was expanded to include six sections—with many subsections—describing in detail the sector's obligations in terms of economic and budgetary discipline. With its introduction, the entire Spanish public sector is now constitutionally obliged to adhere to the no-indebtedness rule and the directives of the European Union. The reform was approved by an overwhelming majority of parliamentary members (more than 90 %) in September 2011, obtaining the support of both conservative and social democratic parties.

After the general elections of November 2011, the conservative Partido Popular won a large majority in Parliament. President Mariano Rajoy's new government immediately launched several measures and reforms in line with the guidelines issued by the European economic authorities. The strong majority enjoyed by the conservatives in both chambers (Congress and Senate) ensured the adoption of all the policies presented by the party, without their having to enter into negotiations with other political forces. Indeed, in July 2012, Spain signed a Memorandum of Understanding (MoU) with the European Commission, expressing its intention to implement a range of measures and guidelines. The formal agreements were specifically designed to face the problems generated by the banking sector crisis and, for this reason, the memorandum focused primarily on the reform and restructuring of this system. However, the Spanish government drew up a complete programme of actions in many other areas. The reforms launched during 2012 and 2013 included a set of policies that adhered to the principles of "economic sustainability" and "rationalisation". Indeed, both terms are repeated frequently in the regulations adopted during that period. In April 2012, Parliament passed the Organic Law 2/2012 of 27 April on Budgetary Stability and Financial Sustainability. The new law was the enactment of the reformed article (135) of the Spanish Constitution and meant all bodies of public administration and government submitted themselves to strict budgetary sustainability and zero debt. This law did not obtain the same degree of consensus in Parliament as the earlier constitutional reform, but the majority enjoyed by the ruling party proved decisive. Clearly, this new regulation meant corresponding changes in budgetary laws, as public budgets introduced an austere programme of cutbacks and downsizing aimed above all at reducing public sector spending.

This package of policies was to have a marked impact on local government, something which we examine in greater detail in the following sections. Yet, undoubtedly, the single measure that was to have the most direct impact on local government was the reform of the Local Government Act by means of the so-called "Law on Rationalisation and Sustainability of Local Administration" (Ley 27/2013). It was passed by Parliament at the end of 2013, more than 18 months after it had first been tabled and with substantial modifications to its original draft. Thus, while some of the initial plans for the transformation of local government were retained in the final reform, others fell by the wayside. The law effectively sets out to reduce the functions and areas of action of municipal governments. Likewise, it promotes a strategy to cutback the number of municipal-based organisations (that is, agencies, companies and inter-municipal associations) and establishes thresholds for the salaries of municipal councillors. However, attempts at fostering amalgamations were eventually associated with extremely soft incentives and the threatened reduction in number of municipal councillors was not included in the final draft. The content and consequences of the reform are analysed below.

Impact on the Local Sector: Fiscal Retrenchment and Political Re-organisation

Local government reforms in Spain unfolded in two waves that took the country in diametrically opposite directions. The first wave—starting in the mid-1980s and lasting until the economic crisis—saw the strengthening of local autonomy; the second, however, reversed this trend. By means of various pieces of legislation and the austerity measures specifically adopted to tackle the financial crisis, central government up-scaled local functions and reinforced their supervision and control.

From the mid-80s onwards, based on the constitutional recognition of local autonomy and the specific tasks decentralised under the Local Government Act , the town halls undertook actions in a wide range of public fields, some of them as the result of legally designated local competences (e.g. land-use, public utilities, transport, sports, some social services), others in order to meet—albeit without no clear legal mandate—citizen demands (e.g. childcare and services for the elderly) (Navarro and Velasco 2016). All in all, municipal activity increased, thanks in large part to the economic expansion Spain experienced from the mid-90s onwards, which also benefited local public budgets. National reforms, first in 1999 and later in 2003, lent further support to the powers of local government authorities within the political system (Alba and Navarro 2003), providing them with access to the Constitutional Court when their autonomy was threatened and reinforcing their executive functions and participatory tools, enabling them to adjust local democracies to the challenges of the new century.

As a result, both the breadth and depth of local agendas were expanded, being assisted in this by the availability of greater economic resources. Indeed, total local public expenditure tripled during the years of economic expansion, that is, 1993 to 2009 (Rodríguez-Márquez and Romera-Jiménez 2014). In 2005, the national government actually drafted a reform that sought to transfer the actual growth of tasks into the legal system and so ensure that Spain's local government enjoyed clearly defined, irreversible powers, together with a guaranteed system of finance to implement their tasks. However, this bill was shelved due to a lack of political support in the final stage of the parliamentary process. Had it been passed, it would have meant the definite institutionalisation of increased autonomy for local government.

It was at this point that the economic crisis hit, ushering in a wave of reforms that led to the retrenchment of municipal capacities and autonomy. As mentioned above, this shift in policy materialised primarily in the guise of three legal instruments: (1) an amendment to the Spanish Constitution of 2011, introducing the principle of financial stability and limiting public budget deficits at all levels of government, (2) the 2012 Law on "Budgetary Stability and Financial Sustainability" and (3) the 2013 "Rationalization and Sustainability of Local Administration Act".

This legislation was all drafted in the context of the financial crisis, which saw Spain apparently heading towards an imminent country bail-out. Eventually, direct intervention was not deemed necessary, but the central government had to accept financial help from the Eurogroup to the tune of 100 billion euros for the recapitalisation of its banking sector. This loan was granted conditional on the future direction of government policy and under strict compliance with deficit targets.

The constitutional reform introduced a clause guaranteeing the principle of financial stability and limiting public budget deficits. This was passed by Parliament in November 2011, during the last months of Zapatero's Socialist Government, with the support of both socialists and conservatives. The subsequent Law 2/2012, implementing this new constitutional provision, provided rules of fiscal stability and financial sustainability. It introduced fiscal discipline mechanisms targeting all levels of public administration (local and regional governments included) and put in place a new early-warning system, aimed at detecting imbalances in public budgets and issuing the relevant recommendations to achieve budget targets. Coercive measures and compliance enforcement were established for sub-central levels of government and the public administration. By so doing, part of the budgeting authority and control was devolved to the central government as it sought to comply with its targets of fiscal consolidation. In parallel with these supervisory measures, conditions for borrowing became considerably more severe. In 2010, Central Government prohibited municipal access to long-term borrowing (Section 14, Decree 8/2010, 20 May) and imposed stricter conditions on short-term borrowing. This measure was extended until the end of 2012. It meant that only local governments in a healthy financial state could borrow and only then for purposes of capital investment without previous authorisation and up to a certain limit.

Other measures in the austerity package adopted by Central Government led to a reduction in the autonomy of the local authorities and restricted their decision-making powers with regard to staffing. For instance, between 2011 and 2015 the hiring of any new personnel was prohibited, as was the filling of posts becoming vacant on the retirement of public employees.

The "Rationalisation and Sustainability of Local Administration Act" also made substantial changes to many aspects of local autonomy. These were justified by the Central Government as a means of limiting what it regarded as excessive municipal spending. This particular narrative maintained that the growing scope of local government actions had resulted in the duplication of tasks and services provided already by other levels of government and in a highly inefficient, unsustainable level of expenditure.

The passage of this bill through parliament was far from easy. Several versions of the draft bill were announced and it underwent major modifications during subsequent parliamentary procedures. Initial announcements regarding the draft legislation were made quite early in the new government's term of office. These basically translated the general narrative outlined in the MoU and in the packages promoting economic sustainability—that is, the reduction of expenditure and the liberalisation of sectors. The new regulations were supposedly aimed at clarifying functions so as to avoid the duplication of powers between different tiers of government, suppressing local entities (in what was a "soft" process of amalgamation), reducing the number of organisations dependent on local entities, while limiting the number of local councillors and their costs. The government initially estimated savings of around 3500 million euros.

Negative responses to the draft bill were immediately registered among opposition parties and groups and many actors in local government. The Ministry of Finance and Public Administration, author of the draft, set out a clearly defined line of action that constituted a direct challenge to the interests of a range of local groups and actors (a list that included associations of local entities and municipalities, political parties and the governments of the autonomous communities and professional associations such as the local civil servants' association), who, in the subsequent legislative process, managed to modify some of the initial proposals. Indeed, the final text of the reform was more moderate than the original drafts.

However, despite the downgrading of its initial goals, the law includes a number of measures that have had a marked impact on local autonomy. First, it devolves some of the tasks performed by local governments (including, social services, health services and others) back to the provincial and regional authorities Second, it obliges municipalities to obtain prior supra-municipal authorisation (that is, from regional and central government) in order to carry out actions in those fields in which the municipalities had previously been active thanks to their ability to "complement" the activity of other tiers of government (namely, education, housing, youth, culture, immigration, etc.). Third, it eliminates the "general competence clause" of the Spanish decentralisation model that granted local governments the possibility to complement the activity of other public administrations in matters of local importance. Fourth, it fixes maximum salaries for councillors and mayors, a matter previously in the hands of the local councils. Finally, it limits the autonomy of local government to choose the legal form of service provision.

The law has generated considerable controversy and, immediately following its enactment, the municipalities, regions and political parties in opposition appealed to the Constitutional Court alleging a clear violation of local autonomy. In March 2016, the Court ruled partially against the law finding some of its articles unconstitutional, particularly those devolving certain tasks to the provinces and regions. The Court held that these tasks belonged to areas for which the regional governments were responsible and, therefore, only they had the right to decide whether they could be transferred to higher tiers. However, the Court endorsed the central government's right to intervene in local matters by means of mechanisms of control and supervision in its attempt to guarantee budgetary stability and financial sustainability.

Following local elections in May and general elections in December of 2015, Spain was left with a complex, fragmented political map. The general election saw a sharp drop in support for the ruling party (Partido Popular), which lost the majority it had previously enjoyed. Likewise, the local elections saw considerable changes in control in the local municipal councils. This shift in the balance of political forces prevented the appointment of a new government and general elections were repeated six months later. Yet, the outcome was no clearer, a situation unheralded in the political life of modern Spain. The Partido Popular eventually formed a minority government and Mariano Rajoy was appointed President of the Spanish Government for a second term, yet now he would have to enter into a complex process of negotiations before introducing any government-sponsored reform measures.

Local Government Reactions. Self-Organisation as a Response to Austerity Measures: Some Data About Catalonia

Local governments are generally considered to be flexible, innovative institutions, with a leadership structure that is capable of initiating change and demonstrating clear strategic thinking (Shaw 2012; Lowndes and McCaughie 2013). In this respect, institutional resilience at this level of government has been shown to be the ability of local authorities to change rather than to continue doing the same thing (Shaw 2012). Therefore, if we consider institutional structure to be both a deliberate design and an unintended consequence of human action and social interaction (Lanzara 1998), local government emerges as an appropriate field in which to explore crisis and institutional change (Baldersheim and Wollmann 2006; Orr 2009). Indeed, in a framework of economic pressure, local government authorities are quite likely to have to face situations in which growing demands for public services have to be met (Overmans and Noordegraaf 2014). The position that local government occupies in the institutional network (i.e. the level of government closest to the citizens) also increases the need to identify specific measures that can address the dual challenge of reducing expenditure while maintaining the effectiveness of community well-being (Claudio et al. 2011).

In describing such measures, Raudla et al. (2013: 12) classify available instruments according to the following categories: (1) instruments for cutting running costs; (2) programme measures (transfers and grants) and (3) investments. With a similar aim in mind, Overmans and Noordegraaf (2014) design a two-dimensional model, in which one of the dimensions is stability and change and the other comprises fiscal and organisational measures. According to their findings, the majority of measures represented temporary adjustments, which may well mean a degree of contradiction between the narrative of the programmes and reality. Here, in order to analyse the behaviour of local governments and their reactions to the economic crisis, we analyse general data from Spain, and examine specific empirical information obtained from Catalonia, one of the 17 autonomous communities.

Table 5.1 shows how local government expenditure for the whole of Spain increased both in absolute terms and as a percentage of GDP between 2007 and 2010. Spending however fell between 2011 and 2012 by almost 16 % (i.e. by around 12,000 million euros). Expenditure continued to fall, albeit more moderately, until 2013, rose again thereafter, before recording another downturn between 2015 and 2016. Local government revenue in contrast presents a less dramatic variation. A fall was recorded between 2010 and 2012, but after that it presented a slow but steady increase. In fact, from 2013 onwards, the values both in absolute terms and as a percentage of GDP are higher than those recorded in 2007. In the case of expenditure, the drop in spending clearly occurred before the reform of the Local Government Act. The comparison of the two dimensions shows that local government revenue has clearly recovered, while spending has fallen—local government spending in Spain today represents a smaller share of total public expenditure than it did before the crisis.

Above and beyond the measures promoted by Central Government, Spain's municipalities implemented other initiatives to reduce their expenditure and to address their fiscal problems. Table 5.2 shows the main

Table 5.1 Local government expenditure and revenue

	2007	*2008*	*2009*	*2010*	*2011*	*2012*	*2013*	*2014*	*2015*	*2016*
LG expenditure (million €)	69,618.0	72,076.0	76,302.0	76,613.0	73,103.0	61,547.0	60,731.0	62,835.0	64,699.0	63,757.0
LG expenditure % GDP	6.4	6.5	7.1	7.1	6.8	5.9	5.9	6.1	6.0	5.7
LG revenue (million €)	66,280.0	66,701.0	70,392.0	69,562.0	64,597.0	64,854.0	66,420.0	68,307.0	69,793.0	70,840.0
LG revenue % GDP	6.1	6.0	6.5	6.4	6.0	6.2	6.5	6.6	6.5	6.4

Source: Based on Eurostat data

Table 5.2 Austerity measures in municipalities with more than 500 inhabitants and their potential impact

		%
Structural measures	Austerity plan [N = 543]	9.8
	Reduction of elected members' salaries [N = 504]	65.1
	Reduction of amounts paid for attendance [N = 543]	56.5
	Reduction in the number of civil servants [N = 543]	19.2
	Reduction in the number of other staff members [N = 542]	46.3
Measures affecting compulsory services	Public street lightening [N = 518]	33.4
	Waste collection [N = 473]	24.5
	Street cleaning [N = 527]	18.0
	Paving and maintenance of streets and roads [N = 512]	18.6
Measures affecting non-compulsory services	Social care [N = 440]	3.9
	Social emergency services [N = 390]	1.5
	Transportation [N = 268]	12.7
	Housing [N = 247]	7.7
	Public libraries [N = 379]	7.9
	Culture [N = 423]	10.4
	Sports [N = 486]	9.7
	Childcare [N = 474]	37.1
	Adult learning [N = 240]	7.1
	Music schools [N = 295]	25.8
Contingency measures	Reduction in overtime payments [N = 491]	52.1
	Reduction in representation allowances [N = 491]	54.2
	Strategies to reduce energy consumption [N = 491]	85.7
	Reductions in funds for investment [N = 491]	51.7

Sources: Based on data drawn from ObsCat7 www.pisunyer.org

measures adopted by the municipalities of Catalonia during the more severe years of crisis—between 2010 and 2013. The actions are listed according to the type of measure (Medir et al. 2017) and their potential impact in budgetary terms. We indicate whether the local authorities did or did not implement austerity measures in specific areas, without focusing on the exact type of measure adopted. Although this information is available for most of the services, our aim here is to trace the global profile of the austerity measures that were implemented. According to Table 5.2, austerity measures of a structural nature were implemented, on average, in 40 percent of local governments. Reductions in the salaries of elected members and in the amounts paid for attending committee or institutional meetings were the most popular actions (65.1 and 56.5 %, respectively). These are immediate and visible responses that are readily perceived and understood by the citizens. However, their impact is not great in budgetary terms. In this category, it should be noted that the reduction in staff affected primarily staff members (46.3 %) as opposed to civil servants (just 19.2 %), probably reflecting different legal regulations. Finally, only 9.8 % of local governments in Catalonia (i.e. 53 out of 563) opted to implement a general austerity plan.

Concerning measures related to public services, responses here varied depending on whether the service can be considered compulsory or not. In the case of compulsory services, the potential impact varies between 18 and 33 % (with the number of municipalities implementing them being correspondingly higher), whereas in the case of non-compulsory services the variation in impact was much wider, ranging from 1.5 to 37 %. Interestingly, the least-affected services were social emergency services and social services in general, while the most severely hit service was childcare. Both cases are perhaps illustrative of the impact of an economic crisis: the low impact on social services illustrates the great need for such programmes in times of crisis as poverty rates soared, whereas the greater impact on childcare services responds to a different logic, namely increased rates of unemployment permit adults to stay at home causing the demand for such services to fall. Finally, contingency measures, such as reductions in overtime payments, were very common, as were reductions in energy consumption in public buildings and facilities, being implemented in 85 % of the municipalities analysed.

These results are very much in line with theoretical expectations. In general, the most widespread measures are cutbacks addressed at making temporary adjustments. In the case of institutional changes, the most common action taken is to reduce the salaries of the councillors, which while being fairly irrelevant in economic terms represents a clear statement of commitment on the part of the political class. In short, such actions contribute to creating a narrative and discourse of reactions and responses to the crisis.

The Autonomy Test: Local Autonomy Under Threat in the Multilevel Governance System

But have the measures implemented by Central Government had an impact on local autonomy in Spain? In seeking to respond to this question, we use the Local Autonomy Index—LAI (Ladner et al. 2016), a comprehensive methodology for measuring local autonomy that basically considers four dimensions: institutional depth, policy scope, financial self-reliance and organisational autonomy.

Institutional depth measures the extent to which local government authorities are autonomous and can choose the tasks they want to perform. In this regard, the reform of the Local Government Act, passed in December 2013, has: (a) reduced the number of compulsory services municipalities have to provide; (b) transferred some of these services to the provincial and regional governments; and (c) eliminated the residual clause of Section 28 of the Spanish decentralisation model that granted local governments the general capacity to act. In short, from this perspective, local autonomy has been weakened.

Policy scope measures the extent to which local governments are effectively involved in the delivery of services in a range of fields (education, social assistance, health, housing, land-use, transport, care, etc.). Here, the reforms have also weakened this dimension of autonomy, limiting local capacity to deliver some of these services, in particular those of education, health and social assistance.

In the case of financial self-reliance, the local authorities have been affected most in terms of their borrowing autonomy. Indeed, the conditions governing borrowing were made considerably stricter during the last years of the period considered. Following the financial crisis, the Central Government introduced legislation in 2010 to reduce public deficit and prohibited municipal access to long-term borrowing (Section 14, Decree 8/2010, 20th of May) and imposed strict conditions on short-term borrowing. This measure was extended until the end of 2012. After that date, only local governments enjoying good financial health can borrow, and then only for capital investment (without previous authorisation) and not over a given ceiling. Heavily indebted local authorities, with amounts exceeding 75 % of their revenue, require external authorisation to borrow, while those exceeding 110 % of their revenue are prohibited from borrowing.

Organisational autonomy has also been weakened. The packages of austerity measures implemented by Central Government imposed certain restrictions on local governments in terms of their decision-making in relation to staffing and local structures. These restrictions affected (i) their autonomy to fix salaries (both for public employees and for councillors and mayors), (ii) their staffing decisions: limiting their possibilities of hiring new employees (which applies to all administrations), (iii) their capacity to create new public entities in certain instances.

In short, the austerity measures adopted by the Central Government have impacted local autonomy in Spain, weakening it in general and undermining all its specific dimensions: institutional depth (by eliminating the "general competence" clause), policy scope (by transferring competences to upper levels of government), financial self-reliance (by introducing financial controls and supervision as a condition for local action) and organisational autonomy (by limiting the scope of self-organisation).

Conclusions

This chapter has both described and analysed the austerity measures adopted in Spain, focusing above all on the impact they have had on local government. It has also sought to interpret them in the light of a theoretical framework that provides a more comprehensive and inclusive vision of the period and its policies. What has emerged is the different forms that these policies have taken in a narrative that has, in many instances, evolved beyond the concrete measures themselves. Thus, the initial reactions to the economic recession—which can be dated to the years 2008 and 2009—saw the crisis as a cyclic failure and, so, the responses took a contra-cyclical Keynesian approach. In line with Hay (1999), the mode of response presented a second degree of intensity, and can be classified as a "response to solve selective contradictions". However, from 2010 onwards, this orientation changed dramatically and the subsequent narrative was focused on the need to make cutbacks and reduce public expenditure.

Even though Spain's local institutions were not especially afflicted by debt problems, they were seen as demonstrating a severe lack of fiscal control and, therefore, a wide range of policies were adopted to correct their supposed dysfunctionalities: first, specific measures to limit their possibilities of running up debt; second, general measures impacting the core of the public sector—a reduction in the number of public employees and a wage freeze; and finally, a complete revision of the local government system and its allocation of functions. The impact of these measures varied. Debt control measures had an almost immediate impact both in material effects and in political impact. But while they affected the operation of the system, they did not redefine the structure or the organisation of the institutional network. However, the Local Government Reform Act was inspired by a very specific vision of the structure and architecture of the public system, though its implementation ran into far more difficulties. Yet, overall, our analysis highlights the resilience shown by local government authorities and stresses their capacity to adapt and to uphold one of their primary values, namely, the ability to respond to local concerns in the provision of local services.

From the perspective of local autonomy, the crisis and the need for fiscal consolidation served as windows of opportunity for Central Government to recentralise, resulting in the degradation of local autonomy. Part of this process of recentralisation was inevitable (Peters 2011), another part was ideological, being implemented through the construction of a specific narrative that placed local governments in the eye of a perfect storm. The austerity measures that the local authorities in Spain were forced to implement meant their having to do less with less, in a framework of recentralising policies and increasing central government control. However, the local authorities' capacity for resilience and adaptation emerged strongly in this period of upheaval. Indeed, Spain's local government managed to find ways to moderate the impact of these recentralising efforts, at least in the short term. The impact of these programmes in the long term, however, remain uncertain and constitute an interesting area for future research.

References

Alba, C., & Navarro, C. (2003). Twenty-five Years of Democratic Local Government in Spain. In N. Kersting & A. Vetter (Eds.), *Reforming Local Government in Europe* (pp. 197–220). Opladen: Leske and Budrich.

Baldersheim, H., & Wollmann, H. (2006). *The Comparative Study of Local Government and Politics: Overview and Synthesis*. Farmington Hills: Barbara Budrich Publishers.

Claudio, E., Oyarce, M., Jones, G., Stewart, J., Travers, T., Oyarce, C. M., & Wei, K. (2011, April). *Redefining Local Government*.

Delgado, M., García, B., & Zubimendi, L. (2017). *La evolución de la deuda pública en España en 2016*. Madrid: Banco de España. https://www.bde.es/f/webbde/SES/Secciones/Publicaciones/InformesBoletinesRevistas/NotasEconomicas/T2/fich/bene1702-nec6.pdf

Hay, C. (1999). Crisis and the Structural Transformation of the State: Interrogating the Process of Change. *British Journal of Politics & International Relations, 1*(3), 317–344.

Hay, C. (2013). Treating the Symptom Not the Condition: Crisis Definition, Deficit Reduction and the Search for a New British Growth Model. *British Journal of Politics and International Relation, 15*(1), 23–37.

Ladner, A., Keuffer, N., & Baldersheim, H. (2016). Measuring Local Autonomy in 39 Countries (1990–2014). *Regional & Federal Studies, 26*(3), 321–357.

Lanzara, G. F. (1998). Self-Destructive Processes in Institution Building and Some Modest Countervailing Mechanisms. *European Journal of Political Research, 33*(1), 1–39.

Lowndes, V., & McCaughie, K. (2013). Weathering the Perfect Storm? Austerity and Institutional Resilience in Local Government. *Policy & Politics, 41*(4), 533–549.

Medir, L., Pano, E., Viñas, A., & Magre, J. (2017). Dealing with Austerity: A Case of Local Resilience in Southern Europe. *Local Government Studies, 43*(4), 621–644.

Navarro, C., & Velasco, F. (2016). 'In Wealth and in Poverty?' The Changing Role of Spanish Municipalities in Implementing Childcare Policies. *International Review of Administrative Sciences, 82*(2), 315–334.

Orr, K. (2009). Local Government and Structural Crisis: An Interpretive Approach. *Policy & Politics, 37*(1), 39–55.

Overmans, T., & Noordegraaf, M. (2014). Managing Austerity: Rhetorical and Real Responses to Fiscal Stress in Local Government. *Public Money & Management, 34*(2), 99–106.

Peters, B. G. (2010). Paying for Government: The Budgetary Process. In *The Politics of Bureaucracy* (pp. 261–293). London/New York: Routledge.

Peters, B. G. (2011). Governance Responses to the Fiscal Crisis—Comparative Perspectives. *Public Money & Management, 31*(1), 75–80.

Raudla, R., Savi, R., & Randma-Liiv, T. (2013). *Literature Review on Cutback Management*. COCOPS—(COordinating for COhesion in the Public Sector of the Future).

Rodríguez-Márquez, J., & Romera-Jiménez, O. (2014). *Un estudio sobre gasto impropio en la Administración Local española*. Madrid: Instituto de Estudios Fiscales. http://www.ief.es/documentos/recursos/publicaciones/documentos_trabajo/2014_03.pdf

Shaw, K. (2012). The Rise of the Resilient Local Authority? *Local Government Studies, 38*(3), 281–300.

Zapico, E. (2012). El presupuesto por resultados ante la crisis fiscal: compatibilizando austeridad y crecimiento. *Presupuesto y Gasto Público, 69*, 53–73.

CHAPTER 6

In the Shadow of Austerity: Italian Local Public Services and the Politics of Budget Cuts

Giulio Citroni, Andrea Lippi, and Stefania Profeti

Introduction

Since the early 1980s, Italian macroeconomic policy has gone hand in hand with the development of monetary coordination mechanisms at the European level. This policy has been characterized by a (more or less explicit) struggle between two opposing coalitions: on the one hand, a public spending constituency composed of the ruling political class, that

G. Citroni (✉)
Department of Political and Social Sciences, University of Calabria, Cosenza, Italy
e-mail: giulio.citroni@unical.it

A. Lippi
Department of Political and Social Sciences, University of Florence, Firenze, Italy
e-mail: lippi@unifi.it

S. Profeti
Department of Political and Social Sciences, University of Bologna, Bologna, Italy
e-mail: stefania.profeti@unibo.it

A. Lippi, T. N. Tsekos (eds.), *Local Public Services in Times of Austerity across Mediterranean Europe*, Governance and Public Management, https://doi.org/10.1007/978-3-319-76225-8_6

has tried to manage economic problems and buy social peace through a combination of frequent currency devaluation and deficit spending; and on the other hand, a technocratic coalition centred around the Bank of Italy (BDI) and its research department, that has been keen on promoting more rigorous, stability-oriented budgetary policies (Radaelli and Franchino 2004).

While the ruling parties originally held a (quasi)monopoly of political and legislative decisions, the BDI enjoyed an unrivalled monopoly of expertise and economic knowledge, together with an excellent reputation among foreign authorities and international organizations (Quaglia 2005).

However, the equilibrium between the two coalitions was reversed in the early 1990s, when the combination of international currency market pressures (forcing Italy to pull out of the exchange rate mechanism—ERM) and the corruption scandals affecting the traditional parties, paved the way for the empowerment of technocrats in governments, and the emergence of a new ruling elite (Radaelli and Franchino 2004). The move towards EMU goes in the same direction, as the convergence criteria established in Maastricht weakened the (formerly dominant) domestic "public spending constituency" (Dyson and Featherstone 1999; Quaglia 2005). Indeed, the need to "stay in Europe" represented an opportunity to dismantle the old system and managed to hold together a new advocacy coalition consisting of technocrats linked to the Bank of Italy, and the rising centre-left which was preparing to govern the country (Hopkin 2012). This coalition's narrative saw the reframing of European constraints as an "external lever to secure results that the domestic political system would have been structurally unable to produce" (Radaelli and Franchino 2004: 945).

Between 1993 and 2001, cabinets led by technocrats such as Carlo Azeglio Ciampi and Lamberto Dini (a former BDI governor and deputy governor, respectively), together with Romano Prodi (professor of economics, President of the state-owned holding company IRI during the 1980s, and former international advisor to Goldman Sachs), fostered a stability-oriented budgetary policy centred on three pillars: the sustainability of public spending, the modernization of the PA and macroeconomic stability. Within such a framework, the recipe for the reform of local administrations and public services consisted of two main ingredients: on the one hand, the greater autonomy and political legitimacy of local governments, through the direct election of mayors and the widespread decentralization of administrative powers; on the other hand, more efficient public intervention through the use of NPM tools such as privatization, the clear-cut separation of political and managerial roles, the contractualization and corporatization of former municipal enterprises and horizontal market integration (economies of scale) in the management and provision of services (Citroni et al. 2016).

The "modernizing" agenda of the 1990s, although codified in a number of laws and in the constitutional reform of 2001, failed to perform as expected in reducing public expenditure and ensuring long-term economic growth. Changes in governmental majorities during the 2000s, together with the absence of sound central coordination and monitoring mechanisms, and the piecemeal re-adaptation of the normative framework to contingent needs, seriously hampered the implementation of structural reforms, thus paving the way for a number of "detrimental side effects" such as the mushrooming of local agencies and corporate bodies (Citroni et al. 2015), the persistent fragmentation of local services delivery (Citroni et al. 2016), as well as a decrease in governments' accountability (Lippi 2011). What is certain, however, is that the reforms introduced in the late 1990s and early 2000s, progressively toughened budget constraints on local governments, through a moderate increase in their financial autonomy and significant reductions in state transfers. In 2007, intergovernmental transfers accounted for two-fifths of sub-national governments' expenditure, whereas that ratio had been three-fifths in the 1990s and three-quarters in the 1980s (Gennari and Messina 2012). Indeed, when fiscal rules were first introduced for local governments through the Domestic Stability Pact in 1999, sanctions initially consisted of cuts in transfers to non-compliant entities, but soon after they also encompassed administrative measures such as restrictions on the purchase of goods and services, and a ban on hiring new staff and on contracting debt to finance investment (Ter-Minassian 2007). In spite of these latter provisions, municipal public debt tripled between 2001 and 2006, rising from 15 billion to 45 billion euros (Banca d'Italia 2007). At the national level, with the exception of certain improvements between 1998 and 2000, general government debt never dropped below 110% of GDP.[1]

However, until the late 2000s and the onset of the global crisis, Italy was not in the same sovereign debt crisis as the other four Portugal Italy Greece Spain (PIGS) countries for at least two reasons: on the one hand, the Italian Treasury had managed a process of gradual consolidation over

[1] See https://data.oecd.org/gdp/gross-domestic-product-gdp.htm

the course of the previous decade; and on the other hand, while the other four countries were heavily indebted to the outside world, Italy was not, thanks to "a relatively conservative banking sector, a large stockpile of domestic savings, and an even larger stockpile of household wealth". So while the public sector was heavily indebted, "those debts [could] be covered by domestic resources" (Jones 2012).

The Austerity Agenda

The Impact of External Demands and Domestic Needs

Since the onset of the economic crisis, there have been three phases in the formulation and framing of an austerity agenda, each one characterized by a specific mix of domestic political requirements and supranational demands. Each of these phases shall now be analysed, with the focus on the said mix overshadowing the framing of policy problems and strategies, and on the role assigned to local governments and public services.

Fire alarms ring in a troubled fire station. Emergency measures in the 4th Berlusconi government (2008–2011)

In 2008, when the global financial crisis started kicking-in in Italy, the centre-right coalition led by Silvio Berlusconi regained power after having been in government during the 2001–2006 period. So far (and contrary to what is normally expected of centre-right coalitions) Berlusconi's governmental majorities had never supported monetarist economic policies, nor had they expressed any pro-European feelings (especially not the eurosceptic Northern League party). Unlike in the past, however, the electoral manifesto of the centre-right was now openly inspired by principles of austerity and financial stability, due to the unlikely prospect of economic growth in subsequent years, and the poor credibility that expansive economic policies would have had (Di Quirico 2010: 4).

Indeed, the Minister of Economy and Finance, Giulio Tremonti, who had already held the same position in previous Berlusconi governments, and who had always facilitated dialogue between the Prime Minister and his pivotal ally, the Northern League, was the only one supporting the new pro-austerity stance. In particular after 2010, when the effects of the crisis had clearly emerged in Italy, Tremonti—who in the past had strongly criticized excessive EU regulation—presented a position very similar to that of Angela Merkel, "calling for yet harsher sanctions to be added to the Stability and Growth Pact for countries failing to meet the targets" (Gualmini and Pasotti 2011: 53). On the contrary, Berlusconi's public discourse was much less coherent, shifting as it did from optimistic announcements to prudent calls for sacrifices when citizens' discontent, caused by the crisis and by unfulfilled promises, began to spread across the country (ibidem). The same ambiguous stance also characterized discourse on local government, with the Northern League calling for stronger autonomy based on fiscal federalism, and with Berlusconi keen to "punish" regions and municipalities for the most part administered by the centre-left. Caught between the need to defend his leadership from public and private scandals, and the difficulty of maintaining the unity of a highly contentious governmental coalition, the Prime Minister was unable to promote, or communicate, a unified, credible anti-crisis agenda (Hopkin 2012); indeed, the perception it gave was that of a government at the mercy of events, only capable of an inconsistent patchwork of emergency measures (Jones 2012).

From late 2010 onwards, European institutions and international observers repeatedly criticized the unsatisfactory performance of the Italian government (Bosco and McDonnell 2012). The situation worsened dramatically in the summer of 2011, under pressure from the financial markets. In August 2011, ECB President Trichet and BDI Governor Draghi wrote a letter to Berlusconi's government, urging it to take due action. "Although not explicitly embedded in a formalized conditional aid program, the letter imposed a policy agenda on the Italian government, going as far as to indicate the specific actions to be implemented" (Sacchi 2015). Among a number of measures for economic growth and fiscal consolidation (including a constitutional reform tightening fiscal rules), the letter requested the large-scale privatization of local public services, stricter control over local expenditure, a strong commitment to abolish or consolidate certain intermediate layers of political administration (such as the country's provincial governments), and actions aimed at exploiting economies of scale in local public services. Similar recommendations had been made previously by the IMF during their annual meeting with the Italian government (Jones 2012).

Berlusconi's inability to comply with supranational requests in the following months led to an increase in criticism not only abroad, but also in Italy itself. In early November, after the collapse of his parliamentary majority, he resigned from office and the President of the Republic, Giorgio Napolitano, appointed former European Commissioner Mario Monti to take his place (Fusaro 2013).

Good pupils deserve to be rewarded. Monti's austerity measures designed to (re)gain credibility abroad

At the time he was appointed, Monti (soon after nicknamed "Super Mario") was President of the private Bocconi University and European Chairman of the Trilateral Commission. He had previously been an adviser to Goldman Sachs and a member of Moody's European Advisory Council. He also held the post of European Commissioner (Internal Market and Competition) between 1995 and 2004 (Bosco and McDonnell 2012: 44). Given his background, some observers maintained that "Monti's ascent to the prime minister's office was certainly a result in part of direct pressure from the ECB and other European leaders" (Hopkin 2012: 45).

The new government led by Monti was an interim one entrusted with the task of dealing with the emergency. It was, to all intents and purposes, a purely technocratic government, with all 18 ministers coming from outside of the world of politics. This government consisted of two private-sector managers, eight university professors and eight senior civil servants, and each was assigned ministerial responsibilities according to his/her specific background (Marangoni 2012). In order to guarantee strict control over European commitments, during his first eight months in office Monti acted as both Prime Minister and Minister of the Economy.

In spite of its non-political nature, the new government gained the support of both the Chamber of Deputies and the Senate on the basis of an overwhelming, cross-party majority (only the Northern League party voted against it): due to the extremely serious economic situation and the need to implement painful measures in the short term, the two main parties—the Democratic Party (PD) and the People of Freedom Party (PDL)—chose to avoid being directly involved and to "keep their hands free" (Fusaro 2013); however, they were forced to support the government, given the financial crisis and "the strong sense of impending danger if action [were not] quickly taken" (Bosco and McDonnell 2012: 53). Initially, the absence of parties was beneficial to Monti's popularity with Italians (Culpepper 2014); however, the "honeymoon" with both citizens and parties ended just a few months later, as the crisis deepened and the government's agenda was implemented.[2]

Monti's agenda religiously complied with the Troika's diktat, following what could be termed the "approach of a diligent pupil": conscientiously

[2] https://www.ft.com/content/fe07930e-7fff-11e1-b4a8-00144feab49a

doing the assigned homework in order to be entitled to certain rewards. The government's belief was that by regaining credibility among its European partners, Italy could obtain greater flexibility in terms of the Stability and Growth Pact rules, so as to enjoy greater room for manoeuvre in regard to policies and investments aimed at economic growth (Stolfi 2013; Giannetti 2013). Of course, there was undeniably a certain affinity between the ECB's demands and Monti's beliefs: in 1992, when Rector of the Bocconi University, he made an appeal to the Italian political class, published in the newspaper "La Repubblica", calling for a more responsible attitude towards budgetary policy, and proposing the constitutionalization of fiscal rules.[3]

As to the contents, Monti's agenda focused on several policy commitments ranging from fiscal consolidation measures to labour market and pension reforms (Marangoni 2012). Spending cuts were meant to be coupled not only with pro-growth measures (such as forms of economic liberalization) but also with the radical streamlining of the state apparatus, including local government and the provision of public services (Giannetti 2013). As to the methods adopted, legislative action was closely coordinated by the executive and by the Prime Minister himself, who introduced (either alone or together with other ministers) around 78% of the bills submitted by government to parliament (Marangoni 2012: 143). The fact that 50% of planned measures were passed by means of emergency decree laws, further testifies to the considerable centralization of the decision-making process (ibidem: 145).

Austerity is a form of therapeutic obstinacy...but an opportunity, too. Renzi's compromise between re-centralization and political negotiation.

Matteo Renzi's cabinet took office in February 2014, after the short-lived, rather unstable centre-left government led by his fellow party member Enrico Letta. Although similar to Monti's programme as far as priorities and policy contents are concerned, Renzi's agenda substantially differs in at least two respects. Firstly, it is the expression of a very political government composed mainly of ministers from Renzi's own Democratic Party (PD). Only the Economic Ministry was assigned to a technical figure, namely the chief economist of the OECD and former director of the IMF,

[3] M. Monti and L. Spaventa, "Quanto costerà entrare in Europa", in La Repubblica, 02/27/1992.

Pier Carlo Padoan. Secondly, for consensus-seeking reasons it marks a break with previous acquiescence to EU requests: in fact, it combines the standard centre-left Europeanist rhetoric with a more combative approach invoking greater national autonomy in domestic policy-making, as well as a more important role for Italy in the formulation of European decisions (Guidi 2015). This was all the more so given that the landslide victory of the PD in the European elections held in Italy in 2014, together with the legitimacy gained in the domestic sphere, and Italy's increased credibility abroad over the previous two years, had given Renzi a certain leverage with which to "raise the stakes" in negotiations with European partners and supranational institutions, to take a more critical approach to the European Union's budget limits, and to ask—for the first time since the onset of the economic crisis—for the review of the austerity paradigm (ibidem) whose efficacy was deemed highly questionable. "Insisting for eight years straight on a cure that does not work is a form of therapeutic obstinacy".[4]

Despite Renzi's apparently different approach to austerity, his policy vis-à-vis local government and public services followed the path previously taken by the Monti government. Nevertheless, two things distinguish the former from the latter: the first is the strong emphasis now being put on the need to reduce the "cost of politics", which was one of the main electoral arguments of the PD's strongest political opponent, the Eurosceptic "Five Stars Movement" (Hanretty and Profeti 2015). Indeed, all reforms, together with the creation of new bodies (agencies, cooperative structures, metropolitan cities etc.), had to ensure that overall expenditure was not affected, and double-hatted positions were not to be rewarded (Bussu and Galanti 2015). The second thing is the new style adopted in centre-periphery relations, which now centred on a peculiar mix of top-down, centralized decision-making (characteristic of the Monti government as well) and flexible bottom-up implementing mechanisms, mostly relying on "disintermediated" political negotiations between central government and local administrators (Di Giulio and Profeti 2016; Bolgherini et al. 2016).

For the first couple of years of Renzi's term in office, European institutions looked with favour on the Italian reform agenda. However, since March 2016 European Commissioners, Moscovici and Dombrovskis have written a series of letters to the Economy Minister, Padoan, setting out

[4] http://www.repubblica.it/politica/2016/02/11/news/renzi_europe_has_taken_the_wrong_road_austerity_alone_is_not_enough_-133189474/

certain conditions for the granting of any further budgetary flexibility, including progress with the Italian government's structural reform agenda. After a referendum had rejected Renzi's proposed constitutional reform in December 2016, and Renzi's consequent resignation, a new letter was received asking the Italian government to formulate additional budgetary measures (constituting a €3.4 billion adjustment to Italy's public accounts), which were to be approved by the end of April 2017 in order to avoid the opening of an excessive deficit procedure. Padoan replied promising a reduction in tax concessions, a stronger battle against tax evasion, and spending cuts limited to less than €800 million. Ninety percent of these cuts concern public administration spending.[5] These measures were approved by the Italian government on 11 April, and are still being examined by the European Commission as we write.

The Puzzle of Austerity Provisions.

Strategies, Instruments and Measures in Search of a Policy Design

Austerity measures affecting LPS have been introduced in Italy through a persistent stream of ad hoc decisions embedded in piecemeal legislation, mainly consisting of Annual Budget Laws (Di Mascio et al. 2013). These have established general provisions or targeted fiscal measures hindering local governments and indirectly involving LPS management and delivery. There is no one, declared austerity design, but an assorted amalgam of instruments all related to two common factors. Firstly, there is an incremental-compromise strategy grounded in the muddling through of politics, which has favoured pragmatic, reactive, short-term decisions related to the occasional policy window. The overall picture is one of an indistinct "less with less strategy", a disjointed, asymmetric form of retrenchment without any stated plan apart from that of shifting fiscal accountability towards lower levels of management. Secondly, policy has combined both across-the-board and prioritized cutbacks (Di Mascio and Natalini 2014; Di Mascio and Natalini 2015): fiscal measures clearly account for the majority of such cutbacks, and involve programme spending cutbacks as well as operational spending cutbacks. Nevertheless, the reorganization of Local Public Service (LPS) arrangements and management has also been included in such reforms.

[5] http://www.corriere.it/english/17_febbraio_02/italy-responds-to-eu-few-cuts-and-fight-against-tax-evasion-b48ae9da-e961-11e6-9abf-27281e0d6da4.shtml

Downsizing and recentralizing: the strategy and measures of the Centre-Right Government (2008–2011)

An initial series of provisions were introduced under the centre-right government that held power from 2008 to 2011. Fiscal retrenchment was promoted in response to the claimed recklessness of local government spending and was consequently designed to limit their spending powers. In 2008, central government abolished the real estate tax that had been the main source of funding for municipal governments. Accordingly, it established an increasing reduction in state funding together with the delegation of new tasks, without covering the costs of such. Other decisions were subsequently taken to rationalize public expenditure: Fiscal Federalism (2009) attempted to make regional governments (and local authorities) more accountable, through the principle of the correspondence of available financial resources to local revenues. Fiscal federalism also imposed the uniformity of local government budgets based on central government criteria and standards for LPS spending. Permanent supervision of local public spending by the Ministry was also introduced. At the same time (2010), the government established the compulsory joint management of LPS in the case of those municipalities with a population of under 5000. Analogously, municipal agencies for the management and delivery of public service could not exist in the case of municipalities with a population of under 30,000. Finally, municipal clerks were directly controlled, once again, by the Ministry of the Interior instead of by local governments and the independent agency for employment was suppressed.

This trend was witnessed in the initial version of the Spending Review, introduced in 2007 as an instrument for development, but which was quickly transformed into a cutback measure in support of central government's provisions from 2008 to 2011 (Goretti and Rizzuto 2013). The Spending Review targeted a reduction in local authorities' costs. The Annual Budget Laws throughout 2009 and 2010 also implemented tough financial cuts "in state transfers to local bodies, calculated in proportion to their population" (Bolgherini 2014: 202). Indeed, the Budget Laws established increasing budgetary cuts for the years 2010, 2011 and 2012 (from 12 to 118 million euros). The 2009 Annual Budget law also introduced a number of general measures weakening local government at the organizational (and symbolic) level: a reduction in provincial and municipal managers (and subsequently the restoration of the "old clerks" appointed by the Ministry of the Interior); the suppression of municipal consortia; and the abolition of state funding of intermunicipal cooperation. In the field of LPS, the municipal *ombudsman* was abolished, mostly as a symbolic measure and with a number of detrimental effects.

The centre-right majority established compulsory competitive tendering for the award of service delivery to Public-Private Partnership (PPP) companies in the public utilities sector, and in 2010 it abolished the second-level entities *Ambiti Territoriali Ottimali* (ATOs) for water and waste management "to save public money, but leaving the system of regulation virtually unattended" (Citroni et al. 2016: 106). Finally, the national water agency was scrapped and its functions were transferred to the energy agency. Social services were also affected by cutbacks, and a reduction in social funding forced municipalities to rely mainly on their own tax revenues (idem: 114), while the government increasingly delegated social care to families and charities, whilst encouraging the privatization of the social services sector (Sacchi 2015).

The Austerity Storm: Monti's interim cabinet's provisions in the light of EU recommendations (2012–2013)

The second wave of reforms (2012–2013) represents the core of the Austerity measures. As of late 2011, Monti's cabinet introduced a range of measures specifically aimed at cost saving, and this was to severely affect management of LPS. The key provision concerned a change in the Constitution based on the "Golden Rules" (the Fiscal Compact) establishing the state's break-even budget. This provision was passed by the Italian Parliament in 2012 by virtue of a change in the Constitution (Article 81) approved by two-thirds of voters in both chambers. This change paved the way for a thorough programme of cutbacks across various sectors, which hindered local government in general, and destabilized LPS in particular (Culpepper 2014). According to the reworked Constitution, municipal deficits or debts are no longer allowed, and further spending on public services is consequently forbidden unless the state covers the cost of such.

A number of cost-saving measures introduced through this austerity package (e.g. the "Rescue Italy" Decree, issued in 2011, and the "Summer Measures" and "Spending Review with unaltered services for citizens", both passed in 2012) specifically impacted local government through further cutbacks and the attempted reduction in the functions of provincial government. At the same time, local social-sector policies were hit by a series of substantial cuts: National Social Fund was drastically reduced once again (Stolfi 2013). Cutbacks particularly affected those funds managed by municipalities: in 2011 and 2012 the fund for dependent and disabled people was suspended, as was the social fund for young people. Again, the Prime Minister promoted certain preliminary, "symbolic" measures reducing the powers of Italy's provincial governments (the "power-hollowing" decree issued in December 2012 reduced state cover of the provinces' financial costs), whilst pursuing their outright abolition in the light of Trichet's recommendations. Indeed, the government provided for the suppression of provincial executive bodies, and reduced the provinces' power, whilst strengthening the compulsory joint management of LPS in the case of the country's smaller municipalities.

Through an incremental decision-making process in 2013, the government streamlined local taxes into a common levy steered by the centre. The new tax encompassed housing (restored, albeit in the state's favour rather than that of local governments), infrastructures and refuse collection. The tax was now fixed (and earned) by the state, but was collected by municipalities, which were free to raise or lower the self-financing cap up to 0.3% (e.g. housing). As a matter of fact, this rationalization implied a process of recentralization and of the delegation of responsibility from the central state to municipal governments. As regards waste, the tariff system was definitively abandoned in favour of a tax system "whereby the price paid by families no longer depends on the quantity of waste produced, but on the size of the house, like it did before the reforms" (Citroni et al. 2017).

So, as far as the management of water, waste and local transport was concerned, while the new territorial districts (ATOs) were now established by regional government, Italy's central government continued to rationalize the system, favouring corporatization and the creation of a limited number of companies by aggregating the multitude of private companies owned by municipalities. This aim was pursued through micro-legislation favouring company concentration, supervision of standards and the restoration of compulsory tender procedures, following the disapproval expressed by the popular referendum held in 2011. However, later decisions which contradicted the result of the referendum and strongly favoured liberalization have been stopped by the Constitutional Court (Citroni et al. 2016).

Austerity continues to do its job: the provisions of centre-left Cabinets (2014–2016)

Finally, the third phase (2014–2016) concerned the centre-left cabinet led by Renzi, and was characterized by episodic, partly contradictory provisions. On the one hand, there was continuity with the direction taken by Monti's government, with the introduction of a series of spending cutbacks (in the 2014 and 2015 budgets). In 2014, the government implemented and supplemented Monti's 2011 provisions (all deriving from Fiscal Federalism enacted in 2011 by Berlusconi's cabinet) regarding the recentralization of Local government spending. This concerned a new plan for municipal spending based on strict state regulation, which also established that LGs' expenditure had to be accounted for on a cash-flow basis instead of on the principle of state transfers. Both measures contributed to hinder and delay the spending capacity of Italy's local governments. On the other hand, central government persisted in promoting the reorganization and rescaling of spending. So, Renzi's cabinet specifically supported (i) the merger of private companies, (ii) compulsory competitive tenders for the award of management services, and (iii) the widening of territorial districts (ATOs) for service management and delivery. In 2016, the government also set limitations on private companies owned by municipalities and working in LPS. The decree law in question aimed to reduce the huge number of such companies (Citroni et al. 2016) by favouring concentrations and capital injections. The government tried to limit the provision of incentives to "large, financially sound" undertakings only, and to create (after several attempts) a consolidated sector of such companies.

As regards the "Social Fund" (Léon et al. 2015), Italy's centre-left governments continued to reduce the total amount of spending through a series of micro-cuts affecting certain specific sub-sectors. The three cabinets proceeded to increase, or reduce, funds for specific social needs in turn.

At the same time, Renzi's government promoted a vigorous rescaling strategy. The "Delrio Act" (2014) re-organized sub-regional governance through a range of measures: (i) provinces were now confirmed as indirectly elected second-tier authorities; their functions were carried out by other territorial bodies such as municipal unions; (ii) intermunicipal cooperation and merger were re-launched; (iii) 9 Metropolitan Areas were created. The government also slackened the constraints on joint management, leaving small municipalities room to arrange intermunicipal cooperation also in a softer way than that dictated by previous legislative provisions. The "Boschi Act" tried to drop all mention of provincial government from the Constitution (Bolgherini and Lippi 2016) and took away powers from regional governments and local authorities, granting these powers to the central state. This attempted amendment of the Constitution failed to be approved by a popular referendum held in 2016, so that the aforementioned rescaling project fell by the wayside.

Coping with Austerity: Citizens and Local Administrations

This section looks at the impact of the austerity policy on local public services, from the perspective of local administrations and citizens. The piecemeal, disjointed nature of the policy-making process implies that on the one hand no linear flow of implementation can be expected, and that on the other hand, any effects are not easily traced. We therefore look at the effects of austerity through the policy instruments lens: the use of authority in order to reduce costs, the attempts to liberalize the markets and the overarching, decisive tool of budgetary cuts.

The use of authority and the transaction costs of cuts

As was noted in the previous sections, a number of provisions were made from 2008 onwards, designed to reduce the "cost of politics" through the abolition (or restructuring) of provinces, of ATO districts for water and waste-disposal services and of municipal corporations, as well as through attempts at rescaling and compulsory intermunicipal cooperation.

Regions in particular have had to cope with the abolition of the former ATO districts for water-supply and waste-disposal services (see previous section), and with the permanent discussion regarding abolition of Italy's provinces. As a consequence, they have had to design new institutional settings for intermunicipal cooperation and service regulation (Citroni et al. 2015). Innovation, experimentation and the elaboration of optimal solutions for local contexts have not been the main criteria for re-regulation, with many regions replicating older models or remaining inactive. In fact, a complex process of redesign and learning has introduced new "transaction costs" in the place of the previous institutional costs.

Similarly, the repeated attempts by governments—especially the Monti and centre-left governments—to reduce the number of municipal corporations in the name of rationalization and of the reduction in the costs of politics have only produced marginal results. An obligation to cut off contractual ties with any companies that do not operate in fields pertaining to the fundamental functions of municipalities has been in place since 2008, and further constraints have been introduced over the course of time. However, the most recently available comparative figures show that between 2014 and 2015, the total number of companies contracted to municipalities actually increased, and it only fell slightly in 2016 (5258 in 2014, 5445 in 2015, 4915 in 2016),[6] despite Prime Minister Renzi's promise in 2014 to reduce such number from 8000 to 1000 in the immediate future.[7] Consequently, Italy's municipalities do not appear to have taken such obligations and threats too seriously—probably also due to the lack of incentives or sanctions. However, a significant burden has been placed on them in the form of compulsory yearly reports they are now required to submit, showing that they intend to rationalize their corporations and companies, and thus reduce their overall numbers. Compliance with this obligation appears to be materializing, albeit slowly and with repeated interruptions, with all the costs this entails for over 8000 municipalities.

Compulsory intermunicipal cooperation, on the other hand, has followed different paths in different fields. In water and waste management (Lippi et al. 2008), a long-standing obligation first established in the mid-1990s was designed to promote industrialization and economies of scale (accompanied by the consequent centralization of political power, and the substantial curbing of attempts at re-municipalization—see below). More recent reforms, as summarized in the previous section, have obliged small municipalities to cooperate in certain fields of their own choice: early research results regarding the southern region of Calabria (Marotta 2015) show that municipalities have so far cooperated either in a mainly formal manner, or in the highly problematic field of social services, where the region's smallest municipalities lack the necessary resources and skills to operate effectively.

[6] State Audit Court, yearly reports on municipal agencies and corporations (*Gli organismi partecipati dagli Enti territoriali*).

[7] Government tweet of 18 April 2014 (user @Palazzo_Chigi); note that the figure of 8000 includes all agencies, associations, etc.

Privatization, competition and regulation: creating markets for want of better options?

The second series of provisions and instruments which have been adopted throughout all three phases, includes market liberalization and regulation. Once again, this is an on-going trend which started in the 1990s (water, waste, transport, health) and the early 2000s (social services): during the 1990s, the separation of service regulation from service provision was intended to create a market for privatization; in the social services, horizontal subsidiarity and planning/regulation have been the key ideas introduced during the 2000s. However, while these reforms were initially framed as being of a substantially technical (economic) nature, since the advent of the economic crisis they have been subject to increasing politicization.

Campaigns against privatization in particular reached a climax in 2011, with the landslide referendum victory of those voting NO to compulsory competitive tendering in the local utilities sector. The campaign (Bersani 2011) was given an initial impetus by the legacy of the early 2000s "Social Forum" movement on international trade and sustainability; it gathered momentum with protests against water privatization; and it culminated in the referendum of 2011, initiated and promoted by an alliance of hundreds of groups comprising NGOs, trade unions, political parties and an extremely heterogeneous mix of cultural, environmental and religious organizations. The referendum called for (and obtained) the repeal of a bill imposing compulsory competitive tendering for all local utilities delivered by municipalities, but the campaign mainly focused on water privatization: mounting tariffs, the involvement of corrupt, greedy multinationals, the loss of democratic oversight, and environmental dangers, represented the key issues at the centre of the referendum campaign.

Successive cabinets have continually tried to either introduce compulsory competitive tendering (Berlusconi, phase 1), or to strongly push for privatization and market competition (Monti, phase 2; Minister Madia, phase 3), while restructuring central regulatory powers. However, no clear design has emerged, no active engagement of local authorities has taken place, and no coordination has been put in place (Citroni and Di Giulio 2016), so that the variations in the degrees of privatization and market creation need to be explained by other factors.

The water sector in particular shows virtually no increase in competitive tendering and private management, with only 3% of the population served by private companies (Citroni et al. 2016); the waste sector reveals stronger market dynamics (around 16% of added value is created by private companies), but this mainly concerns the more innovative fields, such as recycling, rather than the traditional ones (ibid.). Hence, the engagement of private companies seems to be due to their ability to invest in innovation, rather than to any decision by national or local governments to privatize existing services. As we shall see, Italy's municipalities have lost their capacity to invest, and thus it would appear that they are privatizing for lack of other options. Whenever they can, local governments (especially in Northern and Central Italy, where regional and municipal governments possess greater economic and political resources, respectively) prefer to deal with the fiscal crisis by merging to form very large intermunicipal companies, and by having recourse to public-private partnerships (Galanti 2016).

In the social services sector, in terms of nursery school places and places in residential homes for the elderly, private delivery of such services is more clearly on the increase (Citroni et al. 2016). In nursery schools, private delivery amounted to under 7% in 1992, but this was up to almost 40% by 2005, and to 57% by 2012; in residential homes for the elderly, the public quota fell from 45% in 1999 to 30% in 2009 (ibid.): as revealed in the following section, a lack of resources for new investment appears to be the driving force behind this trend. Figures provided by ISTAT (the Italian National Statistics Institute) concerning municipal budgets show that spending on contracts is increasing, while that on personnel is stable or decreasing, as shown in the tables below (Fig. 6.1).

Cutbacks and protests: the origins of a political crisis

All in all, it thus appears that the main driver of change in local services subject to the policy of austerity are budget cuts. Indeed, municipalities have radically restructured their spending: between 2010 and 2015, current primary expenditure was reduced by 12%, and more importantly capital expenditure fell by 25.7% (Monteduro 2016). While there is some hope of a future revival in municipal investment following the "Internal stability pact" provisions, the effects of the aforesaid reduction over the past few years can be clearly seen in the trend towards "privatization for want of better options" described above.

Within this generalized scenario of drastic spending cuts, the availability of resources for services has been badly affected. On the one hand, the

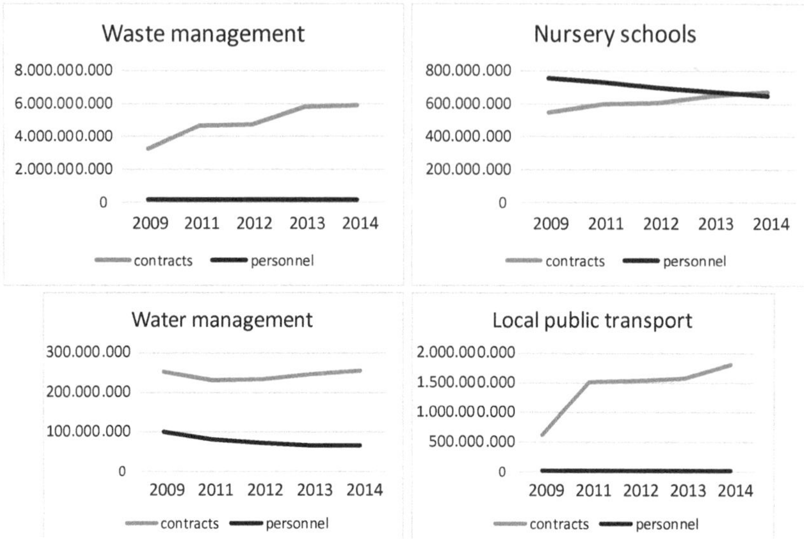

Fig. 6.1 Municipal budgets for local public service. (Source: ISTAT)

tariff systems for the waste disposal and water services have been repeatedly changed, and they offer no certainty or stability of income (Savoldi and Scarpa 2016); on the other hand, and more importantly, the funds transferred by government to Italy's regional and local governments to be used for social services, have been reduced to a pittance. The sum total of the various funds transferred for family allowances, assistance to disabled people, social policy etc., fell from 2.53 billion in 2008 to under 200 million in 2015.[8] User contributions and private services have thus increased, as has the "out-of-pocket" expenses of families for healthcare (which had been steadily decreasing, but is now once again over 21% of total health spending).[9] The regional governments' current spending on health services fell on average by 1.54% every year between 2009 and 2013, and capital expenditure fell by an average of 5.6% each year during that same period. The considerable differences among regions in terms of the incidence of out-of-pocket expenditure on family income have further increased (CREA Sanità 2015). Moreover, a significant number of respon-

[8] https://www.nens.it/archivio/fondi-statali-le-politiche-sociali-una-parziale-inversione-di-tendenza

[9] See data.worldbank.org

dents to a survey reported that they had foregone treatment for economic reasons: 5.6% of them nationwide and 14.7% in Italy's southern regions (ibid.).

At the same time as the reduction in transfers, new accounting regulations have also led to the emergence of "hidden debts" and to the initiation of "pre-bankruptcy" procedures in as many as 146 municipalities since 2012, and bankruptcy procedures in 84 municipalities since 2011.[10] Notably, the "pre-bankruptcy" procedure—introduced in 2012 and aimed at preventing full-blown bankruptcy procedures—entails a number of compulsory budgetary consolidation measures, including increases in service tariffs, cuts to specific welfare measures, and the full recovery of the cost of utilities through user tariffs.

As a consequence of all the aforementioned cuts, which contributed a total of 19 billion euros to national coffers between 2008 and 2015,[11] there has been no systematic, univocal reaction from citizens. However, the politicization of welfare policy has led to strong protests in the form of direct action and legal/illegal self-organization. According to a recent article (Bosi and Zamponi 2015), squatting, the occupation of buildings and theatres for social and cultural initiatives, and innovative "social purchase groups", have resurfaced, grown in size and influence, and expanded to include new social and political strata. These protests have impacted local policy arenas in two ways at least. Firstly, a number of experiments are currently being conducted by municipalities, regarding the regulation of the cooperative use of common goods, and the development of "cooperative agreements" with associations, movements and groups of citizens, in the fields of urban regeneration, welfare, development, the environment etc. (Arena and Iaione 2012).[12] Secondly, the attention raised by the water privatization referendum campaign has led to attempts to re-municipalize water services—most notably in the case of Naples—although no general trend has yet to be identified; of course, the lack of funding for municipalities to be able to buy service companies back from PPPs, is an important factor against re-municipalization, as is compulsory intermunicipal delivery which prevents individual municipalities from stepping back from PPPs.

[10] IFEL Data, http://inchieste.repubblica.it/it/repubblica/rep-it/2016/10/12/news/il_dissesto_finanziario_dei_comuni_italiani-147748161

[11] State Audit Court, Relazione sugli andamenti della finanza territoriale—Esercizio 2014.

[12] For more recent cases and analyses, see http://www.labsus.org/category/patti-beni-comuni/ (in Italian).

The Recentralization and De-institutionalization of LPS Under Austerity

Although it is not the main, specific target of governmental measures, there is no doubt that Italy's LPS have been hard hit by austerity policies, as a consequence of the constant call for the retrenchment of the public sector as a whole, and for an overall reduction in local governments' degree of freedom (as testified by the current dramatic state of municipal governments' finances).

Indeed, the analysis of the austerity agenda reveals that an advocacy coalition calling for budgetary stability, a retrenchment of the public sphere and a change in LPS in the direction of privatization, competition and economies of scale, has been rooted in Italian politics for a long time now. Ever since the early 1990s, several members of the aforesaid coalition, consisting mainly of technocrats and academics who are (to one degree or another) directly linked to Italy's Central Bank, have held prominent positions in Italian governments, and have strategically utilized European constraints to promote change at home, by shifting the blame for unpopular decisions away from themselves. The majority of current austerity measures, including purely fiscal provisions and spending cutbacks, have been envisaged since the 1990s and have been portrayed as "modernization" policies, although their implementation has sometimes failed, or has led to the opposite effect. The onset of the global crisis simply opened a window of opportunity within which to re-launch previous projects, and it provided stakeholders with a new opportunity to urge that reforms be introduced.

Against such a backdrop, since 2008 "austerity" has become a convenient catch-all term encompassing a number of different stakes and political strategies. For example, austerity has provided political actors with the means with which to compete on the political stage (e.g. Berlusconi's centre-right government competing against local governments chiefly administrated by the centre-left; the opposition's use of austerity diktats to dismiss Berlusconi in 2011; or again, Renzi's consensus-seeking rhetoric against austerity). On the other hand, austerity and the imperative nature of reducing costs has paved the way for the rehabilitation of previously unsuccessful or disputed policy initiatives, such as compulsory competitive tendering for the granting of concessions in the field of LPS, the abolition of Italy's provinces and the reduction in the number of elected representative bodies. For this reason, there is no one period of austerity, but rather a sequence of windows opened by different cabinets at different times and based on different rationales. Consequently, it is not easy to identify any one specific recipe for austerity, or its clear effects on LPS; however, certain general conclusions may be drawn here.

First of all, it is worth noting that during the last eight years, austerity has ceased to be of an extraordinary character, and has become "the only game in town" when it comes to dealing with the LPS. As a matter of fact, governments have continued to implement austerity measures regardless of their different ideological positions and of actual policy results. Issue-making has changed, but policy instruments (and measures concerning LPS) have survived with only marginal adjustments made. Furthermore, certain key decision, such as the change in the Constitution, which included the break-even principle in the light of the Golden Rules, have clearly created a political climate for the establishment of permanent fiscal politics, and have framed all subsequent decisions and behaviour in favour of the self-containment and self-reduction of public spending.

Secondly, there has been a lack of visibility with regard to decisions concerning LPS. On the one hand, measures affecting LPS have included various sectoral actions and have been spread out over time, so that the dismantling effect and detrimental impact of austerity has gradually developed away from the public spotlight. The public's perception of changes to LPS has always been extremely limited, with the exception of certain isolated events or specific issues such as the popular referendum held in 2011, which in any case catalysed the general protest against Italy's central government rather than reflecting any specific opposition to the policies at stake. On the other hand, the general public rarely makes a clear-cut distinction between the responsibilities of central and local government, or between decision makers and implementers; rather, LPS users' discontent is likely to coalesce around the last link in the chain, thus encouraging the central elites to concentrate cutbacks and unpopular measures at lower governmental levels.

Last, but not least, austerity measures affecting LPS have produced a series of side effects with strong political implications, as they produce significant changes in relations between different levels of government and between public and private actors. One such side effect is a process of recentralization concealed by cost-saving actions. The economies of scale argument, as well as the rescaling rhetoric, have played a key role here: LPS management units have been the object of an endless process of redefinition in the name of an optimal scale for service delivery. However, such a process has gradually weakened the local capacity of the steering service, since this has relied on the aggregation of a multitude of municipalities characterized by weak planning and control capacities, poor coordinating ability and decreasing funding. Recentralization has also been pursued through the establishment of limitations on staff hiring and retirements, cutbacks, reductions in services and the delegation of new tasks to the local levels without adequate financial cover. All these aspects have strongly impacted the delivery of services and the quality of performance. In the shadow of austerity, central government limits the degree of freedom enjoyed by the peripheral levels, thus increasing the distance between the decision-making arena and LPS users. Moreover, in a situation of enduring fiscal crisis, central government may negotiate the transfer of financial resources with local governments, and in doing so may grant departures from the Internal Stability Pact, or even acknowledge exceptions on the basis of local specificities. In this sense, austerity empowers central government (which holds the purse strings) vis-à-vis the periphery, since it moves intergovernmental relations from institutionalized channels to political—and thus discretionary—ones.

Another side effect concerns the de-institutionalization of LPS management and delivery, in the name of cost saving, and the re-launch of more efficient and inexpensive LPS management. De-institutionalization means undermining codified organizational models and procedures in favour of more flexible, informal arrangements, thus favouring the privatization or liberalization of former municipal settings. However, it also brings with it certain pressures and limitations that force municipalities and local agencies to generate funds through tariff increases, and to outsource service delivery to Non Governmental Organizations (NGOs), charities, families and so on. Certain measures promoting this process of de-institutionalization have paved the way for a redistribution of power between public and private stakeholders. The abolition of ombudsman, the severe reduction of social funds—especially for the disabled and for young people—and, in general, the increasing involvement of private players in place of public ones, have made the system not only more flexible but also more vulnerable to uneven power relations, and more sensitive to local governance arrangements. In a context such as the Italian one, which has traditionally been characterized by strong interregional differences in terms of socioeconomic conditions, administrative traditions and interest-representation mechanisms, this may clearly lead to the exacerbation of territorial imbalances and a variable geography of social citizenship.

Conclusions

This chapter aimed at describing the intentional outcomes and side effects of austerity measures on the domain of LPS in Italy, with regard to the last decade. As illustrated above, internal political dynamics and the alternation of peculiar domestic advocacy coalitions had a strong influence in transferring (and reshaping) external pressures towards austerity. In the process, central government regained power after the "quasi-federalist" wave experienced in the 1990s. As a result, two main effects emerged: a considerable recentralization of decision-making and resource allocation, and a creeping deinstitutionalization of the LPS policy domain.

Recentralization and deinstitutionalization, despite a patchwork, discontinuous nature, have reduced the autonomy of local governments and weakened LPS management and delivery in Italy. While the advocacy coalition supporting the retrenchment of the state in regard to the delivery of LPS remained fairly stable, and has had significant supporters at central and local levels (the President of Italian Republic Giorgio Napolitano, for instance, was a key supporter; likewise, the interest group composed of private companies owned by municipalities, many academics and various influential opinion makers), a similar opposing coalition has never emerged. Municipalities have not proven capable of cohesive resistance, regional governments have tried to negotiate certain trade-offs, unions and consumer associations have focused on other, more clearly visible effects of the crisis (such as unemployment), while the public's attention has been episodic and has focused on a few symbolic issues (such as water supply, in the referendum of 2011). Thus, LPS as a whole have remained bereft of defenders, in a situation that has witnessed a shift towards increasing discretionary powers of central government and the negotiability of resources (and rights) in the periphery. Discretion and negotiability both threaten democratic accountability and contribute to re-politicize social rights and institutions.

References

Arena, G., & Iaione, C. (Eds.). (2012). *L'Italia dei beni comuni*. Milano: Carocci.

Banca d'Italia. (2007, October 30). *Local government Debt—Statistic Series, XVII*(62), 2007.

Bersani, M. (2011). *Come abbiamo vinto il referendum: dalla battaglia per l'acqua pubblica alla democrazia dei beni comuni*. Roma: Alegre.

Bolgherini, S. (2014). Can Austerity Lead to Recentralisation? Italian Local Government During the Economic Crisis. *South European Society and Politics, 19*(2), 193–214.

Bolgherini, S., & Lippi, A. (2016). Italy. Re-mapping Local Government from Re-allocation and Re-Shaping to Re-scaling. In U. Sadioglu & K. Dede (Eds.), *Theoretical Foundations and Discussions on the Reformation Process in Local Governments* (pp. 265–287). New York: IGI Global.

Bolgherini, S., Lippi, A., & Maset, S. (2016). *In mezzo al guado. La governance subregionale tra vecchie province e nuove aree vaste. Rivista Italiana di Politiche Pubbliche, 12*(3), 341–372.

Bosco, A., & McDonnell, D. (2012). Introduction: The Monti Government and the Downgrade of Italian Parties. In A. Bosco & D. McDonnell (Eds.), *Italian Politics. From Berlusconi to Monti.* New York: Berghahn.

Bosi, L., & Zamponi, L. (2015). *Direct Social Actions and Economic Crises: The Relationship Between Forms of Action and Socio-Economic Context in Italy. Partecipazione e conflitto, 8*(2), 367–391.

Bussu, S., & Galanti, T. (2015). Local Governments at the Time of the Crisis. In C. Hanretty & S. Profeti (Eds.), *Italian Politics. The Year of the Bulldozer* (pp. 141–159). New York: Berghahn.

Citroni, G., & Di Giulio, M. (2016). *Dismissioni! E poi? Che fare delle ex-municipalizzate.* Milano: Guerini e Associati.

Citroni, G., Lippi, A., & Profeti, S. (2015). Representation Through Corporatisation. Municipal Corporations in Italy as Arenas for Local Democracy. *European Political Science Review, 7*(1), 63–98.

Citroni, G., Lippi, A., & Profeti, S. (2016). *Local Public Services in Italy: Still Fragmentation.* In H. Wollmann, G. Marcou, & I. Kopric (Eds.), *Public and Social Services in European Countries* (pp. 103–118). London: Palgrave Macmillan.

Citroni, G., Di Giulio, M., Galanti, M. T., Lippi, A., & Profeti, S. (2017). Apprentice Sorcerers. Evaluating the Program Theory of Regulatory Governance in Italian Public Utilities. In I. Kopric, G. Marcou, & H. Wollmann (Eds.), *Evaluation of Reforms of Local Public Services in Europe* (pp. 225–242). London: Palgrave.

CREA Sanità. (2015). *XI Rapporto sanità. L'universalismo diseguale.* Rome: CREA Consorzio per la Ricerca Economica Applicata in Sanità.

Culpepper, P. (2014). The Political Economy of Unmediated Democracy: Italian Austerity Under Mario Monti. *West European Politics, 37*(6), 1264–1281.

Di Giulio, M., & Profeti, S. (2016). Eppur si muove? Il riordino territoriale oltre la crisi. *Rivista Italiana di Politiche Pubbliche, 12*(3), 311–340.

Di Mascio, F., & Natalini, A. (2014). Reform Processes: Performance Management Within Italian Local Government. *International Public Management Journal, 16*(1), 141–166.

Di Mascio, F., & Natalini, A. (2015). Fiscal Retrenchment in Southern Europe: Changing Patterns of Public Management in Greece, Italy, Portugal and Spain. *Public Management Review, 17*(1), 129–148.

Di Mascio, F., Natalini, A., & Stolfi, F. (2013). The Gost of Crises Past: Analysing Reform Sequences to Understand Italy's Response to Global Crisis. *Public Administration, 91*(1), 17–31.

Di Quirico, R. (2010). Italy and the Global Economic Crisis. *Bulletin of Italian Politics, 2*(2), 3–19.

Dyson, K., & Featherstone, K. (Eds.). (1999). *The Road to Maastricht.* Oxford: Oxford University Press.

Fusaro, C. (2013). The Formation of the Monti Government and the Role of the President of the Republic. In A. Bosco & D. McDonnell (Eds.), *Italian Politics. From Berlusconi to Monti* (pp. 78–97). New York: Berghahn.

Galanti, T. (2016). *Sindaci e manager nel capitalismo municipale. Saggio sui vestiti nuovi dell'imperatore.* Bologna: il Mulino.

Gennari, E., & Messina, G. (2012, January). *How Sticky Are Local Expenditures in Italy? Assessing the Relevance of the "Flypaper Effect" Through Municipal Data.* Banca d'Italia Working Paper No. 844.

Giannetti, D. (2013). Mario Monti's Technocratic Government. In A. Di Virgilio & C. Radaelli (Eds.), *Italian Politics. Technocrats in Office* (pp. 133–152). New York: Berghahn.

Goretti, C., & Rizzuto, L. (2013). The Spending Review: Use and Abuse of a Term. In A. Di Virgilio & C. M. Radaelli (Eds.), *Italian Politics: Technocrats in Office* (pp. 188–206). New York: Berghahn.

Gualmini, E., & Pasotti, E. (Eds.). (2011). *Italian Politics. Much Ado About Nothing?* New York: Berghahn.

Guidi, M. (2015). The Democratic Party of Matteo Renzi. In C. Hanretty & S. Profeti (Eds.), *Italian Politics. The Year of the Bulldozer* (pp. 51–66). New York: Berghahn.

Hanretty, C., & Profeti, S. (Eds.). (2015). *Italian Politics. The Year of the Bulldozer.* New York: Berghahn.

Hopkin, J. (2012). A Slow Fuse: Italy and the EU Debt Crisis. *The International Spectator, 47*(4), 35–48.

Jones, E. (2012). *Italy's Sovereign Debt Crisis. Survival: Global Politics and Strategy, 54*(1), 83–110.

Léon, M., Pavolini, E., & Guillén, A. M. (2015). Welfare Rescaling in Italy and Spain: Political Strategies to Deal with Harsh Austerity. *European Journal of Social Security, 17*(2), 182–201.

Lippi, A. (2011). Evaluating the 'Quasi Federalist' Programme of Decentralisation in Italy Since the 1990s: A Side Effect Approach. *Local Government Studies, 37*(5), 495–516.

Lippi, A., Giannelli, N., Profeti, S., & Citroni, G. (2008). Adapting Public-Private Governance to the Local Context. The Case of Water and Sanitation Services in Italy. *Public Management Review, 10*(5), 619–640.

Marangoni, F. (2012). *Technocrats in Government: The Composition and Legislative Initiatives of the Monti Government Eight Months into Its Term of Office. Bulletin of Italian Politics, 4*(1), 135–149.

Marotta, M. (2015). *L'associazionismo obbligatorio delle funzioni dei piccoli Comuni calabresi. Amministrare, 45*(1), 151–162.

Monteduro, M. T. (2016). Riforme istituzionali ed equilibri di bilancio: la finanza locale alla ricerca di un assetto stabile. In G. Arachi & M. Baldini (Eds.), *La finanza pubblica italiana. Rapporto 2016* (pp. 155–182). Bologna: Il Mulino.

Quaglia, L. (2005). *Civil Servants, Economic Ideas, and Economic Policies: Lessons from Italy. Governance: An International Journal of Policy, Administration, and Institutions, 18*(4), 545–566.

Radaelli, C., & Franchino, F. (2004). Analysing Political Change in Italy. *Journal of European Public Policy, 11*(6), 941–953.

Sacchi, S. (2015). Conditionality by Other Means: EU Involvement in Italy's Structural Reforms in the Sovereign Debt Crisis. *Comparative European Politics, 13*(1), 77–92.

Savoldi, A., & Scarpa, C. (2016). Servizi pubblici: i consumatori al centro dell'attenzione. In G. Arachi & M. Baldini (Eds.), *La finanza pubblica italiana. Rapporto 2016* (pp. 185–205). Bologna: Il Mulino.

Stolfi, F. (2013). Back in Europe? Italy, the Troika, and the Chancelleries. In A. Di Virgilio & C. Radaelli (Eds.), *Italian Politics. Technocrats in Office* (pp. 173–187). New York: Berghahn.

Ter-Minassian, T. (2007). *Fiscal Rules for Subnational Governments: Can They Promote Fiscal Discipline? OECD Journal on Budgeting, 6*(3), 1–11.

CHAPTER 7

Austerity Measures and Local Public Services in Cyprus: Coping with Challenges Old and New and Reinforcing Historical Continuities

Andreas Kirlappos, Philippos Philippou, and Kalliope Agapiou-Josephides

Introduction

Cypriot Municipalities have faced retrenchment and fiscal consolidation due to the financial crisis and the adoption of a Memorandum of Understanding (MOU) on Specific Economic Policy Conditionality with the European Commission, European Central Bank and International Monetary Fund ("Troika") in March 2013. Thus, austerity measures have substantially challenged the Republic of Cyprus' (ROC) political, economic and administrative systems. In this respect, investigating the interface between Europeanization and local public services (LPS) constitutes a theoretically and empirically challenging research endeavour. From a theoretical perspec-

A. Kirlappos (✉) • P. Philippou • K. Agapiou-Josephides
Department of Social and Political Sciences, University of Cyprus, Nicosia, Cyprus
e-mail: philipposphilippou@hotmail.com; agapiouj@ucy.ac.cy

A. Lippi, T. N. Tsekos (eds.), *Local Public Services in Times of Austerity across Mediterranean Europe*, Governance and Public Management, https://doi.org/10.1007/978-3-319-76225-8_7

tive, the very logic of Europeanization, *as* a conceptual and analytical framework to understand a complex and dynamic adaptation process in different areas of policies, politics and polity, has found itself seriously challenged by the coercive character of austerity measures. Empirically, the fact that austerity measures outreach their immediately apparent scope of fiscal consolidation, with repercussions for wider public administration and citizens' well-being, has created new dynamics and posed new challenges to LPS.

This chapter contextualizes and analyses the variety of austerity measures and their impact on ROC LPS. It is founded on the theoretical and analytical framework of Europeanization and based on structured questionnaires (50) and semi-structured interviews (40) conducted both upon the agreement and signing of the MOU (2013) and upon its completion (2017) from Mayors, Municipal Secretaries and public servants from the Ministries of Finance and Interiors.

Secondary sources include reports by the Auditor General of the Republic (2000–2016) and European Commission and IMF Economic Adjustment Programme Reviews. In the first place, this work carries out a mapping of austerity measures, their specificities and impact. Secondly, it focuses on whether Learning and Development could prove a parameter operative in reforms in a rapidly changing environment. It examines whether diverse brands of policies and reforms could potentially be transferred via unofficial channels, such as the Learning and Development function of a public administration system.

Specific variables utilized to shed light on the impact of the austerity measures at the local level include the interplay between time and space and along external-internal and centre-periphery dimensions, together with the impact of the past in terms of resources, competencies and local governance-level autonomy. Finally, this work argues that the design and delivery of LPS depend on historical continuities that affect the interplay between central and local government structures and that austerity measures cannot but reinforce them.

The Restrictive Condition of the Cypriot Local Government

The Republic of Cyprus

The ROC is a small island republic that joined the European Union (EU) in 2004 and the Eurozone in 2008. Located at an important geopolitical position at the crossroads of East and West, North and South, it suffers, to date, foreign occupation and political division. It is a unitary state, comprising six Districts, 39 Municipalities and 491 Communities (2017).[1] At a more general level, historical continuities have been generated by the last two historical periods prior to the island's independence generating burdens on its social, political and financial progress (Kirlappos 2016). As we will see, these burdens of the past have long had severe effects on local government, jeopardizing its proper functioning and development.

Ottoman and British Colonial Eras

The basic organization of the local government system of the ROC dates back to the Ottoman era (1571–1878), when the Ottomans established the administrative districts that continue to exist today, that is, Nicosia, Limassol, Famagusta Larnaca, Pafos, and Kerynia. This historical period endowed Municipalities with distinctive characteristics that have since had a crucial role in the operation of local government. These include the firm hierarchical control of the central state via the appointed District Commissioners, along with the precise assignment of a limited list of competencies and restricted sources of revenues (Tornaritis 1972, pp. 6–13).

During the British rule (1878–1960), the condition of the local actors was relatively improved due to some modernizing measures, for example holding the Mayors and the Council accountable for the management of the Municipal budgets (Tornaritis 1972, p. 16). Yet, there was no substantial progress that would significantly strengthen the roles and competencies of Municipalities. As it is explained by Tornaritis (1972, p. 17), this had to do with the fact that during this period, British laws regulating local government reserved many of the provisions of the old Ottoman laws. Both the competencies and financial resources of local authorities remained highly specific, very limited and subject to strict control by the central government. Just like before, Municipalities were overseen by appointed District Commissioners preserving strict administrative control (Markides 2009, p. 186).

[1] This work focuses on the Municipalities that have not been displaced due to the Turkish invasion of 1974 (30) and which remain fully functional local government organizations.

Local Government in the Republic of Cyprus

The first years of the post-colonial period were marked by a series of disastrous events, including the outbreak of intercommunal violence in 1963, the coup d'état executed against President Makarios by the Greek military junta and the consequent Turkish military invasion in 1974. Due to the extremely unusual circumstances that followed, the Council of Ministers decided (1963) not to hold local elections and to appoint instead persons in charge of managing local government (Markides 2009, pp. 348–349). The condition of local government received renewed interest and attention during the 1980s when the adoption of the *Municipalities Law* (1985) and the *European Charter of Local Self-Government* (1988) halted this practice and improved, to some extent, the status of Cypriot Municipalities by providing elements of a more modern legal framework.

While the accession to the EU (2004) instigated institutional adjustment and widespread reform of the political, economic and administrative structure of the ROC, it did not significantly touch local government. Having missed the unprecedented opportunity offered by pre-accession dynamics as a driver of change, the administrative, financial and political autonomy of the Cypriot Municipalities remains extremely limited as it is *de facto* minimized by the burdens of the past and exacerbated by a severe debt crisis. Due to the latter, Cypriot Municipalities face massive debt problems, have restricted means of income and are highly dependent on the central state whose grant constitutes about 40% of their overall budget (Auditor General 2000–2016). Their competencies are still restricted, operating under the administrative control of the central state. Yet, the accession to the EU has highlighted the need for a substantial reform of the local government system, as was the case in other EU member-states, for example Italy (Bull and Baudner 2004, pp. 1072–1073). For this reason, a number of attempts have taken place aiming to reform the local government system. These have been affected by the current economic crisis, the bail-in/bail-out agreement and the consequent imposition of austerity measures (MOU 2013).

Mapping Austerity Measures, Their Specificities and Impact

Due to the impact of external agents, austerity was included in local policies affecting both the multi-level governance relations inside the Cypriot state and the LPS delivered by Cypriot Municipalities. As will be discussed more extensively below, austerity reached LGOs by means of European

Commission recommendations initially and subsequently through the MOU with the Troika. They took the form of fiscal consolidation via severe cutbacks to central government grants to LGOs, recentralization of budgetary discretion by means of a *Fiscal Responsibility and Budget Systems Law* (2014), a law required by the MOU, and a hiring freeze voted by parliament (*Law on the Prohibition of Filling Vacant Positions in the Public and the Wider Public Sector* 2013). They also took the form of compulsory repayment directly by the government via the withholding of state grants to LGOs: (a) of those LGO loans for which the government was guarantor and (b) of Municipality liabilities vis-à-vis central authorities like the water development department. Finally, austerity also characterized proposals for radical structural reforms of LG as put forward by an MOU-required reform study, though the plan was eventually watered down and was not implemented.

As was indicated, the general condition of the Cypriot Municipalities has been restricted both politically and financially, making it hard for them to have a substantial and positive impact on the lives of their citizens. Their competencies in the areas of LPS that fall within the scope of this book are fragmented and shared with central authorities, mainly Ministries and semi-governmental organizations, leaving limited room for Municipalities to operate freely (*The Municipalities Law* 1985). For illustration purposes, we can refer to the water and waste category of LPS. Cypriot Municipalities buy water from central structures (Water Development Department) and sell it to their citizens. Their competence in this area limits their responsibility mainly to implementing tasks such as building and maintaining water supply, sewerage management, waste collection and recycling systems (ibid). Their social policy competencies are of minor scope and are implemented parallel to those belonging to central authorities. Cypriot Municipalities have some social welfare responsibilities, like the establishment and management of retirement homes and charitable institutions but these are not uniformly encountered (ibid). They also have some minor sport and culture competencies, for example organizing and promoting cultural and sports activities (ibid). Finally, Cypriot Municipalities do not have competencies regarding the category of health.

Impact of Austerity Measures on the Institutional Structures of the Cypriot LG

Before presenting the impact of the austerity measures on the LPS provided by the Cypriot Municipalities, we need to explain that the instruments and strategies that promoted them had minimum effect on the institutional structure of the Cypriot local government. Attempts to reform the local government system (National Centre for Public Administration and Local Government 2010) were initially triggered before the introduction of the MOU, indicating that the internal/national level was fully aware of the need to change the way things worked at the local level. Yet, these efforts, which had never really gained traction, were quickly paused since the MOU included a clear provision for the reform of the local level system. In fulfilment of MOU obligations, the government commissioned British experts to prepare new reform reports on the findings of which a new reform plan would be prepared (International Monetary Fund 2014). This plan included proposals for far-reaching institutional reform, substantial reduction and downsizing of the local government actors and an amalgamation of services followed by an amalgamation of local actors (National School of Government International 2014). The Cypriot central authorities agreed to adopt related laws as high priority before the completion of the MOU. In reaction to this, a second, competing study was commissioned by the Union of Cyprus Municipalities (UCM), which was accepted as the basis for reform legislation currently debated in parliament (Dalitis 2015).[2]

In practice, there was only partial completion of this condition, as indicated by the European Commission (2015). One the one hand, the initial reform plan adopted by the Council of Ministers on local government was incomplete since it had a number of shortcomings, such as the inadequate and unclear justification vis-à-vis the rationale of the chosen, new structure and the unclear implementation details (European Commission 2015). On the other hand, there was considerable variation between the experts' recommendations and the executive's decision over the reform of the local government system in Cyprus. This reform plan did not seem to take into account the experts' suggestions that point towards decentralization of competencies and financial means at the Municipal level, thus simply reproducing the balance of power between central and local level. It seems that even within a coercive situation, governments seem to have a degree of freedom to choose the version of policy they consider best suited to

[2] The Ministry of the Interiors prepared the relevant Bills and brought them to Parliament in March 2016. Once again, there was inconsistency between the experts' proposals and the executive's choices with regard to the Bills. Major provisions included mandatory clustering and a non-hierarchical relationship between District and local clusters. The reform proposals triggered new reactions. Since tensions are expected to rise in view of the February 2018 Presidential elections, support for the LG reform bills is expected to further decrease, in fear that local reactions could influence the outcome of the elections.

their situation, regardless of the particular preferences of the international organization exercising coercion (Dolowitz and Marsh 2000, pp. 10–11). Besides the central state structures, which never wanted to lose their control over local government, other mediating factors had a crucial role, which affected the chances of successful implementation of the local government reforms. Despite the high external pressure for local government reform deriving from the MOU and transferred internally via the Cypriot government to Municipalities, there was strong opposition by both political parties and Municipalities to the proposed reforms (European Commission 2014). Regardless of the weak position of the Municipalities vis-à-vis the central structures, it was demonstrated by empirical evidence that the former were in a position to exert pressure, preventing the imposition of reforms that did not constitute a high priority for the latter (Dalitis 2015; Kavkalias 2016). This can be better understood in light of the national characteristics and political dynamics of LG arrangements, where Mayors overwhelmingly rise through the ranks of political party-organizations, are often former government ministers and members of parliament, maintain very good connections to the institutional centre (the Executive and the Legislature) and who come to power in LG on party tickets (Kirlappos 2016). Consequently, delays and inertia were caused, creating an unclear image as far as the centre/periphery relation (Wollmann 2016) and its impact on local autonomy are concerned. As no actual change in the arrangements (e.g. upscaling/recentralization) governing local government and its competencies was observed due to the crisis and fiscal consolidation, it should be noted that Central state structures in Cyprus behaved in a path-dependent manner, revealing their unwillingness to abdicate their control over local government.

Significantly, the ROC legislature and the executive demonstrated greater determination in adopting other, specific and crucial reforms promoted by the MOU that enabled the country to successfully implement its Economic and Adjustment Programme.[3] Thus, our findings verify Ongaro (2014), who notes that fiscal consolidation has become the guiding prin-

[3] The Cypriot government successfully implemented reforms in important sectors for example fiscal consolidation, tax reform, social welfare reform and financial sector reform. Yet, it was not so successful in other areas, such local government, the incomplete health care reforms and the privatization of the Cyprus Telecommunication Authority. See European Commission (October 2015).

ciple of any attempt at administrative reform. Prevailing logic indicates a clear preference for a public sector that spends less, demonstrating measurable results to the operators of financial markets, instead of focusing on improvements in the efficiency, effectiveness and quality of public services that are apparently believed to be unattainable (ibid).

Impact of the Austerity Measures on the LPS of the Cypriot LG

Despite the already existing restrictions in terms of the quantity and quality of the LPS delivered by the Cypriot Municipalities, austerity measures caused noticeable effects that further weakened the potential of Cypriot local government for a positive impact on the daily lives of Cypriot citizens. Empirical evidence demonstrated a serious loss of revenues as a result of the implementation of austerity measures, resulting in a crucial decrease of the Municipalities' already severely limited economic autonomy. Adequate pressure (coercion) had been applied to the ROC since 2010, when the Commission pushed for the adoption of fiscal consolidation measures. This pressure reached its dramatic climax when the newly elected (2013) government of President Anastasiades, based on a centre-right coalition, negotiated and reached an agreement with the Troika in 2013. This bail-in/ bail-out agreement had an immediate and forceful impact on the deteriorating Cypriot banking sector since it imposed both the dissolution of the second-largest Cypriot bank and a one-time bank deposit levy (48%) to the island's largest Cypriot bank (MOU April 2013). It meant significant losses for the Cypriot Municipalities who lost their credits and savings deposited in the two banks. Moreover, there was a massive loss of interest-rate-based revenues, while state reimbursement could not occur due to Cypriot state's dire budgetary situation, its inability to borrow from the financial markets and its dependence on MOU funding.

Two Ministries (Finance and the Interiors) had a key role vis-à-vis the implementation of the austerity policies and local government, respectively. The overall logic of the MOU, which focused on turning the state 'leaner' (Streeck 2013, p. 2), was urgently adopted at the local government level. Despite the financial hardship that this entailed, we noticed relatively modest (public and social) opposition towards the austerity logic and policies of the MOU aiming at the local level.[4] The majority of the

[4] Reactions originated from leftist organizations connected with the opposition party and from groups whose social benefits were running the risk of being decreased, for example the disabled and large families.

Mayors (65%) saw the austerity programme as a window of opportunity to modernize local organizational settings and especially to improve the efficiency of local financial management (structured questionnaires 2013). Conflict was mostly caused due to the (centralizing) reform attempts, and since these were never concluded, opposition to fiscal austerity measures was not as high as might be expected. Across the board, cutbacks by means of new fiscal responsibility legislation and annual government budgets voted by parliamentary majorities admittedly left little room for reaction or successful opposition on the LGOs' part.

The attention of central state politicians, for example the Minister of Finance, consultants and bureaucrats, was clearly focused on substantially reducing local government funding and on improving local financial management, thus securing cost savings (Semi-structured interviews 2013, 2017). While the adopted strategies, instruments and measures of the austerity programme demonstrated in theory a *'to do the same with less rational'* (Osborne and Gaebler 1992), in practice, the implementation of the austerity measures at the local level leads to the manifestation of a *'to do less with less'* rationale with regard to the LGOs and LPS. 'Across the board cutbacks'(Di Mascio and Natalini 2015) were predominantly used by the central structures affecting all local policy areas. As evidenced by the figures (see Table 7.1 below) provided by the UCM (2018, personal communication, 16 January), the state grant allocated to the Municipalities was reduced by up to 40% during the last five years (General Auditor 2012–2016) with further reductions (10%) to the state grants allocated to the Municipalities occurring by the imposition of direct payments towards

Table 7.1 Annual state grant to Municipalities 2009–2017

Year	*Annual state grant Municipalities(€)*	*Compensation grant for losses of professional tax revenues due to the 2003 tax reform (individuals)(€)*
2009	72,170,399	29,166,265
2010	72,354,370	29,165,183
2011	68,795,153	27,701,330
2012	60,976,514	20,528,538
2013	58,082,868	19,912,681
2014	51,093,530	17,501,520
2015	51,130,120	17,501,520
2016	51,130,920	17,501,520
2017	51,157,520	17,545,000

Source: Union of Cyprus Municipalities (2018, Personal communication, 16 January)

the reimbursement of vast Municipal debts to central state authorities, for example water development department (Semi-structured interviews 2013, 2017; General Auditor 2012–2016).

This was combined with further reductions to the funds allocated to the Municipalities for development purposes, with the vast majority of the ongoing or to-be-approved projects being cancelled until further notice (see Table 7.2 below).

These massive spending cuts went hand in hand with a substantial decrease in local revenues, deriving from the effects of the financial crisis and the austerity measures. Thus, the Cypriot Municipalities had crucial reductions in revenues originating from local taxes, such as building permits and occupational taxes. An average reduction of 30% was evident during the last five years (General Auditor 2012–2016), which further reduced local financial means. Local revenues were further decreased due to the citizen's inability to pay their Municipal bills, fees and charges (General Auditor 2012–2016). Even with the return of the Cypriot economy to growth, Municipality revenues remain below their pre-crisis levels (see Table 7.3).

Finally, new laws enacted as a result of the provisions of the MOU, that is, the *Fiscal Responsibility and Budget Systems Law* (2014), introduced a new legal framework that enhanced the budgetary supervision of local government by the central state. The Ministers of Finance and Interiors have been authorized by the Council of Ministers to assess the Municipalities' proposed budgets and to intervene when these are exceeded (ibid). This

Table 7.2 State budget: annual transfers to local authorities, including community councils–district offices 2008–2016

Year	*Transfers to local authorities(€)*
2008	127,159,130
2009	151,607,210
2010	152,302,375
2011	142,435,832
2012	119,610,498
2013	112,041,454
2014	98,000,000
2015	98,000,000
2016	100,000,000

Source: Treasury of the Republic (2009–2017)

Table 7.3 Examples of reductions in Municipal budget revenues

Municipality	*Budget revenues 2010 €*	*Budget revenues 2015 €*
Agios Athanasios	4,716,331	4,453,528
Agios Dometios	5,522,986	3,829,143
Egkomi	6,688,566	6,007,131
Kato Polemidia	5,894,938	4,833,653
Lakatamia	11,967,906	10,782,031
Larnaca	21,408,857	20,731,350
Limassol	45,713,893	38,534,981
Nicosia	33,324,188	29,458,779
Paphos	19,666,912	18,866,682
Strovolos	22,103,026	17,575,076

Source: Auditor General of the Republic (2000–2016)

reduced room for manoeuvre (Ladner 2017), resulting from a lack of resources, seems to further reduce local autonomy, imposing an indirect recentralization of power.

No significant changes were made to the legal framework regulating the defaults and bankruptcy of local public entities as a result of the implementation of the austerity measures. It was this framework (*The Municipalities Law* 1985) that makes no provision for a local government entity's bankruptcy and that allowed reckless borrowing by the Municipalities with the approval of the Council of Ministers and with state guarantees. As a result, the Municipalities' total combined debt became as high as €448,904,248 (Auditor General 2015), with ROC GDP for the same year reaching €17,637,200,000. Several Municipalities could barely meet their obligations. This situation further increased the danger of financial instability since the central government was the guarantor of these loan agreements (ibid). The situation was dealt with on an *ad hoc* basis, with the Ministry of Interior rushing to provide relief with advanced payments of the government grant or footing some smaller bills on behalf of the afflicted Municipalities. The Ministry of Finance, on the other hand, made sure Municipality loans were restructured, or even paid in full when the lenders (foreign and domestic) became anxious, with the Municipalities then paying back the state in smaller installments (Semi-structured interviews 2017).

The impact of the austerity measures on the LPS of the Cypriot Municipalities was in direct correlation with the competencies that the Municipalities enjoyed in these particular fields of policy, indicating the profound impact of the burdens of the past. Cypriot Municipalities demonstrated differentiated responses vis-à-vis the austerity measures imposed by the MOU. It was mostly the more populous urban and sub-urban Municipalities which had a 'reactive' stance, while the smaller and less populous Municipalities that had fewer resources had a more 'inactive' stance. In general, all had to adjust to the cost-cutting rationale of the austerity measures that caused problems both to the proper functioning of the local authorities as well as to the delivery of local public services. Budget constraints compelled Municipalities to concentrate their efforts on decreasing their personnel costs by firing people (see Table 7.4 below) and by reducing their salaries and allowances (Semi-structured interviews 2013, 2017).

A hiring freeze, which included LG, was centrally imposed in 2013 (*Law on the Prohibition of Filling Vacant Positions in the Public and the Wider Public Sector* 2013). An increase of activity in search of more efficient ways of delivering services was apparent, triggering some impact at the organizational level.

Waste

The adoption of a scale economy logic was observed vis-à-vis garbage collecting since clusters were formed as a means of rescaling and reorganization. Hence, neighbouring Municipalities and Communities either adopted these specific instruments during the implementation of the

Table 7.4 Reductions in municipal personnel

Municipality	*Total personnel 2011*	*Total personnel 2015*
Agios Athanasios	79	70
Agios Dometios	86	61
Kato Polemidia	97	60
Lakatamia	144	125
Larnaca	350	318
Limassol	494	393
Nicosia	559	458
Paralimni	180	156
Paphos	255	218
Strovolos	353	283

Source: Auditor General of the Republic (2000–2016)

MOU (24%) or, convinced by their cost-cutting success, started to design their implementation immediately after the completion of the MOU (20%). Empirical evidence showed that the idea for these measures originated from participation in EU programmes and networks, from received training, from participation in local development agencies as well as from private consultants (Semi-structured interviews 2013, 2017).

Other measures aiming at securing efficiency gains include hiring services from the market (contracting out) and reducing the weekly frequency of garbage collecting rounds (General Auditor 2013; Semi-structured interviews 2017). Ironically enough, in some cases, for example Municipality 'ix', spending cuts imposed by the Troika-dictated austerity measures caused the discontinuation of the adoption of modernizing best practices transferred from other EU member-states and ceased the implementation of *Pay-as-you-throw* programmes (Semi-structured interviews 2013, 2017).

Water

Due to both the financial crisis and the austerity measures, the Municipalities faced problems in terms of paying their debts to the Water Development Department. Consequently, the executives decided to impose reductions (10%) to the state grants allocated to the Municipalities so as to repay the vast Municipal debts (Semi-structured interviews 2013,2017). Municipalities also turned their attention to collecting unpaid water taxes and started to adopt additional measures, for example imposing fines and reaching special agreements with citizens concerning the settlement of their Municipal bills. It should be noted, however, that these attempts have so far met minimal success (General Auditor 2012–2016). They also took measures to facilitate payments with arrangements such as payment by instalments, concessions for families facing severe financial difficulties etc. Finally, no additional development projects that would enhance Municipal water supply networks were conducted during this period. (Semi-structured interviews 2017).

Social Services

Empirical evidence suggests that because of the restrictive legal framework and their limited financial autonomy, almost none of the Municipalities was able to plan, implement and deliver large-scale social services. Due to the austerity measures and the consequent limitations imposed on local financial resources, the Municipalities faced important financial difficulties that, in turn, deteriorated the quality of the already limited local social services. A cost-cutting rationale was obvious in the measures taken, including substantial reductions in the operational costs of charitable institutions, Municipal retirement homes and Municipal child day-care services (Semi-structured interviews 2013, 2017). Furthermore, almost all of the Municipalities substantially decreased the number of the local cultural and sporting events organized. The contradiction between the official competence of LGOs on these issues and what happens on the ground did not go unnoticed by the interviewees. They pointed out that the local government shouldered the weight of the social consequences of the crisis and fiscal consolidation, despite suffering a 40% reduction of state funding (ibid), especially since the central government services themselves were referring citizens in need down to the LG level over and above the latter's limited competence.

Nevertheless, almost all of the Municipalities took some local social initiatives in addition to the ones assigned to them by law, in order to assist citizens in need. These initiatives included mostly the so-called 'Social grocery stores' (i.e. Food Banks), cooperation with local church unions and volunteers, fundraising and coupons (Semi-structured interviews 2013, 2017). Finally, in some cases, specialized programmes based on EU-funding have given an additional role to Municipalities. This was observed via the establishment of Municipal Multi-purpose Centres providing citizens with additional social services, for example social inclusion of immigrants and providing care to asylum seekers and the elderly.

Learning and Development: An Unofficial Channel to Change?

Having looked at the coercive channels of policy transfer in the form of external/"Troika" pressure, it would be interesting to investigate whether other forms of austerity policies could conceivably be insinuated via unofficial, 'soft' and, thus, at first glance, 'voluntary' (according to the Dolowitz and Marsh spectrum) channels like learning and development activities, which are essential means for governing and steering formal organizations (Maor 1999, pp. 322–323). It is interesting then for us, in the context of the present chapter, to consider what it means when things like training and learning (e.g. of strategic planning, budgeting, economic management etc) take place during a time of 'hard' imposition of consonant policies like fiscal consolidation, austerity etc. Have austerity policies in particular areas of LPS (i.e. water, garbage and social services) been transferred to Cypriot LG organizations through learning and development activities?

Learning and Development: Underwhelming Impact

Empirical evidence suggests that coercive transfer, in the form of austerity measures, did not necessarily entail change through learning with regard to ROC LPS. Our findings verify Gilson et al. (2009, pp. 33–34) who hold that organizational change is possible *without any background of learning* and that circumstances can often be mostly *fiscally driven.*

Generally speaking, in terms of the Dolowitz and Marsh 'degrees of transfer' spectrum (copying, emulation, mixtures and inspiration), LG in the ROC was not heavily inspired nor has it massively borrowed and transferred policies, tools or procedures through training and best-practice-oriented study-visits. Empirical data showed that the main source of training for the Cypriot LGOs was the training offered by the Cyprus Academy of Public Administration (CAPA) and the UCM in the framework of an EU co-funded project (namely by the European Social Fund). This was the main training activity mentioned by interviewees, as the formalization of Learning and Development (L & D) seems to be almost entirely absent from Cypriot Municipalities.

It is interesting that in a time of crisis with elements of coercion, training reflects some of the priorities of the agenda, conceivably leading to a very particular kind of 'voluntary transfer'; one taking place within a context of fiscal consolidation, which already points to specific directions for action. Verheijen (2007, p. 6) points out the strategic planning and performance management systems aspects of the 2007–2013 EU funding planning period. In fact, the ROC through CAPA has absorbed funds for training projects on these very subjects for the civil service and LGOs. In the context of an EU working within the framework of the Stability and Growth Pact, such emphasis for funding is not without its own significance, especially when considering the cutback-oriented rationale with which strategic planning and budgeting were interpreted and transposed to the ROC level with the *Fiscal Responsibility and Budget Systems Law* (2014).

On the other hand, a transfer of approaches like savings-minded service clustering has taken place, with those involved mentioning study-visits abroad as the provenance of such policies. Given that budgetary constraints outright coerced Municipalities to cut costs, any observer would be hard put to deny any concurrent influence by the austerity policies implemented since 2010 and after 2013 in the form of MOU requirements. In some cases, study visits abroad seemed to trigger the emulation of service clustering, while in other cases, they triggered inspiration, with actual practices being adapted to conditions on the ground (the realities of LG in the ROC). The above also apply to practices like outsourcing services to the private sector, particularly regarding waste collection and management, which is no longer considered taboo for LGOs in Cyprus.

We noticed that the burdens of the past influenced both the intrinsic characteristics and weaknesses of the Cypriot Municipalities and their ability to borrow and transfer policies, tools, procedures from training and best-practices-oriented study-visits. They presented the aforementioned constraints in policy transfer predicted by the Dolowitz and Marsh model, namely, Policy Complexity, Past Policies, Structural Institutional Feasibility, Ideology, Language and Incomplete Information.

Some such features were cited by the interviewees to explain both

(a) the lack of systematic participation in training due to the small number of personnel especially after the hiring freeze (*Law on the Prohibition of Filling Vacant Positions in the Public and the Wider Public Sector* 2013) put in place by the Government and Parliament due to the financial crisis and the MOU requirements, and
(b) the lack of transfer of policies and best practices from classroom training and study-visits abroad in the UK and Greece (University of Nicosia and Institute of Social Innovation 2013, p. 18).

Influence was either entirely lacking or was minimal. Some organizations (e.g. v, iv) were influenced towards a 'positive direction' (sic) in only minor issues due to poor organizational circumstances and trade-union-related difficulties. Others (e.g. xi) mentioned practices like extended operating hours that required political decisions to be transferred to their organization. Finally, a lack of university-educated staff as heads of departments (e.g. vii) was indicated as a factor preventing the proper implementation of what they witnessed during the study visits.

Nevertheless, some local government organizations do report transfer, which they linked to the CAPA Project (50%), for example transfers of ideas (albeit at the level of inspiration and emulation), establishing new inter-municipal 'clusters' for cooperation in waste collection, the enhancement of existing clusters by adding accounts department services and the transfer of customer-service approaches with the use of e-government. Some organizations mentioned how the Strategic Planning elements of the CAPA Training Project were quite transferable to their Municipality because of the huge cost-cutting and restructuring effort that took place in 2012 because of the financial and fiscal crisis.

Our empirical data indicated the counterproductive aspects of fiscally driven change and reform, a tendency already noted by Ongaro (2014), jeopardizing the very prospect of modernization through reform. Due to budgetary constraints, one Municipality (ix.) had to cancel its 'Pay-as-you-throw' (PAYT) pilot programme, which modernized the existing system, reduced costs and per-capita waste production, while increasing recycling levels, and which epitomizes knowledge and policy transfer at its finest. Through participation in Town Twinning programmes, permanent staff became aware of PAYT systems, they investigated on the Internet and they then organized a visit to Belgium where they observed best practices (Tsangarides 2016). Interestingly enough, austerity policies that officially, but it seems only superficially, co-exist with a reform agenda in the MOU caused the interruption of this instance of administrative modernization. Past practices, as well as Structural and Institutional Constraints (Dolowitz and Marsh 1996, 2000) are clearly at play here since they seem to be of immediate relevance to the Cypriot LG framework, with its demonstrably limited capability, path dependence and the sheer weight of the burdens of the past. It refers to the absence of a blank sheet for policymakers who are 'inheritors before they are choosers' since any new programmes must be introduced into 'a policy environment dense with past commitment', which constrains both what can and cannot be transferred and the provenance of the potential objects of transfer (Dolowitz and Marsh 1996, pp. 353–354).

The limitations of copying, emulation, mixtures and inspiration (Dolowitz and Marsh 1996, 2000) are demonstrated in the aborted efforts and in the very prominent constraints to transfer mentioned above, including ideological inconsistency between the organization of provenance and the potential transferring organization (mentioned by Municipality 'v' with regard to the 'corporate logic' in LG).

Europeanization of Local Public Services: Reinforcing Historical Continuities

As was indicated by our findings, the impact of the austerity measures on LPS in the ROC was limited in scope and had a mostly financial rather than an administrative or institutional impact on Cypriot local government. Our findings also indicate that transfer of knowledge via learning and development was quite restricted as well.

Starting with the first analytical dimension (Who), it was clear that the central state structures, for example the Ministry of Finance, complied with the "Troika" view in addressing the crisis (Dellepiane 2015), reproducing their strong gate-keeping role vis-à-vis the Cypriot Municipalities. Empirical evidence also showed that the overly centralized institutional tradition of the ROC filtered attempts to reform LG, acting as a persistence-breeding force (Meyer-Sahling and Yesilkagit 2011, pp. 318–319). For this reason, the reform plans presented by central structures were in contrast to international practice (by not promoting decentralization of competencies and sources of revenues), since the former did not wish to lose control over local government. This strong path-dependence demonstrates the resilience of domestic traditions (Callanan 2012, p. 401) and can be explained by the massive influence that political parties exert over vast parts of the Cypriot society and economy (Zenios 2012) in comparison to their European counterparts.

When the second analytical dimension (What) is concerned, more coercive phases and effects of Europeanization were traced, deriving from the Stability and Growth Pact and the consequent demands for fiscal discipline (Ladi 2013), which were based on entirely different processes and narratives vis-à-vis the 'traditional' forms of conditionality (Ploom 2014). It was clear that the pursuit of fiscal consolidation was the guiding principle, indicating a trade-off between, on the one hand, achieving financial savings and macro-economic stability and the need to carry out modernizing institutional and administrative reforms at the local level on the other (Ongaro 2014). Yet, central state structures asserted their control over institutional arrangements, even introducing stricter central budget supervision (*Fiscal Responsibility and Budget Systems Law* 2014). At the same time, instruments like across-the-board cutbacks and centralized priority setting meant that seemingly mutually contradicting strategies were pursued. Officially, LGOs were asked to 'do the same with less', even though, in reality, the dire financial conditions of their burghers and subsequent needs meant that they were being asked to 'do more with less' (see how organization 'ix' expresses this). While success was minimal, in effect, one cannot but reach the conclusion that the overall financial impact has been one of 'doing-less-with-less'. Hence, any apparent strategic contradiction is resolved: The government in conformity to the MOU clearly aimed at reducing local expenses imposing specific measures, that is, spending cuts. In the end, these diminished the role of the already restricted LPS that Cypriot Municipalities offer, along with an erosion of local government 'autonomy' in terms of institutional arrangements.

As regards the third analytical dimension (When), we observed that the nexus of the transfer of austerity policies in the form of fiscal consolidation through cutbacks/spending cuts can be perfectly described in terms of timing. In fact, it reached the periphery (LGOs) unfettered, straddling the external/internal divide when adequate pressure (coercion) was applied initially by external actors (lending institutions) on the central internal actors (the executive and parliament) and then by the centre on the periphery. It travelled across the centre-periphery divide (Wollmann 2016) by means of budget-related policies which, institutionally speaking, are the centre's prerogative, leading to a further reinforcement of existing power asymmetries in the institutional dynamics, which historically characterize a local government level lacking autonomy of action. ROC governments were reactive in their decision-making regarding the adoption of austerity policies required by external actors, while Municipalities were mostly inactive in the design and implementation of the austerity measures. Nevertheless, a few attempted to be reactive and to negotiate with the central state structures.

With regard to the fourth analytical dimension (How), the dynamics developed during the implementation of the austerity measures reflected the power asymmetry between central state actors and local government. Since no reform of the local government system was enacted, the process was in effect focused solely on achieving fiscal consolidation at the local level. Municipalities (the periphery) simply adopted a cost-cutting rationale in every aspect of their function, much like ROC governments simply succumbed to external pressures due to a lack of alternative options. Based on empirical evidence, it was clear that neither the lenders nor the ROC government had set the reform of the local government as a priority. Given this fact, on the particular issue of reform, the government seemed to have been in a position to effectively bargain vis-à-vis the external actors.

In turn, the Municipalities, with the assistance of parliamentary opposition, and despite the burdens of the past, had bargained with the centre, managing to put contested reform plans on hold. The overall characteristics of the Cypriot political system offer an explanation for this tendency towards stasis. As the elected Mayors overwhelmingly rise through the ranks of political parties, they managed to utilize their very good connections with the political and institutional centre (the Executive and the Legislature) (Kirlappos 2016) to prevent the reform provisions aiming at clustering Municipalities and thereby managed to, in effect, maintain their political positions.

On the other hand, the impact of historical continuities seems to explain the limited influence of the austerity programme on LPS in the ROC. Since the remit of the LG is limited with regard to LPS like water, health and social services, austerity was filtered through the existing arrangements, which offered little room for impact. At the same time, it left the power asymmetry between central and local unchanged, in the sense of division of responsibilities, by not pushing for modernizing reform in the direction of decentralization. New fiscal responsibility and budgeting laws can even be argued to have further reduced local autonomy. Evidence also showed that differences in the 'attributed tasks' (Fleurke and Willemse 2007), personnel and economic capacities among different LGOs acted as mediating factors causing differentiations in the effects of austerity measures on local public services.

Finally, the adopted austerity strategies seem to have an impact even on the democratic process. The external shock triggered by the economic crisis and consequent MOU created an inconsistency between the market logic point of view that places emphasis on fiscal retrenchment on the one hand and citizenship on the other (Schafer and Streeck 2013). As we demonstrated earlier, there was a crucial decrease in the economic autonomy of the political institutions closest to the citizens (LGO) and a clear loss of revenues as a result of the implementation of the austerity measures. These caused additional reductions in the quality of the offered LPS to the citizens, affecting the latter's position and wealth (Morlino and Quaranta 2016, p. 21). This development caused an overall decline in legitimacy as it was expressed via the democratic processes which took place in Cyprus during the implementation of the MOU. All three electoral processes were characterized by a severe decline in voter turnout: 2014 European Parliament elections 43% (2009–59, 4%), 2016 Parliament elections 66, 7% (2011–78, 7%) and 2016 Municipal elections 54, 8% (2011–approximately

70%).[5] A development which is in line with findings by other researchers, suggesting that a decline in legitimacy is possible due to the implementation of austerity measures not only at local/national level but at the EU level as well (Bosco and Verney 2012; Mayer 2013).

Conclusions

In the wider context of economic crisis and the 'most coercive phase of [...] Europeanization' (Ladi 2013), this chapter constitutes a first attempt at mapping the impact of austerity measures on the LPS of the ROC. It highlighted the asymmetrical relations between external and internal as well as centre and periphery divides and the reinforcement of historical continuities at the local level. Austerity measures reinforced government control over LPS but did not help much in promoting long-needed reforms. In terms of L&D, a potentially operative policy transfer channel, as well as an absolutely necessary tool and driving force for successful reforms in a rapidly changing world, transfer was extant but minimal for reasons relating, on the one hand, to the constraining features of the ROC and, on the other, on the prioritization of fiscal consolidation rather than LG reform on the part of the lending institutions driving the current, coercive brand of Europeanization.

This work highlighted the importance of external driving forces, such as the crisis and the MOU, in shaping a top-down transfer of austerity policies in Cyprus LG during the second phase of austerity (2008-present). The main transferred policies focused on rendering the state 'leaner', imposing across-the-board cutbacks on local revenues, for example state and development grants, further reducing the already restricted financial autonomy of the Cypriot local level of government. Austerity measures had a limited impact both on the legal framework regulating default of local government public entities and the overall institutional structure of local government, while it increased central control.

Our findings indicate the importance of institutional paths and historical continuities in terms of resources, competencies and local autonomy that defined the shape of outcomes. Intense gatekeeping by the central government structures meant that austerity policies were simply imposed on the Municipalities. The latter had minimum room for manoeuvre. The attempts to reform local government were filtered by the centralized institutional

[5] Ministry of the Interior-Central Electoral Service (2011–2016).

tradition of the ROC that acted as a persistence-breeding force (Meyer-Sahling and Yesilkagit 2011, pp. 318–319), avoiding international best practice despite apparent external pressures. Yet, in terms of the reforms promoted, and despite central dominance, Municipalities did manage to cooperate with the opposition, successfully avoiding unpopular, *qua* centralizing reform plans.

Key institutional players included the executive, mainly the Ministries of Finance and Interiors and, to a lesser extent, the Legislature. Their overall strategy focused on implementing the provisions of the MOU, especially the ones aiming at fiscal consolidation. These were seen as more important than the need to implement administrative reforms, verifying similar findings by Ongaro (2014). For this reason, attention was focused on imposing austerity measures and not on solving long-lasting institutional problems.

The impact of austerity measures on the LPS was proportional to the competencies that the Municipalities enjoyed in these particular fields of policy, indicating the profound impact of the burdens of the past. Hence, LPS were downgraded due to the external shock triggered by the economic crisis, the consequent MOU and the loss of local financial means, further restricting local economic autonomy. These developments seemed to have caused additional deterioration of the quality of the offered LPS affecting citizens' position and circumstances (Morlino and Quaranta 2016, p. 21). This went hand in hand with a crucial decline in voter turnout in all three electoral processes which took place in Cyprus during the implementation of the MOU indicating that an overall decline in legitimacy was possible due to the implementation of austerity measures at the local, national and EU level (Bosco and Verney 2012; Mayer 2013).

This work demonstrated that the design and delivery of LPS in the ROC depend on historical continuities that affect the centre-periphery divide (Wollmann 2016) in favour of the first one. The implementation of fiscally driven policies lead to further reinforcement of existing power asymmetries in the institutional dynamics and, thus, further restricted local-level autonomy of action. Specific resilient domestic traditions (Callanan 2012, p. 401), such as the close interplay between the wider political system, the political parties and local government have acted as explanatory factors for the limited impact of the austerity measures on the LPS. Further research is needed in order to shed additional light on this interplay.

Finally, Learning and Development was not a particularly operative parameter channelling reform and change, be it austerity-minded or other. Our findings indicated that the degree of policy transfer via learning and development was quite restricted, with rare examples of emulation and a few cases of inspiration. Constraints to transfer exhibited were in accordance with the territorial and temporal dimensions of a small-state public administration system and its limitations (i.e. past policies and structural-institutional feasibility).

References

Auditor General of the Republic. (2000–2016). *Annual Reports 2000–2016*. Nicosia: Audit Office of the Republic of Cyprus.

Bosco, A., & Verney, S. (2012). Electoral Epidemic: The Political Cost of Economic Crisis in Southern Europe. *South European Society &Politics, 17*(2), 129–154.

Bull, M., & Baudner, J. (2004). Europeanization and Italian Policy for the Mezzogiorno. *Journal of European Public Policy, 11*(6), 1058–1076.

Callanan, M. (2012). Domestic Governance Arrangements and Europeanization: The Case of Central-Local Relations in England, Ireland and Denmark. *Comparative European Politics, 10*(4), 399–420.

Dalitis, F. (2015). Reform of the Municipalities with Italian Masters: The Union of Municipalities 'Package for Clustering Gains Ground'. *Philelepheros Online*. Available at http://archive.philenews.com/el-gr/top-stories/885/243496/fakelos-metarrythmisi-ton-dimon-me-italous-maestrous. Accessed 22 Feb 2017 (in Greek).

Dellepiane, S. (2015). The Political Power of Economic Ideas: The Case of Expansionary Fiscal Contractions. *The British Journal of Politics & International Relations, 17*(3), 391–418.

Di Mascio, F., & Natalini, A. (2015). Fiscal Retrenchment in Southern Europe: Changing Patterns of Public Management in Greece, Italy, Portugal and Spain. *Public Management Review, 17*(1), 129–148.

Dolowitz, D., & Marsh, D. (1996). Who Learns What from Whom: A Review of the Policy Transfer Literature. *Political Studies, 44*(2), 343–357.

Dolowitz, D., & Marsh, D. (2000). Learning from Abroad: The Role of Policy Transfer in Contemporary Policy-Making. *Governance, 13*(1), 5–24.

European Commission. (2014, December). The Economic Adjustment Programme: Cyprus 5th Review-Summer 2014, European Economy: Institutional Paper 009 (120p). Luxemburg: Publication Office of the European Union.

European Commission, (2015, October). The Economic Adjustment Programme: Cyprus 7th Review-Summer 2015, European Economy: Institutional Paper 009 (124p). Luxemburg: Publication Office of the European Union.

Fiscal Responsibility and Budget Systems Law. (N.20(1)/2014). Nicosia: Government Printing Office.

Fleurke, F., & Willemse, R. (2007). Effects of the European Union on Sub-National Decision-Making: Enhancement or Constriction? *Journal of European Integration, 29*(1), 69–88.

Gilson, C., Dunleavy, P., & Tinkler, J. (2009). *Organizational Learning in Government Sector Organizations: Literature Review Source: National Audit Office (NAO)*. Available at: http://www2.lse.ac.uk/government/research/resgroups/LSEPublicPolicy/pdf/PPG_OrgLearninginGovLit_review.pdf on 9.3.2013. Accessed 17 Apr 2017.

International Monetary Fund, Country Report 14/180-Cyprus. (2014, July). IMF: Washington, DC. Available at: https://www.imf.org/external/pubs/ft/scr/2014/cr14180.pdf. Accessed 16 Feb 2017.

Kavkalias, G. (2016). Reforming Local Government: The Hidden Traps. *Sigmalive*. Available at http://www.sigmalive.com/news/local/359541/kryvei-pagides-i-metarrythmisi-tis-topikisaftodioikisis#.dpuf. Accessed 4 Sept 2016 (in Greek).

Kirlappos, A. (2016). *Local Government in the Republic of Cyprus: The Limited Europeanization and the Burdens of the Past* (238 p). Larnaca: Vivliekdotiki (in Greek).

Ladi, S. (2013). The Eurozone Crisis and Austerity Politics: A Trigger for Administrative Reform in Greece? *Comparative European Politics, 22*(2), 184–208.

Ladner, A. (2017). Autonomy and Austerity: Re-investing in Local Government. In C. Schwab, G. Bouckaert, & S. Kuhlmann (Eds.), *The Future of Local Government in Europe Lessons from Research and Practice in 31 Countries* (pp. 23–52). Berlin: Nomos.

Law on the Prohibition of Filling Vacant Positions in the Public and the Wider Public Sector. (N.21(1)/2013). Nicosia: Government Printing Office.

Maor, M. (1999). Recruitment and Training of Senior Civil Servants in Denmark and Norway, 1970–1995: The Impact of New public management and European integration. *Current Politics and Economics of Europe, 8*(4), 321–339.

Markides, D. (2009). *Cyprus: 1957–1963* (238 p). Athens: Mesogeios. (in Greek).

Mayer, N. (2013). From Jean-Marie to Marine Le Pen-Electoral Change on the Far Right. *Parliamentary Affairs, 66*(1), 160–178.

Memorandum of Understanding on Specific Economic Policy Conditionality. (2013). Available at: http://www.mof.gov.cy/mof/mof.nsf/final%20MOUf.pdf. Accessed 14 Mar 2017.

Meyer-Sahling, J.-H., & Yesilkagit, K. (2011). Differential Legacy Effects: Three Propositions on the Impact of Administrative Traditions on Public Management

Reform in Europe East and West. *Journal of European Public Policy, 18*(2), 311–322.
Ministry of the Interior-Central Electoral Service. (2011–2016). Nicosia. Available at: http://www.moi.gov.cy/moi/moi.nsf/page16_gr/page16_gr?OpenDocument. Accessed 14 Mar 2017.
Morlino, L., & Quaranta, M. (2016). What Is the Impact of the Economic Crisis on Democracy? Evidence from Europe. *International Political Science Review, 37*(5), 618–633.
National Centre for Public Administration and Local Government. (2010). *Study for the Restructure of Local Government of the Republic of Cyprus.* [in Greek]. Available at: http://www.ucm.org.cy/Project_Card.aspx?ProjectID=10&ProjectCategoryID=61&Language=Greek. Accessed 19 Mar 2017.
National School of Government International. (2014). *Local Government Reform in Cyprus: Final Options Report.* Available at: http://www.moi.gov.cy/moi/moi.nsf/0/D1BB8168615F0DF3C2257D02002F7C52/$file/Local%20Government%20Reform%20in%20Cyprus_Final%20Options%20Report_08%2004%2014.pdf. Accessed 20 Mar 2017.
Ongaro, E. (2014). The Relationship Between the New European Governance Emerging from the Fiscal Crisis and Administrative Reforms: Qualitatively Different, Quantitatively Different, or Nothing New? A Plea for a Research Agenda. *Administrative Culture, 15*(1), 10–20.
Osborne, D., & Gaebler, T. (1992). *Reinventing Government: How the Entrepreneurial Spirit Is Transforming the Public Sector.* New York: Addison-Wesley.
Ploom, I. (2014). Towards Neoliberal Imperialism?Discussing the Implications of the New European Governance Emerging from the Fiscal Crisis and Administrative Reforms for the Identity of the EU'. *Administrative Culture, 15*(1), 21–38.
Schafer, C., & Streeck, W. (Eds.). (2013). *Politics in the Age of Austerity* (240p). Cambridge: Polity Press.
Streeck, W. (2013). The Politics of Public Debt: Neoliberalism, Capitalist Development, and the Restructuring of the State MPIfG Discussion Paper 13/7, Koeln, Max-Plank Institute for the Studies on Societies. Available at: http://www.mpifg.de/pu/mpifg_dp/dp13-7.pdf. Accessed 22 Mar 2017.
The Municipalities Law. (111/1985). Nicosia: Government Printing Office.
Tornaritis, K. (1972). *Η Το π ική Αυτο δ ιο ίκησις Εν Κύπ ρ ω* [*Local Self-government in Cyprus*] (p. 42). Nicosia. The book by K. Tornaritis is self-published Tornaritis: https://www.cyprusbarassociation.org/files/publications/Cyprus_Law_Book_Catalogue_12_07_lq.pdf.
Treasury of the Republic. (2009–2017). *Financial Reports 2009–2016.* Nicosia: Treasury of the Republic.

Tsangarides, H. (2016). *Aglantzia's Pay as You Throw*. Presentation. Available at: http://uest.ntua.gr/cyprus2016/proceedings/presentation/5._tsagarides_pay_as_you_throw_dhmou_aglantzias22062016eng.pdf. Accessed 10 Mar 2017.

University of Nicosia and Institute of Social Innovation. (2013). *Implementation and Evaluation of Learning Activities: Report Submitted by University of Nicosia*, EDEX Educational Excellence Corporation Ltd, and the Institute of Social Innovation. Doc Number: 2579847. Nicosia: Cyprus Academy of Public AdministrationArchive.

Verheijen, T. (2007). Administrative Capacity in the New EU Member States: The Limits of Innovation? *World Bank Working Paper*, No. 115. Available at: http://www-wds.worldbank.org/external/default/WDSContentServer/WDSP/IB/2007/08/28/000020953_20070828155717/Rendered/PDF/405590ECA0Admi1LIC0disclosed0Aug271.pdf. Accessed 2 Jan 2017.

Wollmann, H. (2016). Local Government Reform: Between Multifunction and Single Purpose Organizations. *Local Government Studies, 42*(3), 376–384.

Zenios, S. (2012). *Creative Cyprus: Reform Policy for the 21st Century Cyprus*. Athens: Papazisis (in Greek).

CHAPTER 8

Local Public Services and Austerity Measures in Croatia: Adaptations of the Resilient Social Model Through the Central-Local Power and Blame Games

Ivan Koprić, Mihovil Škarica, and Romea Manojlović Tomań

Introduction

Croatia is a unitary, highly centralized state, with municipalities in predominantly rural areas and towns in predominantly urban areas. Counties are second-tier governments. Fragmentation, limited local scope and autonomy, and scarce local capacities are the main characteristics of the Croatian local government system. Croatia was hit hard by the global economic crisis in 2008. The largest GDP rate drop of 7.4% was experienced in 2009, followed by negative values until 2015. In the period 2008–2014, GDP dropped by more than 12%. The prolonged recession

I. Koprić (✉) • M. Škarica • R. Manojlović Tomań
Faculty of Law, University of Zagreb, Zagreb, Croatia
e-mail: ivan.kopric@pravo.hr; mihovil.skarica@pravo.hr; romea.manojlovic@pravo.hr

A. Lippi, T. N. Tsekos (eds.), *Local Public Services in Times of Austerity across Mediterranean Europe*, Governance and Public Management, https://doi.org/10.1007/978-3-319-76225-8_8

lasted for six years. Economic recovery started at the end of 2014, and it is rather slow.

Many domestic and foreign assessments blame local governments for inefficiency, requesting territorial consolidation. At the same time, several domestic actors are asking for decentralization and regionalization, grounding their requests on the fact that rigid centralization hides inefficiency of overdeveloped but fragmented central state bureaucracy. The economic crisis happened simultaneously with the final stage of the Croatian accession to the European Union in 2013. The accession's influence was twofold: it opened new possibilities for local governments and added to the environmental complexity of local service provision, revealing weak capacities and precarious situations in the vast majority of local governments.

The aim of this chapter is to analyse the influence of the economic crisis on local service delivery, especially in the healthcare and water and waste sectors. We also examine to what extent the harmonization with the EU policy on services of general interest has influenced the changes of local service delivery. The paper takes into consideration (a) Croatian legislation, whose changes have reflected the EU standards and policies; (b) different concepts of domestic political actors and central government's measures; and (c) reactions of various types of local governments to the new situation created by austerity, central government pressures, and European influences. The analysis is based on the neo-institutional theoretical approach.

Local Government in Croatia and Economic Crisis

The Role of Local Government in the Politico-Administrative System

In 1993, Croatia introduced a two-tier local government system. The territorial organization became fragmented, as the number of units quintupled. The local scope was narrowed drastically, local finances were reduced, and the whole system was centralized. The number of local governments increased further in subsequent years (Koprić et al. 2016; Koprić and Đulabić 2018). Today, there are 555 local units, 428 municipalities (*općine*), and 127 towns (*gradovi*), while 20 counties (*županije*) function at the second level, supplementing weak local governments. The City of Zagreb, as the capital, has the dual status of first- and second-tier government. The average number of inhabitants is 6300 (the average rises to 7700 if Zagreb is included), but 71% of local governments (395) have fewer than 5000 inhabitants.[1] Vast disparities among them also exist in terms of developmental indicators and economic capacity (CoE 2016; Jambrač 2017). Genuine regional governments have not been established.

The constitutional amendments of 2000 enabled decentralization in education, social care, health care, and fire service. New competences were granted to 34 towns (only 6% of all local governments) and to counties. Over time, 161 municipalities have taken over certain competences in the fire service. Decentralization reform was evaluated as limited, confusing, and hesitating since it covered but a small part of local governments and did not widen local autonomy (Koprić and Đulabić 2018).

Numerous sectoral laws have undermined local autonomy. Local competences have been narrowed, becoming predominantly executive and technical, without substantive autonomy in conditions of considerable functional overlap among territorial levels, dominant central government role, and excessive supervision over local governments (CoE 2016). The ratio of personnel in the central government and local governments is 87:13. Sectoral laws and rules on financing decentralized functions have created top-down relations between counties and local governments. The establishment of large towns (more than 35,000 inhabitants) in 2005 further complicated the picture of functional overlaps, but enabled these 24 towns to retain a more significant position and autonomy. With the exception of the City of Zagreb, local governments do not perform transferred state functions.

Central ministries, agencies, and other central institutions have established a dense, ever-growing network of loosely coordinated branch offices. Inter-municipal cooperation is mostly limited to co-ownership of utility companies and joint establishment of public institutions for the provision of social services. Strategic and developmental cooperation happens rarely and is not stimulated by national policies (Škarica 2015). Local fiscal autonomy is low, with almost 2/3 of local revenues coming from shared taxes and central budget transfers (World Bank 2014). The amount of central budget transfers is especially high in counties – they make 42% of county revenues.

The Impact of Austerity on Local Government

In 2008, Croatia was trapped in a cycle of deep recession ignited by the global economic and financial crises and prolonged by domestic structural deficiencies. Inadequate austerity policies and delayed or completely absent structural reforms postponed the economic recovery.

[1] There are 274 local governments (49.3%) with fewer than 3000 inhabitants.

In the six years of negative economic trends (2009–2014), GDP dropped by more than 12% and public debt grew from 35% of GDP in 2008 to 85% of GDP in 2014, while the unemployment rate grew from 13.2% to 22.8% in 2012. Budgetary deficit did not fall under 4%. In 2014, the share of people at risk of poverty and social exclusion was extremely high–29.3%.[2] Unfavourable demographic trends were accompanied by a huge emigration wave of predominantly young people, especially after the 2013 EU accession.

The two subsequent governments, led by conservative (Croatian Democratic Community – HDZ) J. Kosor (2009–2011) and social democrat (Social-Democratic Party – SDP) Z. Milanović (2011–2016), had only slightly different ideas of austerity measures that were to be applied to the local government system. The former tried to prepare a comprehensive reform plan, while the later offered a pre-election programme with territorial reform and decentralization as an important component. However, both governments lacked the political will to impose serious structural and territorial reform measures since the two main political parties did not differ significantly in their respective economic and austerity policies.

Croatian public administration reforms have been patchy and bumpy and local government system reforms have not deviated from that practice (Koprić 2017a). Constant but insufficient pressure comes from the EU and the World Bank. The main domestic pro-reform actors include academia, business community, the media, and certain lesser political actors (parties or independents). Budgetary retrenchments at the local level were simply a result of the need to balance the state budget at the time when significant budgetary flow (transfers and grants) towards the local governments took place in conditions of economic crisis, decrease of GDP, and common EU policies.

Local budgets gradually shrunk during the recession (Table 8.1). The total revenues of all local budgets dropped from HRK 23.5 billion in 2008 to HRK 22.1 billion in 2014, with the lowest point of 20.2 billion in 2011. It was a result of general economic decline and falling GDP. The share of local revenues in national GDP remained at 6.7% throughout the period, which amounts to around 15% of consolidated public revenues.

[2] Data on GDP growth rates, unemployment rates, and risk of poverty have been retrieved from Statistical Yearbooks published by the Croatian Bureau of Statistics (https://www.dzs.hr/hrv/publication/stat_year.htm); data on budgetary deficit from Croatian National Bank (https://www.hnb.hr/en/statistics/main-macroeconomic-indicators); and data on public debt from the Ministry of Finance (http://www.mfin.hr/hr/drzavni-proracun-arhiva).

Table 8.1 Local budgets changes (2008–2014)

	Total revenues (in HRK)	*Base index*	*% of change compared to 2008*
2008	23,553,225,507	100	0.00
2009	22,437,331,403	95.26	−4.74
2010	21,118,066,585	89.66	−10.34
2011	20,252,233,199	85.98	−14.02
2012	20,687,119,854	87.83	−12.17
2013	22,166,131,483	94.11	−5.89
2014	22,109,792,677	93.87	−6.13

Source: Authors, based on data from the Ministry of Finance (http://www.mfin.hr/hr/lokalni-proracun-arhiva)

Table 8.2 Equalization grants for decentralized functions (2008–2014)

	Equalization grants for decentralized functions (in HRK)	*Base index*	*% of change compared to 2008*
2008	2,625,433,434	100	0.00
2009	2,767,070,105	105.39	5.39
2010	2,847,740,960	108.47	8.47
2011	2,523,964,728	96.14	−3.86
2012	2,411,281,463	91.84	−8.16
2013	2,222,150,542	84.64	−15.36
2014	2,216,031,739	84.41	−15.59

Source: Authors, based on Decrees on the method of calculating the amount of equalization grant for decentralized functions

Transfers from the state budget to local governments decreased from HRK 1.8 billion in 2008 to HRK 1.5 billion in 2014. Equalization grants for decentralized functions followed a similar trajectory – they decreased from HRK 2.8 billion in 2010 to HRK 2.2 billion in 2014 (Table 8.2).

The changes in the income tax regulations of 2010 (lower tax rates and an increase in non-taxable income share), which were intended to stimulate citizens' personal spending and general economic growth, reduced local revenues by HRK 1 billion. These tax changes met strong and unanimous opposition from the local actors, regardless of their political affiliation. They pointed out that budgetary constraints would diminish their ability to maintain the standards of local service provision. The decrease in local revenues had a substantial negative impact on local public investment and, consequently, on the renewal and modernization of the infrastructure of local public services. While in 2008, local public investments had a share of

2.1% of the national GDP, they dropped to a mere 0.45% in 2014. Insolvency of local governments has become a prominent issue (Posedel and Primorac 2012, p. 331). Nevertheless, local governments are exempt from general bankruptcy rules.

Local governments have partially compensated for the decrease in revenues by borrowing. The rules on local borrowing did not change during the recession; borrowing was allowed only for capital investments, with prior consent of the central government. The total cumulative borrowing limit for all local governments was set at 2.3% (2007–2011) and 2.5% (2012–2014) of real annual local revenues, respectively. In addition, annual amortization repayment by individual local governments could not exceed 20% of its own revenues that is, revenues without transfers and grants. Despite these constraints, direct financial liabilities of local governments grew during the recession from HRK 3.56 billion (804 HRK per capita) in 2008 to HRK 4.48 billion (1046 HRK per capita) in 2014. Annual revenues stemming from borrowing grew from HRK 0.45 billion in 2008 to HRK 1.6 billion in 2014. Many of them reached the borrowing limit and pursued a practice of indirect borrowing via local companies. Indirect liabilities, generated through guarantees for local companies' loans at the time amounted to HRK 7.2 bn (Table 8.3).

As the recession coincided with Croatian accession to the EU, pre-accession funds were propagated as a cure for the unfavourable financial position of local governments. Despite that, the absorption rate was rather low, mostly due to low financial, organizational, and personnel capacities

Table 8.3 Revenues of local budgets stemming from borrowing (2008–2014)

	Revenues stemming from borrowing (in HRK)	*Base index*	*% of change compared to 2008*	*% of total revenues*
2008	447,852,630	100	0	1.9
2009	495,976,357	110.75	10.75	2.2
2010	604,467,902	134.97	34.97	2.8
2011	687,067,033	153.41	53.41	3.3
2012	544,061,124	121.48	21.48	2.6
2013	605,933,087	135.30	35.30	2.7
2014	1,618,179,985	361.32	261.32	7.3

Source: Author, based on data from the Ministry of Finance (http://www.mfin.hr/hr/lokalni-proracun-arhiva)

of local governments (World Bank 2014, 2016). In the period 2011–2014, they received only HRK 311 million (€ 41million) (Ott et al. 2016). However, success indicators slowly improve.

In 2010, two other instruments aimed at strengthening local governments' fiscal discipline were introduced. First, legislation on salaries of local officials was adopted, attempting to harmonize local remuneration schemes. It limited the highest local salaries and total amount of annual salaries in a local government unit (it must not exceed 20% of a local government's own revenues). Despite negative fiscal trends and legal constraints, the number of local civil servants was growing continuously even though no significant decentralization of competences occurred. In the period 2008–2014, local administrative bodies increased their workforce by 9% and public institutions established by local governments by 14%.[3] Second, the *Law on Fiscal Responsibility* was adopted at the end of 2010. It stipulated more rigorous financial supervision of public bodies (including local governments) by the Ministry of Finance. It also introduced personal responsibility of elected officials and other heads of public organizations for the legal and purposeful use of earmarked funds, as well as for efficient and effective financial management and control.

Local governments had hardly any effective instruments for autonomous adaptation to the challenging economic circumstances. As their fiscal autonomy remained low, they were susceptible to general economic trends and central government fiscal measures. The recession highlighted the issues of the ineffectiveness and inefficiency of the Croatian public administration as a whole, its expensiveness, and the fragility of the local government system, which was particularly exposed to critical discourse (comp. World Bank 2014, 2016; CoE 2016; EC 2015). Deficiencies of the Croatian local government system have gained visibility and become a matter of public debate. Despite a solid professional body of literature and participation of prominent scholars, a simplified approach advocating the abolishment of financially unsustainable local governments has been rather prominent in the debate, dominating over promising, but more complex, reform proposals. The disparities in providing local public and social services remained high – disproportion in their investments during this period increased further and their overall provision capacity was diminished (Jambrač 2017).

[3] Data on local budgets, revenues, and expenditures have been retrieved from the Ministry of Finance's reports and calculated by the authors (http://www.mfin.hr/hr/lokalni-proracuni).

Austerity offered a window of opportunity for comprehensive local government territorial, functional, and financial reform. Many reports and academic analyses have suggested structural reform, decentralization, clear delimitation of competences among governance tiers, territorial consolidation, and strengthening of local capacities. Although these goals were included in important national strategic documents (*Guidelines for Decentralization and Territorial Reform*2010; *Strategy for Public Administration Development* 2015), and public expectations were and still are in favour of such a systemic reform, it has not been launched yet. The ruling political coalition remains reluctant. Their reluctance is fuelled by the economic recovery that began in the second part of 2015. Local expenditures increased in 2015 and subsequent years.

The main changes at the local level that significantly mitigated the influence of the economic crisis and the central government's austerity measures on the provision of local, public, and social services have been the following:

- Temporary reduction of investments in local infrastructure during the crisis with an attempt to preserve local service provision on a daily basis,
- More massive borrowing and reliance on loans;
- Better absorption of EU funds and exploring new opportunities for cooperation within the EU;
- Improvement of cost-efficiency and internal savings through betterment of local management (by introducing strategic planning, project financing, performance management, modern financial and fiscal instruments, and similar techniques);
- Innovation and quality improvement in local service provision (public-private partnerships, private and civil sector provision, reliance on self-help, co-production, introduction of various quality management instruments, etc.).

It must be noted that there has not been any deep dissatisfaction of local service users in Croatia. Although local governments provide a circle of public and social services, the majority of welfare services are provided by other governance institutions, mostly under central control. Governance focus during the crisis was on protecting the social position of large groups of people in precarious situations, such as the unemployed, pensioners, healthcare users, and others, and preserving their rights. Austerity measures were designed with an eye on their (dis)satisfaction and attempted to distribute the burden of crisis in a relatively balanced manner, albeit with many deficiencies (Dobrotić 2016).

Local governments contributed to that balance. Adaptation and resilience characterized local governments in Croatia during the crisis. The whole system remained untouched by structural, territorial, or similar measures. It adapted to the new situation using the social balance and welfare needs as an anchor and barrier against any serious consolidation reform. The concept of resilient local authorities, which "adapt, cope, and 'bounce back' when faced with external shocks such as climate change, economic recession and cuts in public expenditure" (Shaw 2012, p. 281), appears to be the appropriate theoretical option to be tested when examining the influence of austerity measures on local governments in Croatia.

Constant betterment in absorption of the EU funds and new opportunities for cooperation within the EU multi-level governance architecture are some of the factors that preserve trust in EU institutions. Croatian citizens are still among the most optimistic with regard to the EU's future and enlargement, with indicators exceeding the EU average. Their trust in the EU institutions is firmer than their confidence in domestic ones (2016 Barometer),[4] which gives added impetus to further internal changes and adaptations of the Croatian public administration, including local governments, to EU standards (comp. Koprić 2017).

Austerity Measures at the Local Level: Examples of Selected Services

Water Services

In the past decade, the list of communal services in Croatia has gradually shrunk, as some of them (gas supply, water and sewage, municipal waste collection and disposal) have been subjected to specific legislation in order to comply with the EU policy on services of general economic interest (Koprić et al. 2016, pp. 206–208). Before the 2008/09 reform, water supply service covered 80% and sewage service 43% of the population. Poor maintenance of water infrastructure and lack of investments resulted

[4] https://eblnews.com/news/croatia/eurobarometer-shows-croatia-hasnt-lost-trust-eu-61012

in inefficient usage of water resources that caused a high leakage rate – more than 40%. Fragmentation of local water and sewage systems and the multitude of local providers (around 150) brought about significant disparities in quality and accessibility of water services and prevented coordinated and efficient investments in infrastructure. Although a significant number of providers were joint companies owned by several local governments, economies of scale were at risk since many of the companies had too small an operational area. Furthermore, water tariffs were kept low, reflecting social considerations of local authorities.

Water sector reform was launched by the *Water Management Strategy* adopted by the Croatian Parliament in 2008. The Strategy proclaimed three main goals: better quality of water services, their wider accessibility, and improved efficiency of water management. In order to meet European qualitative standards of water provision and protection, the comprehensive organizational integration and technical modernization of local water systems, as well as financial consolidation of their operators, were undertaken. As the beginning of the reform coincided with the outbreak of the global economic crisis, austerity significantly influenced the implementation process and the achievement of strategic goals. Although the austerity agenda regarding water services had never been explicitly articulated, many features of the water sector reform resembled its main ideas. However, usual instruments such as budgetary constraints, expenditure cutbacks, and similar austerity measures were not acceptable because harmonization with the EU water directives required public investments on a massive scale. It was estimated that approximately HRK 34 billion (€4.5 billion) should be invested in the construction and rebuilding of water and sewage infrastructure by the end of 2023 (Strategy 2008). In such circumstances, external pressures from the EU were translated into a reform programme according to which domestic actors were expected to do much more with more money as the pre-accession funds became available.

The reform measures were:

1. Territorial re-scaling of water services through the establishment of water service areas (WSAs) as basic units for the provision of water services on a regional scale;
2. Institutional and organizational integration through the establishment of special purpose associations of local governments on the territory of WSAs as separate public authorities, and through the mergers of local providers in order to achieve the principle "one service area – one provider";

3. Financial consolidation of service providers through the principles of "economic pricing" and "full cost recovery" ("users pay"), according to which water tariffs should secure affordability of water services, protection of water resources, and sustainable development of water infrastructure. Prices were expected to be affordable and not to include the costs of inefficient service providers;
4. Better and more efficient management of service providers through the obligatory externalization (corporatization) of water services into separate public companies or institutions; through specialization of providers allowing them to provide only water services; and through the detailed supervision of their activities by the national institutions.

Austerity was used to promote efficiency via structural reorganization, institutional rearrangements, economic pricing, and rational management of service providers.

The reform was incremental. The *Waters Act* adopted in 2009 provided for corporatization and prescribed the basic criteria for the calculation of water tariffs. It moved water services to the supra-municipal level, but local governments remained accountable since special authorities in charge of water services were not established. Liberalization and privatization of water services was explicitly forbidden – only a company or a public institution established and fully owned by one or more local governments could serve as a provider. Local governments were given a three-year period for the establishment of separate public entities for water supply and sewage. By the end of 2014, around 80% of providers had been organized according to the new regulation. Their hesitation postponed the organizational integration of service providers. Corporatization, accompanied by the transfer of property rights over water infrastructure from local governments to providers, diminished local autonomy and emancipated providers from local governments. Furthermore, the central government acquired significant financial and supervisory competences.

Despite proclamations about strict water tariffs control, the burden has gradually been transferred from public budgets to citizens. In the last ten years, the prices have been increasing by an annual rate of 7.5%. The trend is expected to continue. However, they have not yet reached the affordability limit set at 2.5% of the average household income. Tariffs collected by providers and fees for water usage and water protection do not cover operational costs in the sector. Tariffs account for 57% and fees for 18%, while external transfers make 23% of total financing coming to the water sector (World Bank 2016, p. 86).

Completion of the reform was due in 2014/15. In 2014, 20 supra-local service areas were established for the operation of consolidated public providers. They followed county borders with numerous territorial overlaps. The *Water Service Bill* was submitted for public consultation in 2015. However, due to serious conflicts, this draft was later withdrawn. Since the number of water service providers did not decrease (156 in 2015), and voluntary bottom-up mergers did not occur, the formally established service areas remained empty, irrelevant frames. Local resistance prevented effective and timely realization of the reform objectives. Accessibility of water services increased but slightly: 84% of the population were connected to public water supply and 47% to public sewage systems in 2014.

Requirements of the EU water directives have been used as the main reform trigger, but solutions have been shaped, often unilaterally, by domestic actors at the central level. Externally driven reform measures (corporatization of providers, commercialization) have been transposed into national policies, and, despite some difficulties and prolongations, implemented at the local level. Contrary to that, domestically shaped reform objectives (rescaling and integration) have been incorporated into the national legal framework with hesitation and only partially and have not been implemented successfully. The realization of ambitious goals required greater and direct involvement of central bodies that were the main proponents of the austerity reforms. The implementation of reform goals has shifted centre-local relations. Detailed national regulations have narrowed local autonomy in water services provision. Interestingly, no stable focal point for managing the reform has been marked at the central level, allowing the water sector to ramble among the ministries of agriculture, regional development, and environment and energy, depriving the reform of political determination, firm commitment, and clear guidance. It was presented as a set of technical and organizational adjustments to the EU requirements, hiding its political sensitivity. The real institutional hub was the powerful national agency for water management, *Hrvatske vode*. It provided technical assistance to the local actors and channelled the domestic and EU funds downwards. Direct communication between the national water agency and local providers has moved the reform process further away from the political arena and aggravated the possibility of democratic public involvement, rising suspicions of corruption (Zelena akcija 2014).

In 2010, a new, independent national institution for water price regulation (the *Council for Water Services*) was established with the task of harmonizing prices and tariffs and monitoring their conformity to the Government's regulation on minimal prices for water services.

Before the proposal for the integration of service providers in 2015, relevant actors (municipalities and their associations, professional associations of service providers, etc.) had objected mainly to the lack of transparency and participation in drafting the Waters Act and Regulation of Service Areas. In addition, local providers and counties warned about the borders of water service areas, while the *Association for Consumer's Protection* warned about the increase of water tariffs.

The top-down approach has prevented building trust between the national and local actors. Consequently, commitments, ownership over the reform, and mutual understanding of relevant local and central actors have never been achieved. Lack of participation in policy-design and law drafting caused the resistance of local governments and professional associations. Local actors have complained about the "hierarchical system of bureaucratic governance, far from being transparent and participatory" (Zelena akcija 2014).

The Water Services Bill provoked serious conflicts and faced the fiercest opposition. It was eventually unanimously rejected by all relevant actors who complained about the centralization of water management, disrespect for the property of local governments, marginalization of smaller municipalities, etc. Some reform opponents, mostly civic associations dealing with environmental issues, have continued to point out that the reform "paves the way signalises hidden intention for privatisation" promoting negative attitude towards the privatization (Sarvan 2016, p. 312; Zelena akcija 2014, pp. 20–21).

Municipal Waste Management

Municipal waste management comprises communal waste collection and communal waste disposal. In 2000, approximately 80% of the Croatian population were covered by collection of municipal waste. The fragmented system resulted in numerous municipal waste disposal yards – in 2005, there were more than 300 active official landfills and more than 3000 illegal disposal yards. Out of 1.5 million tons of the municipal waste disposed in the same year, only 5% was recycled. Traditionally, the prices did not cover total costs of municipal waste management. They were charged according to household size (in square meters) and this did not include the cost of waste disposal and recovery of landfills (Strategy 2005).

Environmental concerns of domestic actors and harmonization with the EU during the pre-accession period triggered the reform of waste management sector in 2005. The economic crisis changed the perspective on waste. Waste began to be regarded as an economic resource. The new *Strategy of Waste Management* of 2005 finally adopted a strategic approach to waste management sector reform. Its main objectives reflected the goals set by the EU directives: prevention of excessive waste production, reduction of disposed waste, recovery of waste, and development of an integrated modern waste management system.

Waste management reform was only partially affected by the austerity agenda. As the main strategy was similar, *do more with potentially more*, the reform instruments were oriented towards rescaling, reorganization, and modernization of waste management services, efficiency gains, and positive environmental impact. The reform programme comprised: (a) territorial rescaling of waste management, (b) reorganization and corporatization of service providers, and (c) economic pricing of waste collection service according to the polluters pay principle. Liberalization and privatization were also accentuated.

The *Waste Management Plan for the Period 2007–2015* had been adopted by the Government before the economic crisis. It required the establishment of regional waste management centres (RWMC), whose founders would be counties and local governments. RWMCs would serve as the final destination for collected mixed municipal waste that would replace the majority of landfills active at the time. The construction of 13 centres for mechanical biological treatment (MBT) of mixed municipal waste and other waste that was not previously recycled was planned (Plan 2007). The construction and operation of RWMCs were planned via a long-term public-private partnership model: counties would invest in the basic infrastructure while private partners would secure the MBT technology and operate the centres. This approach was promoted by major political parties, private actors in the waste industry, and especially by counties. At that time, various actors, from business community to academia, criticized and demanded the abolishment of counties, which in turn tried to legitimize their role by gaining the new tasks. NGOs, environmental activists, and many local governments were against the adopted model.

The second reform phase began in 2013 with the adoption of the new *Act on Sustainable Waste Management* (ASWM) during the local election campaign. It eliminated municipal waste collection from the list of communal services and was harmonized with the EU standards for the services of general economic interest. Two possible types of provision were provided for: (a) direct provision by a municipal company or public institution established by a local government, or (b) indirect provision via concession to the private company for a period of up to ten years. There were 107 such concessions in 2015, most of them granted to three big private companies. Previous public service of municipal waste disposal was divided into several commercial activities of waste treatment, processing, and disposal. They were fully liberalized. The number of companies with licenses has grown steadily: there were 441 of them in 2016, that is, 42% more than in 2007. Based on the principles of "polluters pay" and "full cost recovery", the prices depend on the quantity of received waste, measured by mass and volume, and the frequency of emptying the waste containers. The practice of price-setting based on household square meters was eliminated by the end of 2016, but 25% of local governments failed to fully comply with the new legal criteria, as they apply the number of household members as the only criterion (Plan 2017).

The reform results are mostly positive. The availability of waste collection has grown in the past decade: in 2005, it was utilized by 93%, in 2010 by 96%, and in 2015 by 99% of the population. The number of active waste disposal landfills has been decreasing: from 305 in 2005 to 135 in 2015. However, waste disposal still dominates among commercial waste management activities. Only 400 local governments (72%) managed to organize separate collection of municipal waste (paper, metal, glass, plastic, textile, and bulky waste) by the end of 2015. The rate of re-use and recycling of municipal waste was 24% in 2015, although the goal set for the end of 2020 is 50%. Despite the increase in the number of recycling yards (from 17 in 2010 to 84 in 2016) with 46 additional mobile recycling units, local governments are still far from meeting the obligations set by the ASWM. The number of waste collection providers remained stable during the reform period (2005–2015): there were 199 providers in 2005 and 203 in 2015 (Plan 2017).

The ministry in charge of environment protection has been the main reform proponent. Besides the Ministry, two other national institutions have played an important role. The Agency for Environment and Nature, established in 2002, is responsible for the database on waste indicators, coordination and supervision in waste management, and reporting on policy implementation. The Environmental Protection and Energy Efficiency Fund, established in 1994, financially supports and coordinates active waste landfills recovery.

A significant part of policy implementation rests on local governments. Although the preparation and adoption of waste management plans were obligatory, only 153 of them adopted such plans by the end of 2013. The law has introduced several fees that should motivate towns and municipalities to intensify their efforts in reducing waste quantities. They have never been implemented since the Fund has not adopted the necessary regulation. The law has not introduced any coercive instruments for local governments. Many municipalities simply ignore their reform obligations. The transfer of reform policy objectives from the centre to the local level is poor. Parallel with closing the landfills, local governments have concluded mutual waste receiving and disposing agreements. The *Association of Towns* has warned several times that separate collection of municipal waste is hardly possible, echoing the situation of small local governments. Small municipalities and towns have also opposed the other reform objectives.

The involvement of counties in municipal waste management has made the already complex, multi-level waste management governance system even more chaotic. Overlapping responsibilities of counties and local governments and weak coordination and project management capacity of the counties have delayed the construction of regional waste centres and led to severe blame games. Only two RWMCs have begun to operate. Delays and stalemates in their construction cannot be ascribed solely to weak local capacities – the concept of regional centres and MBO technology usage have produced stern conflicts between citizens and local authorities as well as between the business community and environmental activists. The locations of RWMCs are a sensitive issue because of real environmental risks. In addition, public protests, based on NIMBY attitude, have effectively prevented necessary decisions. Environmental associations are the main opponents of the RWMC concept. The “Zero Waste Croatia” group consisting of 62 NGOs has consistently advocated against the concept because of its expensiveness and real environmental risks. Public communication and awareness of rising practice is poor, despite the necessity of citizens’ cooperation for achieving the recycling objectives. However, local public communication strategy exists only in rare cases.

After almost three years of delay, the new national *Waste Management Plan* (2017–2022) was adopted by the Government in 2017. Its first draft, prepared by the left-wing coalition in 2015, was not approved by the European Commission. The reasons were general lack of ambition to recycle waste and poor understanding of waste management's preventive purpose. The second draft, prepared in 2016, was never adopted because of the internal conflict within the then right-wing Government. The adopted version has embraced the circular economy approach and the zero-waste concept and emphasized primary selection of waste and its recycling as the vital policy instruments. Recycling centres are to be the backbone of the new system. New orientation has been welcomed by the environmental activists and NGOs but opposed by almost all other actors. Municipalities have complained about their increased responsibilities, counties have feared that their investments in regional waste management centres would become obsolete, while private actors united in the Croatian Association for Waste Management (HUGO) anticipated downsizing of their business activities in waste processing and treatment.[5] The real effects are yet to be seen.

Healthcare Services

Healthcare is organized into primary, secondary, and tertiary sectors.[6] The majority of public healthcare expenses are financed by compulsory health insurance under the Croatian Health Insurance Fund (CHIF), following the Bismarck model (Ministry of Health 2012, p. 159).[7] Local governments and counties are only formally responsible for healthcare infrastructure and capital investments since they receive subsidies from the central budget for these purposes (Koprić et al. 2016, p. 211; Vončina et al. 2007).

[5] http://vijesti.hrt.hr/345491/spor-oko-novog-plana-za-gospodarenje-otpadom

[6] The primary sector encompasses community health centres, healthcare facilities, services providing care for people in their own homes, and institutions providing palliative care. It may also be delivered by private health professionals on a concession base. The secondary sector includes outpatient centres, hospitals, and treatment centres. The tertiary sector includes clinics, clinical hospitals, and clinical hospital centres (Koprić et al. 2016, p. 211).

[7] The CHIF is an extra-budgetary, central government institution. Its director and board of directors are appointed by the Government. A major part of its resources (82%) comes from the compulsory health insurance paid by the employers, self-employed persons, farmers, and pensioners with higher pensions. The rest of the revenues come from the central state budget (11%) and other sources (CHIF 2016, p. 3).

The primary and secondary healthcare services are mainly the responsibility of the counties and certain larger towns, while the central state is in charge of the tertiary sector. Healthcare providers, irrespective of who their owners are, have to sign annual contracts with the CHIF in order to obtain public funds. Such contracts define the costs and payment modes for each health service (Ministry of Health 2012, p. 159), enabling the Government to effectively manage austerity measures in all three healthcare sectors.

The Croatian healthcare sector had been faced with high expenses even before the economic crisis. Efficiency and cost reduction are continuous reform demands (Vončina et al. 2007). The first major reform was implemented in 1993, promoting firm centralization and excessive privatization, especially in the primary sector. The reform of 2001 promoted some decentralization and commercialization, and enabled insured individuals to pay for additional healthcare insurance and obtain better service (Ministry of Health 2012, pp. 147–148).

A comprehensive modernization of the healthcare system was announced in 2008, but it was mostly oriented towards financial stabilization and system efficiency (Džakula et al. 2014, p. 125). It consisted of several measures, including increased citizen co-payment, wider compulsory health insurance coverage, new sources of financing (new imposts or share of taxes that are allocated to the CHIF), and strict fiscal discipline. In addition, different efficiency measures were introduced, such as introduction of information technology in the primary healthcare services, reform of emergency medical service, and introduction of the national waiting list for hospital services (Broz and Švaljek 2014, pp. 55–57; Džakula et al. 2014, p. 125).

Instead of improvements, the reform of 2008 worsened the crisis, with damaging effects for the poorest people (Broz and Švaljek 2014, p. 55). Healthcare expenses grew from 6% of GDP in 2005 to 7.2% in 2010 (Bertelsmann Stiftung BTI 2016, p. 15). The real household healthcare expenditures grew by 13.8% between 2008 and 2010 (Broz and Švaljek 2014, p. 67). The increased co-payment has endangered the basic welfare principles (Ministry of Health 2012, pp. 148–149). The total amount of resources granted to the counties for health care from the central budget has decreased after 2010. Simultaneously, the differences in healthcare grants among counties have grown to the ratio 1:3, without any acceptable reason. Over-politicization of yearly decisions on grants, unrealistic expenditure policy, and inadequate central-local relations in the healthcare sector jeopardize public and users' trust (Jambrač 2017, pp. 206–208).

Despite the austerity measures, the healthcare sector has continued to accumulate debt. The centre-left government of Zoran Milanović launched another round of reform in 2011, when it adopted the *National Health Reform Strategy for 2012–2020* (Ministry of Health 2012). The Strategy was followed by the adoption of national reform programmes for 2014, 2015, 2016, and 2017 and the European Commission's opinion on the healthcare system of 2015 (EC 2015, pp. 73–75). Reduction of fiscal risks was set as the main reform goal for the period by 2018. It was to be realized by a combination of eight measures (mostly directed at the hospital system, introduction of IT, and modern human resource management).[8]

In 2012, the reform was redirected to the indebted hospital system, causing a temporary change in central-local relations. Namely, although counties are owners of secondary healthcare institutions, including hospitals, many of them still lack the administrative, technical, and managerial capacity to govern them. The fact that financing of the secondary healthcare remains the central state obligation has seriously limited the counties' ability to effectively manage their healthcare institutions (Džakula et al. 2014, p. 25).

The purpose of the 2012 *Act on Recovery of Public Institutions* (*Official Gazette* 136/12, 151/14, 27/16) was to provide for temporary centralization of the hospital system by transferring the management rights from the counties to the central state during the entire recovery period plus two additional years. This measure was applied to all the hospitals that did not pay their debts within due deadlines. Nine state-owned hospitals and 25 county institutions (mostly hospitals) were affected by this measure (Bodiroga-Vukobrat 2013, p. 20).

In 2015, the State Audit Office (SAO) concluded that the recovery of the hospital system did not produce the expected results since the affected healthcare institutions continued to accumulate debts (SAO 2015, p. 14). After the parliamentary elections of 2016 and the change of government, the recovery process was officially terminated and management rights were returned to the counties. However, county governors have refused to take over the responsibility for hospitals' debts, arguing that it is the central government, not the counties that should pay the debts since the government decides on grants and regulates the healthcare services. They have advocated for full decentralization, including genuine fiscal decentralization, which would enable them to fully

[8] https://zdravlje.gov.hr/reforma-zdravstvenog-sustava/1491

execute their ownership and managerial rights.[9] These claims illustrate that strong centralization of the Croatian local self-government system creates overlapping competences in the healthcare sector, with a dominant role of the central state, and that such a complex system causes paralyzing and damaging blame avoidance practice.

The most recurrent healthcare reform demands include reduction of expenditures, costs control betterment, financial management improvements, and a higher level of citizen co-payment. Apart from them, reorganization instruments such as temporary centralization of hospital management have been implemented. Thus, the reform strategy is based on the principle of doing the same with less, with instruments that are mostly oriented towards efficiency gains.

All the reforms conducted in the Croatian healthcare sector have had external stimuli. The EU plays the most important role. The latest reform was arranged with the EU as well as with the IMF.[10] External pressure also comes from the World Bank whose loans are indispensable to the Croatian healthcare system. Hence, the World Bank is an active participant in all the reform debates, giving clear guidance about the reform measures (Bodiroga-Vukobrat 2013, p. 24; Zrinščak 2008, p. 129).

These external pressures are being translated into domestic policies created by the Ministry of Health, which, in cooperation with the Ministry of Finance, has designed the austerity measures obligatory for all healthcare institutions, including those owned and managed by the counties. Although healthcare reforms have tremendous effects on citizens "... for many of them policy options were not publicly discussed and no comprehensive implementation plans were developed" (Džakula et al. 2014, p. 123).

Apart from the major centre-left opposition party (SDP), which opposed the reform measures, especially those related to the increasing co-payment and transfer of financial burden to citizens (Bodiroga-Vukobrat 2010, p. 29), the reform was attacked by the unions which blamed the Government for the general lack of transparency in reform design and particularly for the lack of dialogue with thehealthcare professionals (Bodiroga-Vukobrat 2010, p. 29). A small Government collation partner, the Croatian Pensioners Party, also objected to the lack of consul-

[9] http://www.jutarnji.hr/vijesti/hrvatska/zupanije-zele-da-im-se-bolnice-vrate-bez-novih-dugova/105019/; http://www.novilist.hr/Vijesti/Hrvatska/Neuspjela-sanacija-vraca-gubitase-osnivacima-Opce-bolnice-vracaju-se-u-vlasnistvo-zupanija?meta_refresh=true

[10] https://zdravlje.gov.hr/reforma-zdravstvenog-sustava/1491

tations regarding the introduction of health insurance payment for pensioners with higher pensions.[11]

It is interesting that the 2008–2011 reform was not elaborated in a document, but in a PowerPoint presentation posted on the web page of the Ministry of Health (Broz and Švaljek 2014, p. 55; Bodiroga-Vukobrat 2009, p. 23). It is obvious that public consultation, dialogue with the unions and professionals, and reform strategic planning were poor. Response to the crisis was reactive, inadequate, and insufficient.

The situation has improved after the adoption of the National Health Reform Strategy for the period 2012–2020, which comprised the long-term healthcare reform goals. However, criticism for the lack of transparency, dialogue, and participation has remained equally serious (Bodiroga-Vukobrat 2013, pp. 23–24). Moreover, since the then Government treated the hospital recovery programme as an operational (technical) measure, there was no formal public consultation process despite its serious impact on central-local relations and on local governments (Džakula et al. 2014, p. 127).

The lack of appropriate preparations, public consultations, dialogue, research, and reform evaluation are common characteristics of all healthcare reforms in Croatia (Džakula et al. 2014, p. 123). Reform decisions have been reactive – political actors decided only when the problem could not be put aside, with only rudimentary public debate and poor preparation. Consequently, healthcare policy is rarely mentioned in electoral campaigns (Radin and Džakula 2012). Weak preparation is one of the important reasons for the reform failures because the official reform measures could be implemented only partially (Džakula et al. 2014, p. 123). As a result, the reliability, professionalism, and sustainability of the Croatian healthcare system are in jeopardy.

Conclusion

The 2008 economic crisis severely affected Croatia. It provoked various austerity measures in the public sector, local government included. This chapter offers several general conclusions based on an in-depth analysis of three key local policy and provision sectors. The concept of resilient local authority opens appropriate research questions in times of serious crisis and wicked problems that befall local governments. A muddling-through adaptation to the environmental pressures has enabled the

[11] http://dnevnik.hr/vijesti/hrvatska/reforma-zdravstva-docekana-na-noz.html

Croatian local governments to remain untouched by structural, territorial, or similar measures during the economic crisis despite certain austerity measures imposed by the central government. They adapted to the new situation using the welfare needs as a barrier against any serious reform (comp. Hoffmann et al. 2017).

The main external pressure came from the EU and the pre-accession process. However, the EU remains an important motivator of internal reforms since public trust in the Union is relatively firm, above the EU average. Starting from 2014, the European semester has served as an additional channel for elaborating European expectations from the Croatian public sector reforms and of communicating national reform plans back to the EU. The World Bank has been an important external reform driver in the healthcare sector. Although external actors have provided rather clear guidance on the necessary reforms, the implementation has been incremental and hesitating. In contrast to that, reform objectives established by the central government can be much more easily evaded by local governments, as the example of water management sector shows.

When it comes to the centre/periphery dimension of the reform, an increasing centralization can be noticed. Water services have undergone a transformation from communal services to services at the supra-municipal level with direct lines of influence of national bodies on water service providers. Healthcare service is under tremendous influence of the central government, by means of centralized decision-making and huge central budget grants.

The main austerity strategy in the three analysed sectors has aimed at efficiency through financial consolidation and institutional rearrangements. Financial consolidation was attempted mainly through spreading commercialization, transfer of service costs to citizens, resulting in price increase in water services and rising co-payment in healthcare services. Corporatization has taken place in the water and waste sectors. The main measures in the healthcare sector have been connected with savings and fiscal discipline, while structural changes have been neglected, despite local requests for decentralization. These measures have been unsuccessful and financial crisis in the healthcare system is growing rapidly.

The common reform feature is non-transparent policy formulation without proper public consultations, participation, and communication. The overlapping competences of the central bodies and counties (healthcare) and various types of local governments (waste management) trigger the blame-shifting games and blame avoidance. Although commercialization takes place in all three sectors (real prices in water and waste management, co-payment in healthcare), local governments seek a way to preserve the basic social model through various measures, provoking accusations of massive capture practice (Hoffmann et al. 2017).

Efforts to improve local service provision in Croatia have been instigated mainly by the central government, while local governments play the role of passive and hesitant partners. Budgetary constraints are not the main cause of hesitation. Centralization, fragmentation, and overlaps are more important. Sectoral reforms have been faced with inadequate territorial organization. Different institutional and territorial networks have been created in different sectors in order to make necessary reforms possible. General inclination has shifted towards centralization because of the lack of capacities in the vast majority of local governments. However, institutional innovation is not coordinated among the sectors, making the Croatian institutional environment increasingly complex. Croatia needs decentralization and a holistic territorial reorganization in order to make the provision of local public and social services more effective and more efficient.

References

Bertelsmann Stiftung, BTI. (2016). *Croatia Country Report* (32 p). Gütersloh: Bertelsmann Stiftung. https://www.btiproject.org/fileadmin/files/BTI/Downloads/Reports/2016/pdf/BTI_2016_Croatia.pdf

Bodiroga-Vukobrat, N. (2009, May). *Annual National Report 2009: Pensions, Health Care and Long-Term Care – Croatia* (47 p). Analytical Support on Socio-economic Impact of Social Protection Reforms (asisp) on Behalf of the European Commission DG Employment, Social Affairs and Inclusion. http://pensionreform.ru/files/4153/ASISP.%20Annual%20National%20Report%202009%20-%20Croatia.pdf

Bodiroga-Vukobrat, N. (2010, May). *Annual National Report 2010: Pensions, Health Care and Long-Term Care – Croatia* (49 p). Analytical Support on Socio-Economic Impact of Social Protection Reforms (asisp) on Behalf of the European Commission DG Employment, Social Affairs and Inclusion. http://pensionreform.ru/files/4152/ASISP.%20Annual%20National%20Report%202010%20-%20Croatia.pdf

Bodiroga-Vukobrat, N. (2013, November). *Country Document 2013: Pensions, Health Care and Long-Term Care – Croatia* (42 p). Analytical Support on Social Protection Reforms and Their Socio-Economic Impact (asisp) on Behalf of the European Commission DG Employment, Social Affairs and Inclusion. http://pensionreform.ru/files/67452/2013.%20ASISP.%20Country%20Document%202013%20-%20Croatia.pdf

Broz, T., & Švaljek, S. (2014). Financiranje zdravstva u Hrvatskoj: od reforme do reforme. In M. Vehovec (Ed.), *O zdravstvu iz ekonomske perspektive* (pp. 51–75). Zagreb: Ekonomski institut Zagreb.

CHIF. (2016). *Izvješće o poslovanju Hrvatskog zavoda za zdravstveno osiguranje za 2015. Godinu* (27 p). Zagreb: Hrvatski zavod za zdravstveno osiguranje. http://www.hzzo.hr/wp-content/uploads/2016/04/Izvjesce_o_poslovanju_hzzo_za_2015_godinu.pdf?831c2f

CoE. (2016). *Local and Regional Democracy in Croatia* (3 p). Council of Europe. Congress of Local and Regional Authorities.

Dobrotić, I. (2016). Crisis and Croatian Welfare State: A New Opportunity for Welfare State Retrenchment? In K. Schubert, P. de Villota, & J. Kuhlmann (Eds.), *Challenges to European Welfare Systems* (pp. 301–324). Cham: Springer.

Džakula, A., Sagan, A., Pavić, N., Lončarek, K., & Sekelj-Kauzlarić, K. (2014). Croatia Health System Review. *Health Systems in Transition, 16*(3), 1–162.

EC. (2015). Macroeconomic Imbalances. Country Report Croatia 2015. *European Economy* (112 p). Occasional Paper 218. http://ec.europa.eu/economy_finance/publications/occasional_paper/2015/pdf/ocp218_en.pdf

Hoffmann, D., Miošić-Lisjak, N., Prkut, D., Stubbs, P., Šalaj, B., Zelić, D., & Zrinščak, S. (2017). *Naša zarobljena mista: Istraživački izvještaj studija kvalitete lokalnog javnog upravljanja u Hrvatskoj* (131 p). Zagreb: GONG.

Jambrač, J. (2017). Funkcionalna decentralizacija u Hrvatskoj: petnaest godina poslije. *Croatian and Comparative Public Administration, 17*(2), 189–216.

Koprić, I. (2017). European Administrative Space – Myth, Reality, and Hopes. In I. Koprić & P. Kovač (Eds.), *European Administrative Space: Spreading Standards, Building Capacities* (pp. 31–54). Bratislava: NISPAcee.

Koprić, I. (2017a). Reform of the Croatian Public Administration: Between Patchy Europeanization and Bumpy Modernization. In P. Kovač & M. Bileišis (Eds.), *Public Administration Reforms in New Eastern European Union Member States: Post Accession Dimensions of Public Governance Convergence and Divergence* (pp. 339–388). Ljubljana: Faculty of Administration, University of Ljubljana & Mykolas Romeris University.

Koprić, I., & Đulabić, V. (2018). Evaluation of the Decentralisation Programme in Croatia: Expectations, Problems and Results. In I. Koprić, H. Wollmann, & G. Marcou (Eds.), *Evaluating Reforms of Local Public and Social Services in Europe: More Evidence for Better Results.* London: Palgrave Macmillan.

Koprić, I., Musa, A., & Đulabić, V. (2016). Local Government and Local Public Services in Croatia. In H. Wollmann, I. Koprić, & G. Marcou (Eds.), *Public and Social Services in European Countries: From Public and Municipal to Private Sector Provision* (pp. 201–215). London: Palgrave Macmillan.

Ministry of Health. (2012). *Nacionalna strategija razvoja zdravstva 2012–2020* (96 p). Zagreb: Ministry of Health. https://zdravlje.gov.hr/UserDocsImages/dokumenti/Programi,%20projekti%20i%20strategije/Nacionalna%20strategija%20zdravstva%20-%20za%20web.pdf

Ott, K., Bronić, M., & Stanić, B. (2016). Pomoći Europske unije županijama, gradovima i općinama od 2011–2014. *Newsletter Instituta za javne financije, 105*, 1–13.

Plan. (2007). *Plan gospodarenja otpadom u Republici Hrvatskoj za razdoblje 2007–2015. godine*. Official Gazette 85/2007.

Plan. (2017). *Odluka o donošenju Plana gospodarenja otpadom Republike Hrvatske za razdoblje 2017–2022*. Official Gazette 3/2017.

Posedel, P., & Primorac, M. (2012). Modelling Local Government Unit Credit Risk in the Republic of Croatia. *Financial Theory and Practice, 36*(4), 329–354.

Radin, D., & Džakula, A. (2012). Has Anyone Seen It? Health Care in Croatian Elections. *East European Politics and Society, 26*(1), 189–212.

SAO (2015). *Izvješće o radu Državnog ureda za reviziju za 2015. godinu* (84 p). Zagreb: Državni ured za reviziju. http://www.revizija.hr/datastore/filestore/71/izvjesce_o_radu_za_2015_v2.pdf

Sarvan, D. (2016). Upravljanje vodnim uslugama kao faktor teritorijalne integracije lokalnih jedinica. *Croatian and Comparative Public Administration, 16*(2), 295–319.

Shaw, K. (2012). The Rise of the Resilient Local Authority? *Local Government Studies, 38*(3), 281–300.

Škarica, M. (2015). Suradnja hrvatskih jedinica lokalne samouprave – rezultati i pouke empirijskog istraživanja. In I. Koprić, M. Škarica, & B. Milošević (Eds.), *Suradnja i oj u lokalnoj i regionalnoj samoupravi* (pp. 253–292). Zagreb: Institut za javnu upravu.

Strategy. (2005). *Strategija gospodarenja otpadom Republike Hrvatske*. Official Gazette 130/2005.

Strategy. (2008). *Strategija upravljanja vodama*. Official Gazette 91/2008.

Vončina, L., Džakula, A., & Mastilica, M. (2007). Health Care Funding Reforms in Croatia: A Case of Mistaken Priorities. *Health Policy, 80*(1), 144–157.

World Bank. (2014). *Croatia Public Finance Review: Restructuring Spending for Stability and Growth* (160 p). http://documents.worldbank.org/curated/en/532211468245997938/Croatia-Public-finance-review-restructuring-spending-for-stability-and-growth

World Bank. (2016). *Croatia Policy Notes 2016: Restoring Macroeconomic Stability, Competitiveness and Inclusion* (120 pp). http://documents.worldbank.org/curated/en/876601468000628285/pdf/103938-WP-P156959-PUBLIC-Croatia-Policy-Notes-2016-EN.pdf

Zelena akcija i projektni partneri. (2014). *Naša voda – analiza upravljanja vodnim uslugama u Hrvatskoj* (68 p). Zagreb: Zelena akcija.

Zrinščak, S. (2008). Zdravstvena politika. In V. Puljiz, G. Bežovan, T. Matković, Z. Šućur, & S. Zrinščak (Eds.), *Socijalna politika Hrvatske* (pp. 119–162). Zagreb: Pravni fakultet.

CHAPTER 9

The Bumpy Road of the Externally Transferred Austerity Agenda in Albania and Its Fragmentary Effects on Local Public Services

Visar Dizdari, Arjeta Troshani, and Elvisa Drishti

Introduction and National Background Classification

In the new global economy, austerity is fast becoming a key instrument of achieving and preserving economic stability through fiscal security. Investigating austerity is a continuing concern within the field of fiscal stress and cutback management, be it at the central or local level (Scorsone and Plerhoples 2010). In the setting of recent developments, subsequent

V. Dizdari (✉)
Faculty of Educational Sciences, University of Shkoder "Luigj Gurakuqi", Shkoder, Albania
e-mail: vdizdari@unishk.edu.al

A. Troshani • E. Drishti
Faculty of Economy, University of Shkoder "Luigj Gurakuqi", Shkoder, Albania
e-mail: atroshani@unishk.edu.al; edrishti@unishk.edu.al

A. Lippi, T. N. Tsekos (eds.), *Local Public Services in Times of Austerity across Mediterranean Europe*, Governance and Public Management, https://doi.org/10.1007/978-3-319-76225-8_9

to the fiscal crisis, the issue of austerity has received considerable critical attention as a means to address public debt unsustainability. Since the transfer from the central to the local government is experienced more acutely – with regard to the provision of local public services – the bearings they have therefore on the citizens' day-to-day life make it a fairly tangible object of research.

The changes experienced from the financial crisis over the past years remain unprecedented and many times authors have considered it as the largest recession since the Great Depression. When considering such effects on a fragile and young free market economy such as Albania, the public management approaches pursued signify the heart of understanding and projecting the economic and social prosperity of this nation.

Despite the fact that Albania diverges significantly with regard to population, economic standard, and actual political status, and apart from the fact that each of the Central and Eastern Europe Countries have experienced their own individual brand of transition (Mitra and Matlay 2004), it has lagged a comparable economic and political track with other post-communist countries along the decades following the Second World War (Cook 2010; Lehmann and Muravyev 2010; Savić and Zubović 2015).[1] The impact of this paucity is reflected also in contemporary post-communist public management and public services practices. In the venue of a global financial crisis, Hungary, Romania, Serbia, Latvia, and Ukraine called for international bailouts; however, Albania eluded the International Monetary Fund's (IMF's) involvement since, at the time (2008–2010), the country was facing economic growth and the government reduced general expenditures by a quarter. As a result, diverging from the paths of other Balkan and post-communist countries, Albania avoided the external shock but it was the post-crisis impact that stalled growth and provoked domestic and external vulnerabilities.

There are patterns, as we will show in this chapter, in the democratic governing coalition mandate (2005–2013), where the retrenchment is quite distinguishable but in such fashion that incremental adjustments, in the form of corrective actions, rather than radical change were followed. On the other hand, subsequent to the 2013 governmental elections, the left-wing coalition launched a set of radical reforms arguing that in times

[1] The author investigates these post-communist countries: In Europe: Bulgaria and Romania, Czech Republic, Hungary, Poland, Slovak Republic, and Slovenia; and in the Former Soviet Union: Latvia, Lithuania, and Estonia.

of extraordinary fiscal stress, as the financial crisis and mounting debt levels proved to be, cutbacks must follow on. Interestingly enough, most of the reforms were not agreed by political consensus by the centre-right parties. On the other hand, the rhetoric proposed by the post–2013 left-wing coalition supported by the unusual parliamentary majority that granted them the 2013 win, reassured this force that the incurred meaningless electoral cost of wide-ranging overhauls was to be ignored.

However, being an ongoing process, many aspects of the impact of the austerity measures are yet to be seen, and we believe that the externally and internally induced cutbacks in local public services embody a long-term trend and not merely a rebound to transitory macroeconomic conditions imposed by the financial crisis for the Albanian case. In the case of Albania, austerity has been mainly triggered by direct and explicit external forces, resulting in voluntary policy transfer or what classifies as mimetic isomorphism (DiMaggio and Powell 1991) since compliance with the EU standards before the external shock and avoidance of the external shock spill over to other member countries was recommended by international agencies and supranational institutions. Domestic forces have had their share on this matter as well since political parties managed to handle the Territorial Administrative Reform as a political dispute which failed to gain widely held approval in 2009.

Little is evidenced academically about the dynamics of local public services under the new era of austerity in Albania and no previous attempts to investigate such process domestically, let alone to provide cross-national comparisons, were made. Also, the word "austerity" per se is quite absent from the wide political, economic, or social discourse, which makes it difficult to collect information that is explicitly related to austerity measures. As a result, this chapter seeks to contribute to a wider debate on public management research in the age of austerity in general and to the local public services performance evidence particularly for the Albanian case, a representative post-communist context.

In what follows, we have used a qualitative methodological approach which consists of the arrangement of clear statements in a narrative form to address four analytical dimensions, that is, who, what, when, and how, enriched with a defined set of verbal descriptors in order to provide a comparable base with other Chaps. in this book (Schneider and Wagemann 2012).

The overall structure of this chapter takes the form of five sections, including this introductory one. The remainder of the chapter proceeds as follows: The second section includes a comprehensive chronological laying out of the austerity agenda in Albania and looks at how the programme of financial consolidation and structural reforms has evolved pre and post the effects of the financial crisis hit the economy in the context of the political forces/coalitions that steered such endeavours. The third section reviews public borrowing and fiscal deficits as the main reasons that persuaded the change in territorial and fiscal austerity. Ever-rising debt levels peaked at 72.7% in 2016, leading to divergences from the advised fiscal consolidation measures and gradual debt reduction. The fourth section presents Territorial and Administrative Reform as the most radical (de jure) programme completed by the Government of Albania in terms of the local unit's self-government and decentralization. Finally, the conclusion and discussion give a brief summary and critique of the findings.

The reader should bear in mind that it is beyond the scope of this study to provide a comprehensive review of all the political developments and discourses about issues such as the removal of the debt ceiling law or the territorial administrative reform and, instead, the key milestones and measures have been called into attention.

The Austerity Agenda in Albania: A Programme of Financial Consolidation and Structural Reforms in the Context of Major Political Events

Prior to the global financial crisis, Albania was one of the fastest-growing economies in Europe, albeit starting from a low baseline. After 2008, echoing the Eurozone situation, the annual real growth initially halved, to deteriorate to the very minimum (2013: 1%) (INSTAT 2016). Furthermore, macroeconomic imbalances in the public sector emerged, and the declining rate of growth was complemented by rising levels of poverty and unemployment. Notwithstanding the fact of a much needed austerity agenda in such an aggravated situation, only after the 2013 government elections did it became part of political discussions – the year in which the new coalition of left parties won the elections after two consecutive centre-right governments.

In 2005, the coalition, led by the major centre-right Democratic Party (DP), after eight years in opposition, won a significant parliamentary majority. The first cabinet of Prime Minister (PM) Sali Berisha formed after the elections implemented a neoliberal programme based in the principles of small government and public savings, reduction of current expenditure, tax cuts, new privatizations, and public investments in large infrastructural projects. The government continued the lending arrangements with the IMF and World Bank (WB) initiated since 1991 when Albania became a member of those international agencies. In January 2006, a three-year arrangement was sanctioned and sought to prepare the country for graduation from IMF-supported programmes. The disbursement of the loan under the Poverty Reduction and Growth Facility Agreement was conditioned upon continued macroeconomic stability supported by fiscal consolidation, the enhancement of growth potential, the pursuit of a reform agenda, including improvements in revenue administration, declining levels of public debt relative to GDP, financial market development, civil service, and expenditure management (IMF 2006). Throughout the three years of the programme, Albania maintained macroeconomic stability, improved its debt sustainability outlook, and made progress with structural reforms. The growth rate rose around 7.5% and the budget deficit reduced to 5% of the Gross Domestic Product (GDP), in line with the programme targets. Due to the good financial performance, Albania graduated in January 2009 from the IMF programme funds. The favourable economic climate continued in these years, and the government was able to raise the wages and pensions. In fact, public sector wages had an overall 50% increase (2005: 7.5%; 2009: 17%). Pensions had a yet more eminent annual raise and in 2009 the average pension in urban areas was 50% higher than in 2005, while in rural areas it doubled. Nevertheless, pensions remained low in terms of absolute value and purchase power. The rate of unemployment slightly decreased (1% in three years) and the rates of poverty decreased by more than 5% for those falling into the "poor" (2005: 17.9%; 2009: 12.5%) and "very poor" (2005: 3.3%; 2009: 1.2%) income categories (INSTAT 2016).

The previous economic achievements served as the battle flag of the 2009s DP electoral campaign. The centre-right coalition led by DP was the winner of these elections but did not have a parliamentary majority, so it entered in a government coalition with a small left party, Socialist Movement for Integration (SMI). The cabinet formed the second consecutive cabinet led by the leader of DP, Sali Berisha, soon had to face economic difficulties. The effects of the Eurozone crises had already arrived in Albania. Due to an underdeveloped financial system and limited financial exposure to international markets, Albania did not directly face the banking crisis. Kickert (2012) considers the banking crisis as the initial phase of the global crisis, where banks and other key financial institutions faced difficulties. In the second phase, the economic crisis emerged after the financial one and led to drastic falls in GDP and employment. The fiscal crisis is the final phase that arose when the budget deficits the governments had (and the gross state debts that had accumulated) came to be seen as excessive. Despite evidences of economic difficulties, such as the annual real growth halved (2008: 7.5%; 2009: 3.4%), accompanied by an increased rate of poverty (2008: 12.4%; 2012: 14.3%) and unemployment (2008: 13.2%; 2012: 16.4%), the government of Prime Minister (PM) Berisha initially denied the inevitability of interventions for realignment with the new order. In front of the opposition criticism with regard to economic policies, the government argued that, in times of global crisis, when most of the Eurozone countries were going through an economic recession, the low positive annual growth of Albania was a sign of decent economic policies.

Previous research on cutback management reveals that retrenchments take place in a series of stages (Raudla et al. 2013). First, public entities deny the need for change and delay cuts. After this initial denial stage, the first round of small cutbacks is typically applied. In analogy, the second cabinet of PM Berisha was not fully convinced of the gravity and duration of the difficult economic situation (stage 1), and the measures were insignificant (stage 2), for example the decision taken in 2009 to not pay public servants the 13th wage introduced in 2007, which was replaced with an "end-of-year reward." Other small cuts in operative expenditure were also made such as the removal of the postponement of holidays on weekdays when the earlier dated on a weekend.

Due to the weak domestic demand associated with fiscal loosening (especially along the 2013 electoral year), the financial situation aggravated. Public debt increased, from about 60% to about 70% in 2013, including unpaid bills and government arrears linked with the contract signed by the public administration. Moreover, the deficit for 2013 was about 5% of GDP (IMF 2014). It was in this situation of economic slowdown that the 2013 government elections were held. The left pre-electoral coalition formed by the Socialist Party (SP) and SMI (transferring into opposition only three months before elections) won an unusual parliamentary majority and created a new government led by the head of SP, Edi Rama. The new government claimed that the crisis was more severe and persistent than expected and it needed difficult public finance and structural reforms. As previous governments had done before when in receipt of control, the Rama government demanded a large loan from the

IMF. The first signs of the austerity agenda became evident in 2014–when a three-year arrangement with the IMF was approved – which combined with a number of important structural reforms, including public finances management, pensions, and local government reforms. Such reforms were generated by the external-internal transfer of austerity, levered by the pre-conditions of EU admittance, as a supranational institution, and implied a strict budgetary discipline, savings in current expenditure, and a strengthening of the tax base.

The Rama government that promoted these reforms did not make explicit the term of financial austerity but rather showcased it as a large programme of reforms that sought the modernization and consolidation of institutions. Also, the austerity programme undertaken by the government, rather than imposed externally, is justified with the presumed abusive transfers and unjustified expenses done by the precedent centre-right government.

A strong parliamentary majority allowed PM Rama to undertake severe public finance and structural reforms supported by the IMF, WB, and EU. The consolidation included both expenditure and revenue measures. The most important operational measure applied by the central government was hiring and pay freeze. In Albania, the period of pay freeze in the public sector (except for the police forces) has been explicitly fixed: a three-year pay freeze (at the previously increased level) and the abolition of the "end-of-year reward" was foreseen from 2014 to 2017. Reduction of staff has not been applied as a cutback measure. However, the government has opted for reorganization to reduce the expenditure side of the budget. Public Administration Reform was initiated in 2013 and strived to reorganize or substantially reform the public agencies. In addition, the 2014 Territorial and Administrative Reform included the abolition of more than 300 small municipalities. A very important expenditure measure was a reduction of loss in electricity distribution by improving the collection rate and reducing energy theft. Programme measures have proved to be the largest expenditure reductions amongst the cutbacks share in OECD countries. The most frequently targeted areas for savings have been health care, pensions, welfare, and infrastructure (OECD 2012). Health care expenditures were slightly reduced in Albania, but the pension reform shifted the retirement age to 67 for men and 65 for women, which was associated with a limitation of pension indexation subject to inflation (a requirement under the pension law).

Apart from pensions, cuts were made in other social security benefits. The overall public social expenditure was constricted by cuts in two social assistance programmes: (i) the Social Assistance Program (SAP) and (ii) the Special Needs and Disabilities Pension (SNDP). The government intended to reform the social assistance system (a Social Assistance Modernization Project was financed by World Bank for the years 2012–2017) to prevent abuses and evasion and by improving the screening of social benefit programmes; the left coalition government expected to reduce the number of recipients by 20% by 2016. Both schemes were reviewed in 2014, and the number of beneficiaries of SAP reduced by 20,321 families and those of SNDP by about 1000 (SHSSH 2014). Capital investment cuts targeted the public infrastructure investment projects, in particular the highway constructions projects of the former government.

Revenue measures were numerous. As a rule, governments relied more on increasing the rates of existing taxes rather than introducing new ones (Kickert et al. 2013). In Albania, the increase in excises was a major tax measure that raised taxes on luxury goods, cigarettes, wine, beer, alcoholic beverages, energy drinks, tobacco, and grease. The circulation tax increase, equivalent to an increase in fuel price was significant, making the fuel price at the pump throw the highest in the region. Also, the increase in corporate income tax rate was significant (from 10% to 15%). The rate of standard value added tax (VAT) was not increased, but several VAT exemptions were abolished. At the same time, the government introduced a progressive income tax system on salaries (the former tax system, implemented by the centre-right government, was a flat income tax of 10%) with rates of 0%, 13%, and 23%. This system, called by socialist leaders "fair taxation", was an important element of the electoral programme of the left.

To date, the progress towards the establishment of a fully functioning market economy, an essential EU requirement, was modest in fields such as formalization attempts and electricity sector reformation; slight growth improvements that were outweighed by high unemployment are evidenced. Public borrowing has not met any reduction and the substandard implementation of public investments is perpetual (European Commission 2016).

In what concerns local government and local public services criteria aligned with the strategic purpose of pressing forward Albania's EU compliance progression, the STAR2 interventions funded further consolidation of institutional and administrative capacities of local governance units to improve the local service delivery quality and enhance good governance through citizen-oriented and participatory decision-making (RAT 2016).

Public Borrowing and Fiscal Instability

In this section, we will address the main reasons that persuaded the change in territorial and fiscal austerity in Albania, debt and fiscal deficits. Public sector borrowing has risen from 59.5 (2009) to 64.6 (2013) and peaked at 72.7 (2016)[2] as a percentage of GDP. This poor performance of the national accounts has contributed to further deviations from the fiscal consolidation measures and gradual debt reduction advised by international agencies (IMF 2016).

Central government election years have proved to be authentic hazards with respect to public finances patterns at the national level. In 2013, during the first two quarters, an investigation of the WB figures alerted that Albania's public debt declined at 63.8% due to heavy borrowing requirements at a time when other South Eastern Europe countries had lower public debt and higher growth rates. In absolute terms, the public debt increased by 43 million Albanian Lek (ALL). The DP, to justify the ever-rising debt-to-GDP ratios sanctioned, in October 2012, removed the 60% debt-to-GDP ceiling, a limit imposed by the Organic Budget Law in 2008 and, at the same time, it continued to increase public sector wages and pensions. The WB warned that the removal of OBL threatens the country's further economic growth and exit out of control. The same pattern regarding public debt can be witnessed in the first quarters of 2017 from the governing socialist coalition side. In current times, to manipulate the public sentiment for the upcoming government elections in June 2017, the public administration wages have increased in March and so did the pensions and transfers. More specifically, the 2017–2019 medium-term budget, approved by the parliament, increased public sector wages by 10% following a pension increase confirmed by the Minister of Finances, Arben Ahmetaj. The funds allocated for such an undertaking are the largest in the post-communist Albanian fiscal policies history and are planned to increase by 500 million ALL per year.[3] Local government wages are also agreed to increase by 7% and the funds have to be covered by own revenues (Ministry of Finance 2017b), indicating that further coercion of local

[2] We used 2009 and 2013 as points of reference due to the fact that central government elections were held in these years. June 2017 is the date for the upcoming elections but data on the first and second quarters are not yet available. The major changes in central and local public finances have happened in government election years.

[3] In other words, starting from 2017, the funds for such an increase reach 1 milliard ALL, in 2018: 1.5 milliard ALL, and for 2019: 2 milliard ALL.

government units' own revenues is to be experienced in the next years. Regarding pensions, a 1.4 milliard ALL fund is approved, which is planned to start in 2019 while transfers such as compensation for ex-political prisoners and expropriation of landowners are projected to increase for the next three years. For expropriation, the 2017 fund is planned as 4 milliard ALL, while for 2018, this reaches 5 milliard ALL. Upsurges are projected also for compensation for ex-political prisoners in the medium-term budget programme at 2 milliard ALL, similar to the one in 2016.

In addition, the Minister of Finances' press conference on the 28 March 2017 confirmed the commencement of a fiscal amnesty period valid until the end of the 2017 and which will include full conditional and unconditional cancellation of businesses fines and tax payments, at the national and local level for the arrears falling between the 2011 and 2014 fiscal years. Also, other tax obligations including business fines, the failure of submitting reporting papers, obligations payable at customs, etc., will be written off (Ministry of Finance 2017c).

Figure 9.1 reveals that at least the primary deficit, for the first time in the history of Albanian fiscal policy, was within the financially sustainable constraints mandated by the Maastricht Treaty and its descendant, the Stability and Growth Pact. It is comprehensible that what the governing

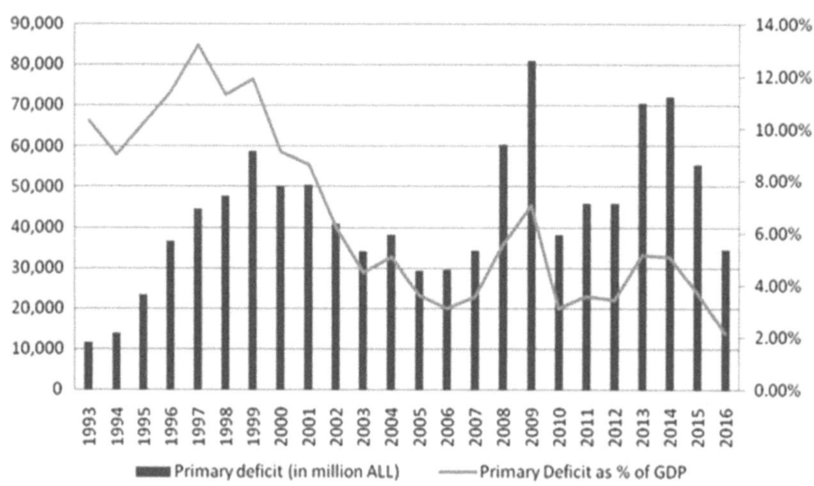

Fig. 9.1 Primary deficit in absolute and relative value to GDP. (Source: Open Data Albania 2017)

fiscal authorities look after throughout the pre-elections quarters is the diffusion of a deceptive *fiscal illusion* amongst electorates. The explanation for running such fiscal policies can be associated with the opportunistic approach to the *political business cycle* (Nordhaus 1975; Nordhaus et al. 1989), which contends that political parties behave as vote-maximizes while voters are non-rational – do not have all the required information – since they are generally myopic and recurrently overestimate the advantages of deficit-financed government expenditures in the present time (e.g. transfers, pensions, electoral spending, and public sector wages) while undervaluing the future tax burden. Political parties, in order to win the elections, engage in economy-stimulating activities only when the elections are about to happen to the cost of future unemployment and inflation. However, Legrenzi and Milas (2010) argue that a burden of fiscal consolidation dependent entirely on taxes can impose serious negative effects on the economy and Alesina and Ardagna (1998) similarly found that fiscal consolidations carried out on tax increases alone are short-lived, unlike fiscal consolidations based on spending cuts.

The mounting amounts of debt imply that the Albanian economy qualifies as a dynamically inefficient case, which indicates that an increase in current debt has no implications for future surpluses and there is no such thing as the "promise to pay back debt with future surpluses." Reasonably, there are dramatic consequences for the Keynesian stabilization policies: politicians approve to increase deficits through recessions but do not come to an agreement to increase the primary surplus when the recession has ended. It should be pointed out that the most important point in terms of public debt measures is the fact that the local government units are not allowed to use the borrowing option as a measure of keeping public debt levels under control.

The Territorial and Administrative Reform

After winning the election in June 2013, the left-wing coalition initiated the process of the new TAR and the Minister of State for Local Government, Mr. Bledar Çuçi, piloted this undertaking under the coordination of the Support to Territorial and Administrative Reform (STAR) project implemented by the United Nations Development Programme and funded by the United States Agency for International Development (USAID). Technical guidance and support has been provided throughout the process by local and international experts' teams.

There were a number of actors who acted as enablers and catalysed the whole TAR process. The European Commission country progress reports, within the framework of the strategy devised to tackle the main challenges for the EU enlargement agenda, clearly advised that with respect to local governance, there is a lack of economical sustainability due to small Local Government Units (LGUs) (EC 2012). Furthermore, the decentralization and TAR preparation process were assessed to have weak progress and that substantial financial and human resources inefficiency, lack of local public services (LPS) delivery, failure of strategic alignment, and transparency-oriented funding have hindered the coordination between central and local government (EC 2013). The OSCE presence in Albania played a crucial role in fostering such reform. The Head of the European Union Delegation to Albania, Ambassador Ettore Sequi, pointed out that the collection of revenues, strategic planning, human resource management, financial control, transparency, as well as a high number of staff with temporary contracts in local government units should be of particular concern to the reformation (OSCE 2013).

Decentralization reform has evolved since a new Constitution was approved in 1998. The salient decentralization stage was the approval of Law No. 8652 on 31 July 2000, "On the organization and Functioning of Local Government," which consents the local government units' rights and authorities in conformity with the 1998 Constitution and the European Charter for Local Self-Government, ratified by the Government of Albania in 1999. The approval of the Law on Local Government gave room to other laws that regulated the local government activities and consolidated the autonomy, that is, Law No. 8653 "On the Territorial and Administrative Reform" based on which the local government units, 65 municipalities and 309 rural communes, were established as public services provision units.

Law No. 8652 defines three types of local authorities' functions: exclusive, shared, and delegated. The (i) *exclusive functions* include infrastructure and public services,[4] local economic development,[5] social, cultural

[4] In more detail: (a) the construction, rehabilitation, and maintenance of city streets, pavements, and public squares; (b) water supply; (c) sewage system; (d) waste management; (e) urban public transportation, (f) public lighting; (g) parks, gardens, and public places; (h) service decor; (i) cemeteries and burial service.

[5] In more detail: (a) preparation of programmes; (b) regulation and functioning of public markets and trade network; (c) small business development; (d) veterinary services; (e) protection of local forest, pastures, and natural resources.

and recreational functions,[6] and order and civil protection.[7] The (ii) *shared functions* are types of functions that local governmental units exercise in common with the central government.[8] The municipalities also have (iii) *delegated functions,* which, by law or agreement, are delegated from the central government to the local government units. These delegated functions include the administration of Civil Registry offices and the National Registration Centre. The local offices and their expenditure are covered by the state budget.

Local authorities encounter difficulties in the management of different services, such as water supply, sewage, and waste management, mainly due to lack of financial resources to develop and maintain local infrastructures and an unclear approach with regard to decentralization of the supply of these services. The implementation of shared functions in pre-university education, social services, and public order and civil protection has progressed, while shared functions in primary healthcare services have fallen far behind. The ambiguity concerning the delegation of powers between central and local government and insufficient transfer of funds from central government to cover the additional costs have affected the provided services' quality by local units.

The sources of local government units' funds are own revenues (tax on small businesses, fees, and fines), intergovernmental transfers, revenues from shared taxes, local tax on immovable property, and local borrowing.

Small businesses' tax was transferred to local government units in 2003 and until 2005 was the most import local own revenue, despite the fact that the collection rate was very low (14–21%). Further revision to the national tax system converted the small businesses' tax into small businesses' profit tax. Revenues from this tax are collected by the central tax administration unit to be then transferred to local budgets. Local fees are

[6] In more detail: (a) preservation and promotion of local historical and cultural assets and management of relevant institutions (b) organization of recreational activities and management of relevant institutions; (c) administration of social services, such as asylums, orphanages, day care, and homes for the elderly.

[7] In more detail: (a) maintaining public order to prevent administrative violations and enforce the implementation of municipality acts; (b) civil protection.

[8] The shared functions include: (a) maintenance and operation of pre-university education facilities located in the jurisdiction; (b) primary health service system and the protection of public health; (c) social care, reducing poverty by administering the economic assistance funds and ensuring the functioning of the relevant institutions; (d) public order and civil protection; (e) environmental protection.

another constituent of the local, own revenue structure. Revenues from fees have grown rapidly over the recent years and represent a large share of all own, local revenues. Collected fines do also provide a financial source of the LGUs' own revenues. However, the main sources of funds are inter-governmental conditional and unconditional transfers from the central government.

Before 2002, the conditional grants were the central LGUs' source of revenues, but, in 2002, a substantial step as to fiscal decentralization was the adoption of the concept of unconditional transfer for local governments in the Law on State Budget. From this year on, the size and share of unconditional transfer enlarged considerably.

The year 2006 marked the introduction of competitive grants which sought to increase the funding performance and objectivity in local government investments; in 2010, custody for the conditional fund management passed to the Regional Development Fund. The competitive grants awarding procedure has been criticized over the past years for political favouritism.

Local funds are also supplied with shared taxes[9] and the tax on immovable property. Regarding the latter, in 2008 was approved Law No. 9869 "On Borrowing of Local Government," but the credit issued to LGUs is very low. Furthermore, the Ministry of Finance, on account of the high level of public debt existing in the country, has imposed several restrictions on local borrowing.

An important reform carried out in 2001 transferred public assets to local government units by granting them the right to administrate and develop such assets.

Local authorities do not have appropriate financial resources or local revenues commensurate with their own and shared functions. Small LGUs rely on financial assistance from the central government. Extreme fragmentation of local authorities has resulted in a lack of capacities for collecting some revenue sources.

Among the main issues that have concerned the local public government agenda in the last decade in Albania are decentralization and public spending cuts. "The existence of a great number of small local government units have increased the overall administrative cost of governing and management of the local government and made it difficult provision of services with high quality and effectiveness" (MSLG 2015).

[9] LGUs receive a share of the motor vehicle tax.

On 31 July 2014, the Parliament adopted the Law on TAR, and in 2015, the Government of Albania (GoA) completed a radical programme of TAR. The output of the reform translated into a contraction in the number of LGUs (former "Urban Municipalities" and "Communes") at the first level of government from 374 to 61, and also abolished the "Communes." The existing number of regions remained stable at 12 regions.[10]

The aim of TAR was to improve the efficiency and effectiveness of public administration at both the national and local levels, to improve the quality of local public services, and to encourage more balanced socio-economic development (USAID 2017). TAR is perhaps the most prominent step with regard to local public services in the history of post-communist Albania. The scope of this reform emerged from the need for improved LPS cost efficiency and wider access (MSLG 2014). This step sought to pave the path for the upcoming local elections that were held in June 2015. From a historical perspective it is worth mentioning that the existing territorial division, that of 1992 which followed the collapse of the Communist Regime in 1991, did not reflect the pace of the new economic, social, demographic, and infrastructural developments (USAID 2017).

The 2014 TAR provoked stormy debates because it changed the administrative and electoral structure of the country; the opposition accused the Government of having been driven only by electoral considerations (Council of Europe 2015). In the course of the TAR, the political polarization in Albania further deepened. Although the parties did agree, in principle, on a reduction in the number of LGUs, the opposition, led by the DP, strongly criticized the reform, making reference, in particular, to the dissection of the new municipalities' boundaries as purposefully favourable to SP and its associates.[11] The DP boycotted both the ad-hoc parliamentary commission intended for the TAR discourse and the parliament for five months, until the European Parliament led a reconciliation mission in December 2014, which reached a settlement between the opposition and the Government.

[10] At the second level of government, Albania is divided into 12 regions (Qarqe): Berat, Diber, Durres, Elbasan, Fier, Gjirokaster, Korce, Kukes, Lezhe, Shkoder, Tirana, and Vlore.

[11] Mr. Lulzim BASHA (Mayor of Tirana until June 2015, Democratic Party) raised this issue in a letter addressed to Congress' President Frecon on 27 October 2015. The Democratic Party also published a document titled "Albania: Local Government under attack", in which it criticizes the "gerrymandering and malapportionment of mandates in the new territorial division."

At the same time, the Congress welcomed the implementation of the new Law on the "Organisation and Functioning of Local Government," containing, among other provisions, procedural safeguards for an inclusive process of the drawing of future territorial boundaries, an issue which was hotly debated between the Government and the opposition prior to the elections. Based on this fact-finding mission, which was organized for the first time in the framework of its post-electoral dialogue, the Congress encouraged the Albanian authorities to focus on a broader electoral reform, addressing, in particular, the de-politicization and professionalization of the election administration and the issue of voters residing de facto abroad (this concerns about 1 million Albanian citizens).

Events such as migration, technological progress, the external shock to economic growth from the financial crises, and the attainment of the official candidate country for accession to the EU altogether externally induced the need for territorial and fiscal cutbacks in order to tackle the widening gap between the perceptions of citizens in terms of LPS and the existing ones. This step also sought to implement the recommendations for fruitful application of the decentralization legislation, policies, and reforms from international agencies' programmes such as USAID. The latter, via its extensive work with local governments has been playing a crucial role with regard to the (i) establishment of efficiency, transparency, and accountability of local government operations; (ii) improvement of local government management and oversight of public utilities in order to provide LPS in line with EU standards; and (iii) to the strengthening of the capabilities of the GoA and local governments to plan and manage urban and regional growth (USAID/Albania 2017).

Territorial reform has brought difficulties in service delivery. The Association of Albanian Municipalities[12] (AAM) claims different issues of which the most important addressed the adoption of an appropriate structure for the new, expanded territories. The existing staff in the municipalities' central offices lacks the experience of managing rural and urban areas, which was previously covered by the 5–13 employees in administrative units (prior communes) dismissed due to the merging process (AAM 2016b).

Municipalities encounter delays in the new transferred functions produced by interruptions in the drafting and approving of relevant regulations and guidelines for ownership transfers of assets and inventories. The

[12] A local governments association that represent the interest of municipalities vis-à-vis the central government.

AAM highlighted the need for faster delegation of new functions' provision such as preschool education, sewage and drainage system, fire brigades, forests and pastures management, water supply, etc. Specifically, the lack of funds for salaries and social insurance for preschool staff, educators in Cultural Centres, and child support services in primary education has been a recurrent dispute. Correspondingly, AAM claims that funds are minimal for the maintenance of the rural road network. An additional query has been the shifting of the water supply functions, as in many municipalities this process is not finalized, coordinated, or managed properly and problems such as non-supply of drinking water, misuse of public assets, and theft or substitution of assets have been met.

TAR is one of the most discussed reforms. The political opposition and AAM have reacted mainly through press releases and statements. The former has claimed that the new territorial division is not accompanied by progress in the decentralization process and is used mainly for electoral profit by the left coalition.

In a press release, AAM claimed that the funds transferred by the central government in 2016 were not realistic, did not meet adequately the LGUs real needs, and did not stimulate economic development and social cohesion. Furthermore, the LGUs allocated budget was not reflecting the post-reform situation and did not respond to the implementation of new functions by municipalities (AAM 2015). The same concern was claimed for the budget of 2017 (AAM 2017).

The mechanism of unconditional funds transfer is a major concern for municipalities. The Regional Development Committee, an institution controlled by the central government and set up to review and select infrastructure project applications from municipalities, in July 2016, agreed upon the allocation of 97.5% of funds to projects submitted by municipalities won by the majority, leaving only a 2.5% for the opposition ones. The AAM contemplates this mechanism as unfair and based on political affiliations and demanded that this mechanism must come to an end, as that way, the conditional funds would be delivered proportionally to all 61 municipalities (AAM 2016a).

The territorial consolidation advocated the creation of bigger local government units which have larger capacities to exercise a wider range of functions. Therefore, the reorganization and rescaling of LPS sought to foster the efficiency gains generated by territorial consolidation since the reduction in the number of LGUs was expected to increase the efficiency of local government by lowering administrative costs. Following the

Financial Crisis, in 2009 and onwards, the (unconditional) transfer cuts imposed further reductions of up to 30%, on average, of local funds (Ministry of Finances 2017a). The levels of central unconditional granting to local authorities have been fluctuating around 13 million ALL[13] and are projected to increase by 0.250 million ALL on an annual basis. At first glance, TAR gives the impression of a reform austerity but on closer consideration, one can easily find much compliance to the fiscal austerity agenda as well. Regarding the decentralization process, the transfer of additional responsibilities for delivering day-to-day public services to larger LGUs should allow the national government to focus more of its energies on the strategic, legislative, and policy-making functions of the state – including the goal of balanced territorial development.

This legal and institutional process, however, has been associated with two main financial endeavours. First, the underfunding that has characterized the local government units in general and along the 2009–2014 post-shock period in particular made it impossible to fulfil the citizens' demands for better public services, and this need for more revenue from the central government translated to an increase of the unconditional transfers. As a consequence, the year-on-year growth of the unconditional grant increased (2014:12.5 billion ALL – 5%[14]; 2016:16.5 billion ALL – 6.5%). Levitas and Stafa (2015) also argue that the downward instability of the unconditional grant has resulted in progressive erosion of the revenue generated by local tax collection. Second, the delegation of new functions currently being provided by state-owned institutions has, in 2016, been transferred to LGUs but is initially being financed by conditional grants.

An attempt to associate such changes with Hood's (2010) established scenarios, which stemmed from the new public management approaches in the post-crisis "cold fiscal climate" indicates similarities with the "do more with less" strategy of the local management. The first element of this strategy is the highlighting of efficiency gains from economies of scale of transferred functions. Second, even though both the unconditional and conditional grants increased at least in the first stages of the TAR, the increment is judged by local authorities insufficient in confronting the needs and services that the local governments deliver and not responding to the implementation of new functions by municipalities.

[13] Exchange rate 1 euro = 132 ALL.

[14] As a percentage of the central government tax and customs revenue.

TAR evaluations of its medium- and long-term outputs are yet to be seen in the upcoming years but an initial assessment gives the impression of an intermediary strategy between the re-engineering of public service reform and system redesign courses of action. TAR is a policy instrument that in terms of the austerity process qualifies as a "soft" or "by recommendation" category of austerity – oblique and indirect. When the Albanian economy was hit by the Post-Financial Crises shock and entered the 2010–2012 recession, the Ministry of Finance designed a set of instruments in order to stipulate the much needed coercive fiscal policies which would drive fiscal policies in the middle term since restrictions are also planned for the upcoming years (MSLG 2014).

Figures 9.2 and 9.3 give a detailed overview of the local government revenues and transfers and the main indicators. The unconditional transfers have reached their peak value in 2009 and by the time the country entered the recession in 2010, a sharp decline can be noted. As the economy was preparing to enter the growth part of the economic cycle, a growing trend of unconditional transfers followed. Interestingly, the LPS transfers maintained a rather stable growth. When the latter are disaggregated in Fig. 9.3, they in fact reveal that the only transfer responsible for such growth was "social assistance." This is explainable by the fact

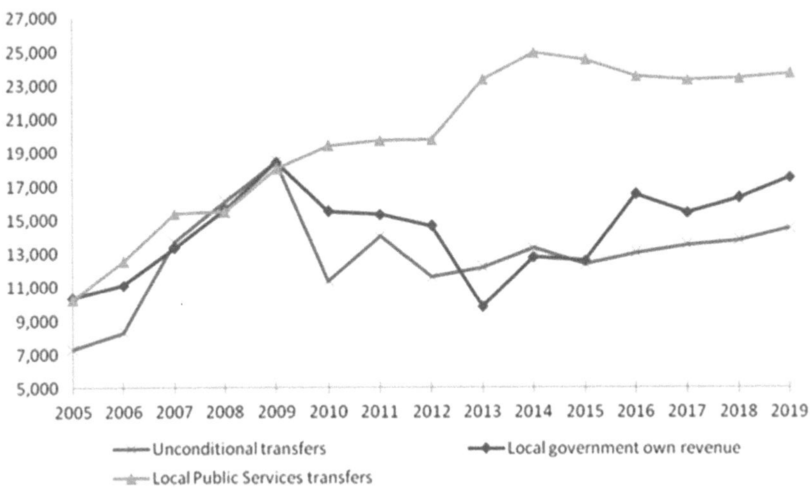

Fig. 9.2 National local government units funding by source. (Source: Ministry of Finances 2017b)

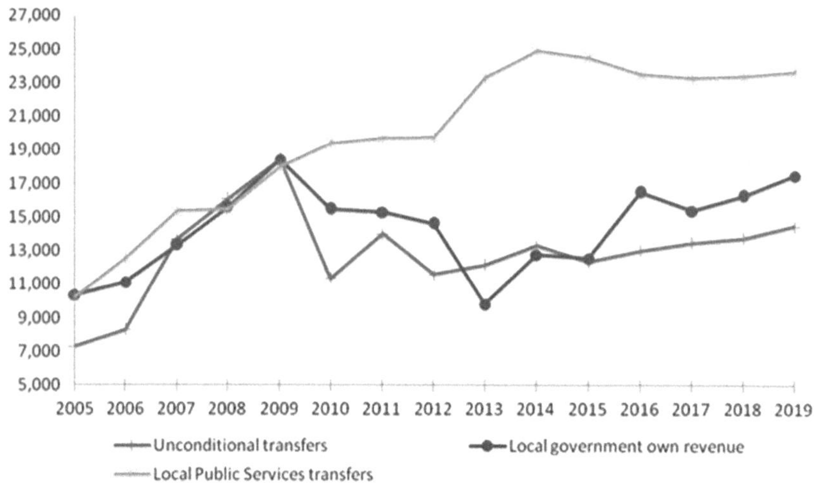

Fig. 9.3 Disaggregation of LPS transfers (by year). (Source: Ministry of Finances 2017b)

that the 2008 financial crisis had a major implication in terms of demographic mobility. It is estimated that as many as 73,231 people returned along the 2009–2011 time horizon, the majority being men (50,311), aged on average between 25 and 34, from the neighbouring countries that were mostly affected by the crisis, Greece and Italy. The highest return flow is observed in large cities, such as Tirana, Fier, and Vlora (MSLG 2014). It is worth pointing out that the "compensation for ex political prisoners" voice increases only during times of electoral campaigns, namely in 2009 and 2013 – years of governmental elections – once more resembling the Political Business Cycle.

Following the implementation of TAR, a fact-finding mission has been commenced by the Congress of Local and Regional Authorities of the Council of Europe in February 2016 within the Congress' post-electoral dialogue agenda and the 30th Congress' Session. The reporter, Jos Wienen, Netherlands (EPP-CCE), provided his remarks on the matter of the TAR implementation following the 2015 local elections in Albania, articulated his concerns about the information absence from the side of the 61 newly established municipalities about their new competences, and involved budgetary uncertainties, inherited financial burdens at the local level, and workforce reduction.

Discussion and Conclusions

This study set out to assess the dynamics of the adaption of the austerity agenda with regard to local public services for the Albanian case. Restructurings aimed to tackle fiscal stress and cutback management in Albania, for example territorial administrative reform, have been levered via an external conditionality. The European Union and other supernatural agencies, such as the IMF, WB, and USAID, require economic cohesion if the accession of Albania as a new member is to be achieved. Therefore, the transfer of austerity was triggered by direct and explicit external forces, resulting in voluntary policy transfer or what classifies as mimetic isomorphism.

At the first stage of retrenchments, during 2009–2013, the right-wing government was not fully convinced about the gravity of the situation and adopted an incremental strategy, with slow and small decisions. Only after the elections of 2013, when the economic conditions worsened, the strong parliamentary majority allowed the left-wing government to undertake severe public finance and structural reforms supported by international institutions. This stage seems to be characterized by a more centralized and systematic decision-making process, aiming for medium and long-term sustainable solutions. The mixture of adopted instruments includes across-the-board cuts, revenue measures, and efficiency gains (such as the administrative-territorial reform). However, the impact of the austerity measures is still hybrid and we believe that these externally induced cutbacks in local public services embody a long-term trend and not merely a rebound to transitory macroeconomic conditions imposed by the financial crisis for the Albanian case.

The transfer of austerity measures from the central to the local government in general and local public services in particular was more eminent among the left-wing coalition government with the introduction of territorial and administrative reform and another set of radical reforms, which, albeit not agreed to by political consensus by the centre-right parties, reflected, for the first time, an acceptance of the electoral costs that such wide-ranging overhauls are associated with.

It was also shown that, regarding debt, the current level of around 73% of GDP is quite problematic with regard to the fiscal consolidation measures and gradual debt reduction advised by the IMF. The removal in October 2012 of the 60% limit imposed by the Organic Budget Law in 2008, which sought to converge domestic public finances with the path devised by the Stability and Growth Pact, raised many questions about the ability to meet the EU admittance preconditions. Elections have proved to be the actual hazards in terms of public borrowing and similar patterns, from all the governing forces, of the opportunistic approach to the political business cycle, were pointed out above.

The study is limited by the fact that the austerity reforms are still ongoing and at an early stage in terms of the medium- and long-term impact of the austerity measures on local public services. There are incontestable features of the "do more with less" approach that emerged in this investigation, even an increase in both, conditional and unconditional, transfers after 2015 occurred but, then again, the increment was insufficient to confront the needs and did not respond to the implementation of new functions by municipalities. However, it is worth recalling that the underfunding characterized local government units before the reform and many aspects of the territorial and administrative reform are yet to be weighed. Finally, the political discourse between governing coalitions and the opposition revealed that the hidden political agenda rather than the public good comprise the evidenced shortcomings of the management of such radical changes.

References

AAM. (2015). *Deklaratë për shtyp: Qeveria redukton me 1,3 miliarde leke buxhetin per bashkite; ulje diskriminuese dhe kercenim i sherbimeve publike*. http://www.aam.org.al/qeveria-redukton-me-1-3-miliarde-leke-buxhetin-per-bashkite-ulje-diskriminuese-dhe-kercenim-i-sherbimeve-publike, 17 Dhjetor.

AAM. (2016a, September 21). *Association of Albanian Municipalities Contests Central Government Policies and Attitudes Toward Local Government*. http://aam.org.al/en/association-of-albanian-municipalities-contests-central-government-policies-and-attitudes-toward-local-government

AAM. (2016b, November 26). *Organizational Structures a Persisting Challenge*. http://aam.org.al/en/organizational-structures-a-persisting-challenge

AAM. (2017). *Njoftim për shtyp: Reforma territoriale dhe decentralizimi nen hijen e buxhetit vendor per vitin 2017*. http://www.aam.org.al/reforma-territoriale-dhe-decentralizimi-nen-hijen-e-buxhetit-vendor-per-vitin-2017, 5 Janar.

Alesina, A., & Ardagna, S. (1998). Tales of Fiscal Adjustment. *Economic Policy, 13*(27), 488–545.

Cook, L. (2010). More Rights, Less Power: Labor Standards and Labor Markets in East European Post-communist States. *Studies in Comparative International Development, 45*(2), 170–197.

Council of Europe. (2015). *Observation of Local Elections in Albania*. Strasbourg: Chamber of Local Authorities.

DiMaggio, P., & Powell, W. W. (1991). The Iron Cage Revisited. Institutional Isomorphism and Collective Rationality in Organizational Fields. *American Sociological Review, 48*(2), 147–160.

EC. (2012). *Albania Progress Report*. Brussels: European Commission.

EC. (2013). *Albania Progress Report*. Brussels: European Commission.

European Commission. (2016). Albania 2016 Report.

Hood, C. (2010). *Reflections on Public Service Reform in a Cold Fiscal Climate*. London: 2020 Public Service Trust-ERSC.

IMF. (2006). *Albania Country Report*. s.l.: N. 06/54.

IMF. (2014). *Albania Country Report*. s.l.: N. 14/78.

IMF. (2016). *Albania: Selected Issues*. Country Report No. 16/143.

INSTAT. (2016). In: s.l.:Institute of Statistics.

Kickert, W. (2012). State Responses to the Fiscal Crisis in Britain, Germany and the Netherlands. *Public Management Review, 14*(3), 299–309.

Kickert, W., Randma-Liiv, T., & Savi, R. (2013). *Fiscal Consolidation in Europe: A Comparative Analysis*, Brussels, EU Commission: COCOPS Report, Deliverable 7.2.

Legrenzi, G., & Milas, C. (2010). Spend-and-Tax Adjustments and the Sustainability of the Government's Intertemporal Budget Constraint. *CESifo Working Paper*, No. 2926.

Lehmann, H., & Muravyev, A. (2010). *Labor Market Institutions and Labor Market Performance: What Can We Learn from Transition Countries?* Quaderni DSE Working Paper, No. 714, Volume http://ssrn.com/abstract=1681525

Levitas, T., & Stafa, E. (2015). Policy Paper: Creating an Equitable, Transparent, and Predictable Unconditional Grant Formula. *Discussion Draft: Planning and Local Governance Project (PLGP) in Albania*.

Ligj nr. 8652, datë 31.07.2000. Për organizimin dhe funksionimin e qeverisjes vendore. *Fletorja zyrtare e Republikës së Shqipërisë*, 2000, nr. 25, Tiranë, pp. 1269–1299.

Ligj nr. 9869, datë 04.02.2008. Për huamarrjen e qeverisjes vendore. *Fletorja zyrtare e Republikës së Shqipërisë*, 2008, nr. 18, Tiranë, pp. 644–653.

Ministry of Finance. (2017a). *Pagat e administratës publike rriten 10%, një tjetër shpërblim i reformave të suksesshme*. Tirana: Ministry of Finance.

Ministry of Finance. (2017b, March 23). The budget in years. http://www.financa.gov.al/al/raportime/buxheti/buxheti-ne-vite

Ministry of Finance. (2017c). *Fshirja e detyrimeve, përfitojnë 200 mijë tatimpagues. Afati deri më 31 Dhjetor 2017*. Tirana: Ministry of Finance.

Mitra, J., & Matlay, H. (2004). Entrepreneurial and Vocational Education and Training: Lessons from Eastern and Central Europe. *Industry and Higher Education, 18*(1), 53–61.

MSLG. (2014). *General Report of the Local Government Situation in Albania*. Tirane: Office of Minister of State for Local Government.

MSLG. (2015). *National Crosscutting Strategy for Decentralization and Local Governance 2015–2020*. Tirana: Ministry of State for Local Issues.

Nordhaus, W. D. (1975). The Political Business Cycle. *The Review of Economic Studies, 4*(2), 169–190.

Nordhaus, W. D., Alesina, A., & Schultze, C. L. (1989). Alternative Approaches to the Political Business Cycle. *Brookings Papers on Economic Activity*, (2), 1–68.

OECD. (2012). Restoring Public Finances, 2012 Update. *Special Issue of the OECD Journal on Budgeting*.

Open Data Albania. (2017). *The Budget Deficit in the Years 1993–2016*. s.l.: Open Data Albania.

OSCE. (2013). OSCE Presence Helps Albanian Government Start Administrative and Territorial Reform. *OSCE Presence in Albania*, 17 October.

RAT. (2016). *Reforma Administrative Territoriale Website*. s.l.: Reforma Administrative Territoriale.

Raudla, R., Savi, R., & Randma-Liiv, T. (2013). *Literature Review on Cutback Management. COCOPS–(COordinating for COhesion in the Public Sector of the Future)*.

Savić, M., & Zubović, J. (2015). Comparative Analysis of Labour Markets in South East Europe. s.l., *Procedia Economics and Finance*, 388–397.

Schneider, C. Q., & Wagemann, C. (2012). *Set-theoretic Methods for the Social Sciences: A Guide to Qualitative Comparative Analysis*. Cambridge: Cambridge University Press.

Scorsone, E. A., & Plerhoples, C. (2010). Fiscal Stress and Cutback Management Amongst State and Local Governments: What Have We Learned and What Remains to Be Learned? *State & Local Government Review, 42*(2), 176–187.

SHSSH. (2014). *Raporti vjetor*. Tiranë: Shërbimi Social Shtetëror.

USAID. (2017, July). 2016 CSO Sustainability Index Scores for Central and Eastern Europe and Eurasia. U.S. Agency for International Development Washington, DC, 20th Edition.

USAID/Albania. (2017). *Planning and Local Governance Project*. Tirana: USAID/Albania.

CHAPTER 10

Conclusions: The Direction and Entity of Austerity in Mediterranean Local Public Services

Andrea Lippi and Theodore N. Tsekos

During the grave financial and economic crisis afflicting Europe since 2008, Southern European countries have been severely affected by a wave of austerity. Austerity policies have taken different forms, depending on each country's specificities. However, it would seem that local governments have been particularly hit by austerity measures in all of the countries concerned. This chapter offers a summary of the main findings from the preceding case studies, which will enable us to draw up a general typology of the patterns of austerity in local services provision in Mediterranean Europe.

A. Lippi (✉)
Department of Political and Social Sciences, University of Florence, Firenze, Italy
e-mail: lippi@unifi.it

T. N. Tsekos
Department of Business and Public Administration, Technological Education Institute of Peloponnese, Kalamata, Greece

A. Lippi, T. N. Tsekos (eds.), *Local Public Services in Times of Austerity across Mediterranean Europe*, Governance and Public Management, https://doi.org/10.1007/978-3-319-76225-8_10

Summarizing Evidence: Similar and Dissimilar Austerity Paths

This section examines our principal findings and the different paths that Local Public Service (LPS) has taken for each of the countries affected by austerity policies considered in this study.

The sovereign debt crisis that affected **Greece** in early 2010 resulted in three Financial Assistance Agreements (stipulated in 2010, 2012 and 2015), which have had a serious impact on Greece's local governments and the provision of LPSs in that country. Austerity policies included extensive spending cuts, reductions in staff numbers, decreasing wages and operating costs, rescaling through closing and downsizing local government units, together with the extensive centralization of fiscal policy and control mechanisms. However, municipal spending did not seem to be a significant cause of the country's indebtedness since, at its very highest point, it only represented 3.09% of the Gross Domestic Product (GDP), one of the lowest levels in Europe. As a result of the crisis, local governments had to deliver a multitude of social programmes with much reduced resources. To accomplish this, municipalities had to utilize social economy and volunteering tools. Moreover, not only are these instruments inappropriate for efficient public policy-making, but there were also accusations that such means were being used by local mayors for their own clientelistic purposes.

The sovereign debt crisis has meant that **Portugal** has had to bear the impact of increasing borrowing costs since 2010. The country's request for financial aid from the European Union, the European Central Bank (ECB) and the International Monetary Fund (IMF) meant that Portugal would have to implement austerity measures focusing on fiscal consolidation, in an attempt to reduce public spending. Even though Portugal's public debt problems do not seem to be due to local authorities' spending and financial imbalances, the adjustment programmes inflicted exceptional budget cutbacks on local governments, facilitated long-awaited structural reforms, and imposed increased central supervision as a prerequisite for loans from central government. While the reforms were induced by supra-national institutions, Portuguese authorities obtained the necessary margins by which to fine-tune the specific measures to be adopted. Many of these policies remained for some time in the agendas of the two main political forces before passing through the window of opportunity opened by the adjustment programme. Successive governments developed strategies of blame avoidance, based on the argument that reforms had been externally imposed, in an attempt to encourage public acceptance of the austerity measures.

In **Spain's** case, during the financial and economic crisis, an extensive range of austerity measures were introduced that reduced local government autonomy through municipal reorganization and the readjustment of local service provision, with the declared aims of financial sustainability and public spending rationalization. Nevertheless, during the early phase of the crisis (in 2010), the dominant political narrative considered the country's local government system as a part of the solution, that is, as a key agent in the implementation of its Keynesian economic stimulation policies. However, although figures showed that Spain's municipalities had never been an important source of debt, after 2010, they came gradually to be considered the main component of the crisis. Therefore, the austerity policies put forward by the central government, as a precondition for a Euro-group loan in 2012, restricted local governments' powers and decision-making functions, and impacted staffing and the provision of local facilities. In general, the most widespread measures have been cutbacks.

For many years, policy-making in **Italy** had been dominated by the conflict between a 'public spending constituency' constituted by the ruling parties and a technocratic coalition in favour of fiscal consolidation and centred on the research department at the Bank of Italy. In 2011, under pressure from the financial markets, the ECB, the Bank of Italy and the IMF forced a policy agenda on the Italian government, albeit not in the shape of any formal agreement, requiring the tightening of fiscal rules, the large-scale privatization of local services, centralized controls over local expenditure and a radical rearrangement of the political-administrative apparatus, including the provision of local public services. Reforms were presented as prerequisites for further budgetary flexibility, thus constituting a sort of 'indirect conditionality' without any formal agreements or Memorandum of Understanding (MoU). Severe cutbacks proved substantially detrimental to local governments and undermined provision of LPS. Constitutional provisions prohibited municipal deficits and supplementary expenditure unless covered by the State. Measures have been taken to reduce the 'cost of politics' through the elimination of provincial governments and municipal corporations, a reduction in the total number and earnings of councillors and attempts at compulsory inter-municipal cooperation and rescaling. However, constitutional reform was rejected by a referendum held in 2016, and consequently the rescaling plan was shelved. The majority of the adopted measures had been on the political agenda since the 1990s and were reintroduced in the name of the economic crisis. Successive governments implemented austerity policies regardless of their different ideological positioning. Austerity policies generated a covert recentralization process that reduced local government power in favour of central government.

The institutional, political, economic and administrative reforms initiated by the accession of **Cyprus** to the EU have not affected local government to any great extent. However, LGS were heavily affected by the austerity policies triggered by the bank sector crisis in 2012 and implemented through Cyprus' MoU with the EU, ECB and IMF. Such policies took the form of fiscal consolidation by means of local government cutbacks and the recentralization of budgetary decisions, while the proposals for far-reaching structural reforms set forth in an IMF study were mitigated. Despite the external pressure for local government reforms in the wake of the MoU, there was strong opposition from both political parties and municipalities. The dynamics of this process led to fiscal austerity but without any structural reforms that could cause any conflict between central and local government. While the proposal revealed a '*do the same with less*' strategy, the 'across the board cutbacks' that were widely deployed in all local policy areas prove that the end result was a 'doing-less-with-less' situation.

In 2009, **Croatia** entered recession triggered by the global financial and economic crisis. During this recession, local government budgets were reduced while the high costs and the instability of the local government system were criticized in political discourse. Consequently, the economic downturn created a 'window of opportunity' for local government reforms; however, even though they had previously been included in governmental strategy and policy, such reforms have not been implemented. Austerity policies consisted of financial consolidation and institutional rearrangements. The main drivers of reform were external pressures, mainly from the EU during the pre-accession period but also from the World Bank. In spite of the fact that external actors offered clear policy guidelines, implementation has been uncertain and incremental due to the fact that specific reform measures have been shaped domestically. The overlapping powers of the central, state and local governments have led all parties to adopt blame avoidance tactics, thus depriving reforms of the required political commitment while hiding their political dimensions and presenting them simply as technical adjustments to EU requirements. However, reforms have more recently been associated with changes in centre-periphery relations, with an increasing centralization of power now discernible.

In the case of **Albania**, austerity was triggered by immediate, overt, external influences, since policies initially designed to bring the country into line with EU standards and subsequently to prevent external economic risks from arising were recommended by international institutions. Nevertheless, domestic political forces were also involved in shaping reforms, within the framework of internal electoral and political rivalry.

Since 2005, the centre-right government has implemented a neoliberal programme based on public savings, a reduction in current expenditure, tax cuts and privatization, but also public investment in large-scale infrastructural projects. Such policies derived from lending arrangements with the IMF and the World Bank. As a result, a positive economic climate was initially established, permitting the Albanian government to increase wages and pensions. During a second phase, however, Albania was hit by the Eurozone crisis, leading to a substantial reduction in GDP, increased unemployment and a rising public deficit. The centre-right government initially denied the gravity of the financial situation and the unavoidability of reforms and adopted an incremental strategy consisting of limited measures. Conversely, a new left-wing coalition government in 2014 admitted that the crisis – which it accounted for, however, as a result of the excessive spending of the previous government – was very serious and required financial and structural reforms together with a new IMF loan. Lending conditionalities implied strict budgetary discipline. Austerity reforms were generated by external-internal interplay, influenced chiefly by IMF policies but also by pre-accession EU conditionalities. The most important measure aimed at reducing public debt is the ban on local governments' borrowing. The clear characteristics of the reforms show that 'do more with less' logic prevailed. What at first sight appears strange, but which is easily accounted for within a clientelistic environment, is that civil servants' wages and pensions increased prior to the June 2017 election.

Systematizing Evidence: Dimensions of Policy Transfer

The aforementioned narratives reveal extensive cutbacks in local government, together with the overall downsizing of the LPS system. In addition to certain specific results, a number of generalizations may be made in regard to the analytical dimensions of the observed policy transfer: the reference here is to the aforementioned emergent factors driving austerity policy across countries. The focus is on the dynamics of external pressure for, and the resulting internal reaction to, an austerity 'recipe', characterized by adaptation/rejection by central governments and/or local authorities.

The path towards retrenchment, and the subsequent downsizing of LPS, can thus be analysed by examining types of policy-making approaches and their corresponding outcomes. This analysis is based on the evidence available regarding four questions, namely: (a) the point of departure in terms of the fiscal framework and policy legacy of reform; (b) the institutionalization of austerity and the external/internal divide; (c) the emerging types of policy transfer; and (d) the 'shopping basket' of austerity strategies and tools.

The Fiscal Framework and Policy Legacy of Reform

As previously mentioned, the economic crisis has affected Mediterranean countries at different times and with varying intensity. Some countries, like Greece and Portugal, have been rocked by a sudden, dramatic fiscal crisis. Those countries' fragile structural position, and the unsustainability of their public finances, has overwhelmed them. Likewise, the increased public debt of Spain, Italy and Cyprus has undermined their credibility. On the other hand, EU newcomers (e.g. Croatia) or candidates (e.g. Albania) have entered a cycle of recession driven by the globalization of crises and policies.

Consequently, national political agendas have called for measures to reduce public expenditure and to promote cutbacks, although the timing and types of choices in question have varied considerably. According to the study by Silva and Bucek (2014) that we mentioned at the beginning of this book, variance was the main emergent topic regarding the inputs and outcomes of austerity. Timing, designs, intensity and typology of external pressures, together with each political system's propensity to agree to 'recipes' – and the subsequent ability to react to such recipes at the domestic level – are all variables that have accompanied and influenced the basic framework of austerity. Nevertheless, as far as regards the 'Old Southern Four', the crisis emerged following a lengthy period of economic decline which the public was, mostly, well aware of, while in the other cases it emerged during periods of limited economic stability (Cyprus) and contained fragility (Croatia) or partial growth (Albania).

Furthermore, there is the question of policy legacy relating to public sector performance and local government reforms. For example, in Greece the legacy of patronage in relation to the State has negatively influenced the opinion held by supra-national agencies. Consequently, the innovative process of decentralization experienced in previous years was overshadowed by this 'bad reputation'. Similarly, in Portugal and Spain the increased fiscal deficit associated with the considerable fragmentation and small size of municipalities adversely framed the reputation of local authorities despite their actual performance. This is also the case of Croatia, where fragmentation and static economic performance has overshadowed the local public sector, which has experienced deliberate centralization since the 1990s. A negative policy legacy concerning decentralization (i.e. scandals) has also proven detrimental in the case of Cyprus, where the imposition of measures was also framed by previous debt crises. Finally, Italy's enterprising decentralization and devolution programmes implemented up until 2001 were both overshadowed by a gradual trend towards recentralization driven by the public-spending constituency of ruling parties and a technocratic coalition.

The Institutionalization of Austerity and the External/Internal Divide

More importantly, austerity has been institutionalized in different ways, depending on the type of promoter.

On the one hand, austerity policy was adopted through agreements made with supra-national institutions (e.g. the Troika of European Commission, European Central Bank and International Monetary Fund). In these cases (Greece, Portugal, Spain and, later, Cyprus), institutionalization corresponded to a claimed coercive isomorphism. The MoUs and corollaries have been of crucial importance and have deliberately moved the political system into a new era. They have been more dramatic and influential in the cases of Greece and Portugal compared to those of Spain and Cyprus. These are cases of institutionalization through agreements, whereby institutionalization has been governed by conditionality.

On the other hand, Italy, Croatia and Albania have avoided EU conditionality and experienced seemingly softer measures. The politics of fiscal retrenchment entered the agenda incrementally through stepwise provisions and moral suasion (letters, promised agreements, deterrence strategies). No specific agreements were signed by this second cluster, but Europeanization was incisive all the same. Gradual change also included postponement and hypocrisy. The cases of Albania and Croatia both proved significant. Central governments initially attempted to avoid austerity, and they approached the question of fiscal retrenchment at a later stage, after national elections had been held. This ambiguous mix of compliance and delay consequently led to a piecemeal policy emerging in both countries, as well as in Italy, while ambiguity led Cyprus' government to ban social protests, as was also the case in Greece.

Furthermore, incremental austerity paved the way for symbolic politics. The Parliaments of Spain and Italy approved changes to the Constitution, in 2011 and 2012, respectively, based on the Fiscal Compact Treaty and the principle of 'no debt' strictly framing national politics and intergovernmental relations. Local governments and LPS were overwhelmed by this U-turn.

To sum up the situation then, what we have are two clusters based around a hard or a soft policy transfer approach (Benson and Jordan 2011): 'austerity by prescription' and 'austerity by recommendation', respectively. Greece and Portugal come within the first cluster, while Italy, Croatia and Albania come within the second. Spain and Cyprus, on the other hand, share certain features of both, and thus can be situated in between the two clusters.

Austerity by prescription implies the importation of designs, strategies and tools. Austerity by recommendation pertains to the oblique, piecemeal construction of domestic austerity policy in the light of specific external pressures, including deeper-rooted normative isomorphic change driven by professionals, experts and academics.

Overall, to what extent did policy transfer occur thanks to external influences or to domestic interests? We have acknowledged that external influence has been decisive almost everywhere. Italy is the only country where external agents have not explicitly dictated the austerity agenda. Italy's political system 'internalized' external pressure by appointing a former European Commissioner, Mario Monti, as Prime Minister. A technocratic constituency of academics and experts pushed the political system towards fiscal retrenchment from within.

In the Spanish case, external influences have been less significant since the domestic interests of central government vis-à-vis local authorities have obscured inputs from abroad. Similarly, the Portuguese government has adopted a blame avoidance strategy that takes advantage of external pressures to hit LPS.

Elsewhere, external agents have been instrumental in providing legitimacy to domestic institutions. Supra-national experts have replaced the weak advisory role of technocrats in Greece and have addressed Cypriot planning. Croatia's weak policy was, however, decisively inspired by supranational experts. Likewise, the austerity agenda in Albania overlapped with the EU's advice on admission.

Overall, the issue of Europeanization affected developments in different ways throughout the Mediterranean. Countries were deeply concerned about the risk of losing EU membership. As we have shown, Europeanization was the main driver of the political debate that led to the introduction of austerity measures in Cyprus. In the case of Albania, the issue was that of expected EU admission, while Europeanization represented a threat for Croatia. Also in the case of the 'Old Southern Four', the political mantra of 'staying in Europe' legitimized the introduction of austerity measures.

Types of Policy Transfer

What type of policy transfer may thus be considered as the driving force of austerity? While Albania's case is one of mimetic isomorphism, where policy-makers were pressured from outside into imitating others' examples, a number of austerity designs belong to the 'coercive isomorphism' category or were influenced by normative isomorphism.

In the case of the Mediterranean countries, four different forms of behaviour can be identified:

(i) a passive (strictly mandatory) policy transfer, where LPS were subjected to strict measures imported from outside and reinforced by the national government's decisions;
(ii) a resistant policy transfer, where (painful) acceptance has been accompanied by domestic opposition and the political will to adjust external input to internal needs and limits;
(iii) a reshaped policy transfer, where domestic opportunities surpassed international requests, offering room for domestic actors to internalize global discourse into national political practice;
(iv) a voluntary policy transfer, where a trade-off between acceptance and pursued stakes is embraced by national (but not local) policy-makers.

Thus, the typology offered by Bennett (1991), which is discussed in the theoretical chapter, may help support this interpretation. Evidence suggests that Portugal's policy transfer corresponded to the so-called *penetration* type: vertical, passive, characterized by the mandatory acceptance of coercive isomorphism and blame avoidance on the part of central government. At the opposite end of the spectrum, we have Albania's mimetic isomorphism, which corresponds to *emulation* in Bennett's typology: 'voluntary' austerity in search of EU admission. The trade-off between measures and expected awards was considerable. Both cases belong to the 'imported austerity' category (see Chap. 2).

All the remaining cases belong to the 'constructed austerity' category and are situated in the middle of the austerity spectrum. Greece, Croatia and Cyprus attempted to slow down, from below, those impositions decreed from above. This was a case of either 'not implementation' behaviour or biased implementation (Croatia and Greece) on the one hand, or strong political bargaining through the protests of municipalities (Cyprus) on the other. Policy transfer consisted of a compromise (more in Cyprus and Croatia than in Greece) in the face of domestic resistance and supranational demands. Bennett calls this *harmonization*, that is, the search for a *muddling through*: endogenous readjustments to exogenous *stimuli*, in other words. It is not necessarily proving successful (in Greece, for example), but the search for a compromise has been evident.

Finally, there is the case of reshaping, where the policy transfer has occurred thanks to its domestic interpretation as a *window of opportunity*. Spain and Italy both witnessed the opportunistic behaviour of central government, which took advantage of austerity to launch a programme of recentralization. This was also the case in Croatia and Portugal, albeit to a lesser extent. This is what Bennet calls *networked and brokered policy transfer*, where local policy entrepreneurs, domestic political brokers and eminent advisors re-interpret external pressure to encourage internal acceptance: in other words, global discourse generates local practice.

Indeed, the evidence would suggest that austerity has opened a window of opportunity for domestic politics almost everywhere, encouraging and empowering central government to reduce local autonomy and limit LPS management and delivery. It has left room for the promotion of other policies and for the adoption of recentralization. The Spanish case dramatically shows how central government adopted a blame-and-shame strategy to divert blame from the central state to LPS. In general, one of the most important findings of the present work is that austerity gave central governments an extraordinary chance for recentralizing power.

The institutional path towards recentralization was stepwise and surreptitious in Italy and Croatia, whereas it was explicit and sudden in

Greece, Spain and Portugal. However, in all cases austerity has represented an opportunity to promote the redistribution of power between the centre and the periphery, through the recentralizing, rescaling and downsizing of local autonomy.

The Shopping Basket of Strategies and Tools

According to Christensen's concept (2012) of global discourse leading to local adaptations, the design of austerity varies considerably. Christensen deals here with what is termed a 'shopping basket' of austerity policies. An examination of the global range of instruments dictated by supra-national recommending bodies reveals that national strategies adopted in order to reduce the powers and scope of LPS have been differentiated and contingent. This 'shopping basket' is evident from the recurrence of three different types of approach: (i) the delaying and selecting of certain tools rather than others (Croatia and Greece); (ii) piecemeal, sectoral legislation overshadowing any broader, comprehensive approach, with a focus on certain specific aspects only (Italy); and (iii) the bargaining of tools with the recommending bodies (Cyprus).

This does not mean that the consequent effects were accommodating or ineffective. On the contrary, it means that the various combinations opened the way for *many austerities:* one set of standardized tools, but various different implementations of those tools. This is a case of allomorphism: the interpretation from below led to the adjustment of the toolkit to suit local situations, through specific policy mixes concerning those strategies and instruments to be adopted.

As regards strategies, we know that governments have downsized LPS through reduction in public expenditure, autonomy, organizational capacity and service delivery; however, this occurred in different ways and to different extents. The majority of the countries in question adopted a '*do less with less*' strategy. This was true in the case of the Old Southern Four. The Croatian government, on the other hand, promoted austerity under the umbrella of 'do the same with less' through the pursuit of 'efficiency gains'. Albanian policy-makers tended towards a 'do more with less' approach in order to stress the organizational and financial capacity of the LPS system. Finally, Cyprus' approach was more ambiguous than that of the other countries concerned. The government officially claimed that it aimed 'to do the same with less', as in Croatia, but in practice it adhered to the 'do less with less' or even 'do more with less' approach, since the country's municipalities were practically forced to make an enormous effort to maintain the expected standards.

As asserted by Kickert et al. (2013), evidence shows a 'rational, comprehensive strategy' adopted in Portugal, Spain and Greece, that is, goal-oriented measures assembled in order to pursue efficiency, and an 'incremental-compromise strategy' adopted in Cyprus, Croatia, Italy and Albania, that is, muddling through to promote efficiency and preserve consensus at the same time.

As regards the tools employed, what was witnessed was *political assemblage*, as McCann and Ward (2013) point out, that is, the hybridization of the suggested set to give different, specific local combinations (Table 10.1). The set of available instruments is examined in the theoretical chapter and has been discussed at length in the literature (Kickert et al. 2013; Overmans and Noordegraaf 2014; Di Mascio and Natalini 2015). Scholars have subdivided the instruments employed into two categories: 'pure fiscal instruments' designed to reduce costs and save money, such as cutbacks and the freezing of public expenditure and reforms; and 'organizational instruments' to re-launch NPM, such as privatization and outsourcing, and the elimination or restriction of services.

While pure fiscal tools have generally been adopted by all of the Mediterranean countries, organizational reforms have only affected certain countries and in very different ways. In all countries, fiscal consolidation has meant public spending cuts, wages freeze and a freeze on hiring. More importantly, the LPS system has been downsized almost everywhere by 'across the board' cutbacks. Selective cutbacks on LPS have only been registered in Spain, Greece and Portugal. Organizational reforms have implied incentives for privatization, rescaling, amalgamations, inter-municipal cooperation, and the territorial rearrangement of LPS delivery. This is a complementary set of instruments that is employed extensively, but in a less incisive manner than the fiscal measures mentioned.

Table 10.1 shows that the plethora of tools is widespread and scattered. It reveals that Portugal has implemented the most varied set of tools, while Croatia and Albania have concentrated on a subset thereof. There are certain commonalities that ought to be pointed out here.

The first concerns the intensity and distribution of tools. Some countries, such as Croatia and Albania, have been more committed to budget cuts than others. More importantly, they have mixed 'old' financial instruments with proposed 'new' provisions. Secondly, budget cuts and limits to public expenditure in the case of the 'Old Southern Four' have been much harsher and more widespread than elsewhere. Furthermore, EU conditionality and

Table 10.1 Mix of tools for the seven countries

	Transfers	*Expenditure*	*Fiscal supervision*	*Revenues*	*Borrowing*	*Functions*	*Rescaling*	*Management and delivery*	*Staff and salaries*
Albania		Severe cutbacks for health care, social assistance and disabilities	Supervision of budget	Increased state revenues, excises and taxes on goods, increased VAT and fuel tax	Limit to borrowing		Abolition of more than 300 municipalities, amalgamation and inter-municipal cooperation	Privatization	Three-year pay freeze, abolition of end-of-year reward and postponement of retirements
Croatia	Decreasing transfers	Reduction of public expenditure	Financial supervision by the Ministry of Finance	Increasing revenues on income	Limit to borrowing with respect to revenues, 20% of revenues to limit annual amortization		Rescaling for delivery, integration of municipalities and merger of providers	Full cost recovery, corporatization, self-sustainability and PPP	Limits to salaries according to 20% of revenues
Cyprus	Cutbacks to grants, up to 40%, additional reductions	Recentralization of budgetary discretion and compulsory repayment	Supervision by the Ministry of finance and interior, and recentralized budget	Decrease in local revenues				Contracting out, reduction of waste collection and reduction in social services provisions	Hiring freeze

(*continued*)

Table 10.1 (continued)

	Transfers	*Expenditure*	*Fiscal supervision*	*Revenues*	*Borrowing*	*Functions*	*Rescaling*	*Management and delivery*	*Staff and salaries*
Greece	Reduction and economic recovery programme for indebted municipalities	Reduction of spending, across the board cutbacks, ex-ante control of spending and double entry system	Operational plans, observatory, fiscal supervision, budgeting under control and central audit committee		Limit to borrowing through standards to interests payment and debt		Amalgamation of municipalities and reduction to 30% of municipal corporations	Dismissing, outsourcing and privatization	Freezing recruitment, reduced personnel, replacement of only 20% of retirements and reduction of fixed-term contracts
Italy	Reduction in transfers and retrenchment for social services	Spending review and across the board cutbacks	Supervision of local public spending by the Ministry	Abolition of housing tax, new revenues for waste and new recentralized housing tax		Delegation of tax collection without recovery	Inter-municipal cooperation, amalgamation, metropolitan areas and downsizing of provinces	Compulsory competitive tendering for LPS	Reduction of councillors salary, suppression of ombudsman and clerks in place of managers
Portugal	Reduction of grants and state transfer	Across the board cutbacks	Central supervision on municipalities and corporations	Abolition of local taxes	Limits to borrowing	More functions without recovery	Amalgamation of corporations, inter-municipal cooperation and metropolitan areas		Reduced staff 2% and reduction of positions at least 15%

Spain	15% reduction of state transfer	Across the board cutbacks	Control and fiscal supervision and authorization from regions and province before of deciding		Zero debt, no long-term borrowing and restriction in the short term	Upscaling of functions	Reduction of agencies, inter-municipal coop. and municipal enterprises, amalgamation and reduction of municipal entities	Reduction of functions for LPS and limits to the choice for the legal form of LPS	Frozen pensions, reduction in salaries for employees, mayors and councillors, prohibited hiring and no substitutions after retirement

agreements have led to a standardized set of choices for EU members. Nevertheless, while Portugal and Greece (and Spain to a certain extent) have diligently and passively adopted the mix of instruments, Cyprus and Italy have been more creative. Thirdly, there is the matter of timing. On the one hand, the adoption of austerity by prescription (hard transfer) was concentrated in a given phase. Austerity by recommendation (soft transfer), on the other hand, has been adopted over a lengthier period, or even later, than the former types.

Effects and Reactions: Towards Patterns of Austerity for LPS

As previously mentioned, austerity has been detrimental to LPS across Mediterranean Europe. Nevertheless, there has been a certain variance, as displayed by the contributions published in this book. Different outcomes can be clustered, and Table 10.2 attempts to summarize the emerging trends. Four patterns of austerity can be identified, representing different combinations of the following dimensions: legacy, institutionalization (by prescription or recommendation), types of transfer (penetration, emulation, harmonization and networked) and strategies (rational comprehensive vs. incremental compromise), together with their expected effects. A column on the right of Table 10.2 shows the outcomes that have emerged.

1. *Pure austerity policy (top-down)*

The first cluster includes 'pure austerity' transfers. It covers austerity measures institutionalized by prescription through a rational, comprehensive strategy and associated with a 'less with less' approach. This is the case of Portugal and Greece, even though Greece has been less passive than Portugal in the adoption of austerity measures. Nevertheless, both share the most incisive degree of external pressure, generating a top-down policy. As a result, both have suffered detrimental impacts, with a substantial downsizing of LPS' autonomy and of the management and delivery of LPS.

2. *Moderate austerity policy (more top-down than bottom-up)*

A more moderate austerity policy has been adopted in Spain and Cyprus. This represents a harmonized, 'by prescription' policy transfer, where external input has been softened and reshaped by domestic

Table 10.2 Policy transfer and impacts compared

	Legacy	*Institutionalization*	*Policy transfer*	*Strategy*	*Expected effect*	*Outcomes*
Albania	Economic growth and fragmentation	By recommendation	Emulation (soft)	Incremental compromise	More with less	Recentralization
Cyprus	Strong local politics and debts	By prescription	Harmonization (hard)	Incremental compromise	Less with less	Bargaining
Croatia	Fragility and centralization	By recommendation	Harmonization (soft)	Incremental compromise	Same with less	Resilience, recentralization
Greece	Decentralization and patronage	By prescription	Harmonization (hard)	Rational comprehensive	Less with less	Reduced autonomy, poverty
Italy	Fiscal constituency and decentralization	By recommendation	Networked (soft)	Incremental compromise	Less with less	Deinstitutionalization; lack of accountability
Portugal	Fragmentation and good performance	By prescription	Passive (hard)	Rational comprehensive	Less with less	Victimization, reduced autonomy
Spain	Fragmentation and good performance	By prescription	Networked (hard)	Rational comprehensive	Less with less	Recentralization, reduced autonomy, resilience

dynamics, even if such have proven more detrimental than the external ones. Bottom-up relations within the State have combined with the top-down stimuli. Rational, comprehensive and incremental strategies have been mixed, and the range of tools – partially bargained and reshaped – is less standardized than elsewhere. The effects on LPS have been detrimental but have also been the direct result of domestic politics and not only generated by global discourse.

3. *Oblique austerity policy (more bottom-up than top-down)*

There has also been what can be termed 'oblique policy-making', where domestic opportunities and behaviour have rendered austerity policy more national than international. This approach incorporates both top-down and bottom-up pressures, to produce somewhat ambiguous, 'oblique' behaviour on the part of national politicians It entails austerity through recommendations, networked and brokered transfers and a strategy of incremental compromise by means of stepwise, sectoral and delayed policy-making. Italy and Croatia both belong to this cluster.

4. *Evocative austerity policy (bottom up)*

This final type is where allusive austerity has been witnessed, that is, austerity through recommendations, a strategy of incremental compromise and a form of policy transfer based on emulation. The Albanian case fits into this cluster. Austerity here is seemingly voluntary, and the mix of instruments is merely inspired by austerity, while the real goal remains that of Europeanization.

Apart from the question of variance, there are also a number of common features which ought to be examined.

The first of these concerns recentralization. Recentralization is the most evident side effect observed everywhere. It was broadly foreseen by the literature, and there is evidence of it in seven countries. In Mediterranean Europe, apart from improving (or otherwise) financial performance, austerity triggered a process of recentralization. In Italy (but also in Portugal, Cyprus and Spain), recentralization also implied the de-institutionalization and politicization of rights. This means that austerity contributed towards dismantling institutions and replacing them with political bargaining and concessions by the centre; in other words, favours took the place of rights.

A second commonality is directly related to the first, and concerns the loss of autonomy and the increase in the degree of supervision. This engendered 'victimization' in the case of Portugal's local governments but 'resistance' in Greece and Cyprus. In general, the loss of autonomy strongly diminished the autonomy of local authorities as a whole and, in particular, led to a reduction in LPS. The loss of autonomy is particularly evident if we look at the austerity mix: limits to borrowing, public expenditure retrenchment and across the board cutbacks, fiscal supervision together with rescaling and privatization, all represent attempts to reduce the freedom of local government. The loss of autonomy is not only a pursued effect but also a side effect, since the blame avoidance approach by central government is like 'sweeping the dust under the carpet'.

A third concern is that of the reactions to austerity measures. As the chapters examining austerity in Croatia and Spain point out, the loss of autonomy led to resilience on the part of local authorities, which took the form of self-financing schemes and exit strategies. Resilience is maybe the only positive side effect found in this comparison. Local governments tried to resist through innovation and survival strategies. Also, in the Italian case, a similar survival attitude can be seen. In search of an escape route, 'non-implementation' emerged in Greece and Croatia, while political bargaining with the centre was witnessed in Cyprus. In general, as mentioned in the Cypriot chapter, no 'learning from below' was found following austerity policies, but only downsizing.

Fourthly, some contributors have raised the question of legitimacy in the adoption of policies of budgetary cuts, and of the diminishment of legitimacy both before and after austerity. This is also the starting point: the lack of credibility in Mediterranean Europe with regard to financial performance has overwhelmed the citizens of those countries. There was already a serious problem with local authorities' accountability in many of the countries examined here, but austerity has proven more destructive than therapeutic. As the Italian chapter shows, post-austerity the problem of accountability is worse than it was before.

Consequently, the political protest is deserving of analysis here. Opposition by municipalities and agencies managing and delivering LPS was globally weak, isolated and delegated to social and political actors. Beyond the vehement protest by the association of municipalities in Greece, together with late isolated protests by mayors in Albania, municipalities suffered the imposition of austerity measures without reacting in any significant way. Local Public Services have been totally ignored in the political debate: provisions for reductions in organizational and financial capacities were included in a broad debate on welfare. However, any specific focus on the crisis and the restrictions of rights at local level has been overshadowed by the debate on the same problems at the national level. Austerity policies were political actions taken at national level, that generated problems at local level, but were only discussed and problematized as national issues, with no local representation to be seen. LPS provision was considered an epiphenomenon almost everywhere, despite its incisive, crucially important role.

Drawing Conclusions: Convergences, Divergences and the Role of Ideas

The preceding description of the main findings from the country reports shall now be followed by our attempt to systematize the different trajectories and narratives, to draw conclusions regarding the observed dissimilarities and commonalities, and to classify the forms, modalities and consequences of austerity.

To begin with, one basic common characteristic that emerges is that despite the different levels of indebtedness and soundness of public finances in the countries selected for the present study, all have been heavily impacted by the effects of the crisis. In some cases public debt, in others the vulnerability of the banking system, or trade imbalances and productivity problems, or various combinations of all these factors, constitute the Trojan horses that transferred the USA-originated crisis across the Atlantic to Europe and into the Mediterranean.

A second trait is that, perhaps after an ephemeral prelude of Keynesianism, all the countries in question have turned, via different political paths and for different reasons, to the stock recipes of neoliberal orthodoxy, namely, the policies of austerity.

A third feature common to all the cases considered here is that in one way or another, the institutional and financial remedies used to deal with the crisis' effects were also administered to local governments and affected local public services.

In addition to these generic similarities, a number of significant differences were discerned.

A first clear difference regarding the diffusion of austerity throughout Mediterranean Europe is that some countries had to plea for international loans, while others did not. Those countries requiring international financing, applied to institutions such as the European Union, the European Central Bank, the European Stability Mechanism and the International Monetary Fund and, in doing so, had to sign agreements and MoUs with the lending organizations. In these cases, austerity policies were imposed through conditionality clauses included in the agreements and the MoUs. Greece, Portugal, Cyprus, Spain and Albania (which repeatedly applied for, and received, IMF loans) fall into this category. In all cases such policies had been unsuccessfully promoted for decades in the respective countries, by international organizations and national elites, before passing through the windows of opportunity generated by the crisis.

On the other hand, those countries that did not have to request external loans, such as Croatia and Italy, were influenced through rather different channels, such as political pressures, technical consulting and the transfer of dominant ideas by political think tanks, prominent experts and research centres.

The institutional and political paths followed by the individual countries led to diversified set-ups and final results. For example, countries like Croatia and Cyprus, both of which relatively recently went through the EU pre-accession process, experienced different effects at local government level. Due to the specific institutional arrangements, the political balances in each country, as well as the interplay between national and local elites and the European authorities during negotiations, Croatia managed to rearrange local institutions, whereas Cyprus failed to do so.

Austerity-driven reforms focused on three levels of intervention: firstly, spending cutbacks; secondly, the reorganization of powers and functions; and thirdly, rescaling and amalgamation processes. While the ingredients of the 'recipe' were the same in all countries, the exact mixture differed from one country to another. In Greece, for example, a very significant rescaling programme drastically reduced the number of municipalities, which was not the case in other countries such as Spain, where amalgamations failed, as they were not compulsory, but, on the contrary, were associated with ineffective incentives; likewise in Italy, where a rescaling plan was rejected by referendum. In Portugal, on the contrary, even during the crisis, new powers were devolved to the country's local authorities.

The reduction in the number of municipal corporations and agencies was unsuccessfully promoted in Italy, whereas in Greece, it had been effectively achieved during the previous, pre-crisis period under the influence of EU programmes and within the framework of a centre-periphery conflict, as a means of weakening Greece's local elites.

Local governments were actually overspending in some countries (for example, in Italy, where municipal public debt tripled in five years) and were directly targeted by austerity policies as a result. Conversely, in other cases (Spain, Portugal and, to some extent, Greece), local authorities were not the main sources of public deficit. However, even in these latter cases, against a background of blame avoidance tactics, central governments denounced the spending excesses of LGs and promoted spending-cut reforms, which they have, in fact, attributed to pressures from the lenders within a 'there-is-no-alternative' situation.

The main tools for sound financial management at the local level were spending cutbacks instigated through the establishment of obstacles to borrowing money, which, in some cases, were inscribed in the Constitution, as well as the central state's re-introduction of previous restrictions and controls over local government spending.

Reforms of powers and responsibilities moved in two opposite directions. In some cases (such as Portugal and Italy), local government powers were increased – albeit with decreased funding as a rule – while in other cases there was a tendency towards greater centralization.

Amalgamations and sound financial management represented the long-lasting strategy of domestic forces, such as parties, think tanks, etc. that had identified windows of opportunity through which to promote their policies during the crisis, whilst blaming external forces for that crisis. In all of the cases considered here, reforms resulted in the restriction of local operational capacities and autonomy. As regards the increasing social problems due to the crisis, LG was burdened with dealing with them, in virtue of their proximity to such problems and their greater flexibility compared to central structures. They managed to deal with the resulting situation through the utilization of the social economy and NGOs.

In some cases (e.g. Spain, Italy under the Berlusconi government, and Greece during the first months of the Papandreou government), the initial response to the emergence of the crisis was the adoption of Keynesian policies. But then again, as Joseph Stiglitz puts it (The Guardian, 10/10/2013), 'after the financial crisis everybody was a Keynesian – but not for long enough'.

While political cleavages do not appear to play a decisive role in the overall prevalence of austerity policies, there are certain significant differences in the trajectories followed towards the ultimate predominance of austerity. The NPM-inspired ideas that were divulged by international organizations and think tanks and which prevailed, in the main, during the

1990s, in most cases, were not fully implemented as policies due to the fierce resistance at national level from ideologically and politically opposing coalitions, composed not only of left-wing parties but also of right-wing, clientelistic blocs as well as local groups and networks. The crisis has led to the renaissance of such ideas and of the corresponding policies presented as unique remedies to the problems of public finances. However, in cases such as that of the socialist Zapatero government in Spain, the centre-right Berlusconi Government in Italy (mainly under the influence of the populist Northern League party) and, for a brief initial period, Papandreou's socialist Government in Greece, attempts were made to combine moderate reforms with expansionist financial policies in response to the radical neoliberal recipes promoted by the European and national 'austerity coalitions', including the IMF. Albania represents a unique case in that while implementing the IMF's programme, both centre-right and centre-left governments have opted to increase public sector wages and pensions, following a combination of demand-driven policies and clientelistic considerations, despite the disagreement of the lenders (the IMF and the WB).

Nevertheless, in spite of discernable political differences and implementation disparities, the overall conclusion is that a final convergence can be observed: both centre-right and centre-left governments ended up by adopting rather similar policies originating at the international level.

Contrary to the political cleavages of governing parties, that have been mitigated by the imposition of external conditionalities on domestic policy-making, the centre-periphery antithesis appears to have had a greater impact on the austerity arenas. During the pre-crisis period, in the name of New Public Management principles, such as those of efficiency and effectiveness, and following the directives of the EU, OECD, IMF and other international institutions, there was a steady tendency to devolve powers and resources towards the local level. In contrast, during the crisis, for the reason that the local government was considered, not always correctly, as an administrative level spending overly, the central state tried in a variety of ways to limit municipal powers. Municipalities, in response, have adopted strategies to overcome these attempts and to maintain their competencies. Such dynamics, particularly in the case of the centralized Napoleonic states, rearranged the traditional division of power and influence on policy-making between central and local political-administrative elites.

Finally, it can be concluded that in the development of the forms of 'treatment' designed to deal with both the causes and the consequences of the crisis, ideas mattered a lot. Early recommendations for austerity were made in the late 1990s, in a number of countries exposed to the risks of extended bloated public sector and/or excessive public spending, under the influence of neoliberal orthodoxy combined with the ideas emanating from the gurus of New Public Management. The second wave of neoliberal policies came about 15 years later, during the economic and financial crisis, frequently after a brief period of Keynesian responses to the crisis. In this second phase, severe sovereign debt and solvency problems emerged in many countries, including those of Mediterranean Europe, followed by the fervent defenders and promoters of austerity deploying far more efficient methods of persuasion, such as urgently needed loans accompanied by disbursement conditionalities. Therefore, during this second phase, austerity policies were broadly accepted and implemented, even by centre-left governing parties that, in general, had opposed them in the 90s, albeit with certain prominent exceptions, such as the German SPD under Schroeder and the British Labour Party under Blair. Despite the different methods adopted, and despite the different results obtained, in these two periods, there is a clear continuum linking them. The thin red line connecting the late 1990s and the early 2010s consists of ideas, that is, the diachronic ideological cleavage between monetarist policies on the one hand and expansionist and re-distributional policies on the other. A cleavage that goes back to the antithesis between Keynesian and Austrian economic ideas.

All in all, two recommendations for policy-makers can be made on the basis of the foregoing reasoning.

The first is that global recipes – in this case neoliberal recipes – have failed. Global discourses and hard, top-down policy transfers from supranational experts and agencies have failed when adopted at local level. Domestic opportunities for reshaping or biasing are excessively influential, generating side effects and offering other local actors the opportunity to pursue other goals. In addition to the intentionally detrimental impact of austerity policy on LPS, one significant side effect has been that it has weakened such services even further.

Secondly, the findings of this study suggest that LPS have been neglected at all levels when adopting and implementing austerity measures as the end of the line. No specific attention has been paid by policy-makers, experts or academics, whereas LPS represent the most important manager of social rights. Consequently, we have shown that LPS need to be addressed through a specific focus at both the political and the scientific level.

References

Bennett, C. J. (1991). Review Article: What Is Policy Convergence and What Causes It? *British Journal of Political Science, 21*, 215–235.

Benson, D., & Jordan, A. (2011). What Have We Learned from Policy Transfer Research? Dolowitz and Marsh Revisited. *Political Studies, 9*, 366–378.

Christensen, T. (2012). Global Ideas and Modern Public Sector Reforms: A Theoretical Elaboration and Empirical Discussion of a Neo-Institutional Theory. *American Review of Public Administration, 42*(6), 635–653.

Di Mascio, F., & Natalini, A. (2015). Fiscal Retrenchment in Southern Europe: Changing Patterns of Public Management in Greece, Italy, Portugal and Spain. *Public Management Review, 17*(1), 129–148.

Kickert, W., Randma-Liiv, T., & Savi, R. (2013). *Fiscal Consolidation in Europe: A Comparative Analysis.* COCOPS Report, Deliverable 7.2., Brussels, EU Commission.

McCann, E., & Ward, D. (2013). A Multi-disciplinary Approach to Policy Transfer Research: Geographies, Assemblages, Mobilities and Mutations. *Policy Studies, 34*(1), 2–18.

Overmans, J. F. A., & Noordegraaf, M. (2014). Managing Austerity: Rhetorical and Real Responses to Fiscal Stress in Local Government. *Public Money and Management, 34*(2), 99–106.

Silva, C., & Bucek, J. (Eds.). (2014). *Fiscal Austerity and Innovation in Local Governance in Europe.* Farnham: Ashgate.

Index[1]

A
Accountability, 9, 30, 51, 56, 91, 117, 123, 137, 208, 233, 235
Across the board cutbacks, 36, 149, 158, 161, 220, 228–231, 235
Adjustment, 6, 10, 30, 38, 41, 64, 73, 74, 78–80, 83, 99, 107, 110, 123, 135, 144, 178, 194, 218, 220, 227
Aggregation, 86, 136
Allomorphism, 40, 227
Annual real growth, 196, 198
Austerity
  agenda, 17, 43, 98–102, 134, 176, 180, 193–214, 224, 225
  by inspection, 35
  instruments/measures, 4, 6–8, 12–17, 26–28, 31, 41–43, 56, 63, 66, 73–92, 97–100, 102, 106–110, 112, 113, 120, 123, 125, 134, 135, 137, 141–163, 167–189, 195, 213, 214, 217–219, 225, 232, 235, 240
  by recommendation, 35, 224
  state, 6, 28
Autonomy (local), 14, 17, 29–31, 42, 78, 98, 100, 102, 104–106, 111–113, 147, 151, 160, 161, 169, 177, 178, 226, 227

B
Bailout, 8, 17, 54, 62n1, 63, 68, 69, 74, 75, 84, 103, 194
Best practice, 14, 39, 66, 153, 156, 157, 162
Blame avoidance, 36, 91, 186, 188, 218, 220, 224, 226, 235, 238
Blame shifting, 33, 188
Borrowing, 56–59, 73, 83, 104, 111, 151, 172, 174, 196, 200–203, 206, 214, 218, 221, 229–231, 235, 238
Budgetary constraints, 156, 157, 171, 176, 189
Budgetary discretion, 145, 229

[1] Note: Page numbers followed by 'n' refer to notes.

A. Lippi, T. N. Tsekos (eds.), *Local Public Services in Times of Austerity across Mediterranean Europe*, Governance and Public Management, https://doi.org/10.1007/978-3-319-76225-8

Budgetary stability, 101, 103, 106, 134
Budgetary supervision, 3, 150
Bureaucracy, 30, 49, 50, 76, 168
non-Weberian, 51

C

Capital investments, 104, 111, 172, 183, 200
Central and Eastern Europe Countries, 194
Central government, 1, 3, 13, 17, 18, 28, 30, 32, 35, 39, 43, 59, 61, 65, 74, 78–80, 83, 85, 88–90, 96, 97, 100, 102–107, 111–113, 122, 124, 126, 127, 135–137, 143, 145, 151, 154, 161, 168, 169, 172–174, 177, 183n7, 185, 188, 189, 199, 201, 201n2, 205, 206, 208n12, 209, 210, 210n14, 218–220, 222, 224, 226, 235, 238
Centralism, 49–51
Centralization, 76, 77, 83, 99, 100, 121, 129, 179, 184–186, 188, 189, 218, 220, 223, 238
Centre-periphery relations, 122
Civil parishes, 76, 85–87
Civil servants, 60, 100, 110, 120, 221
Clustering, 146n2, 156, 160
Coercion/coercive, 3, 7, 31, 39, 104, 142, 146–148, 154, 155, 158, 159, 161, 182, 201, 211, 226
Commercialization, 178, 184, 188
Commodification
Compulsive competitive tendering, 125, 130, 134, 230
Conditionality, 9, 17, 30, 69, 73, 158, 213, 219, 221, 223, 228, 237, 239, 240
Consolidation, 5, 10, 61–63, 117, 133, 175, 199, 200
Constitutional reform, 102, 104, 117, 119, 123, 219
Constitutionalization of fiscal rule, 121
Contractualization, 117
Contra-cyclical policies, 112
Co-payment, 12, 184, 186, 188, 189
Corporatization, 52, 117, 126, 177, 178, 180, 188, 229
Cost
-cutting, 29, 152–154, 159
efficiency, 174, 207
of politics, 122, 128, 219
reduction, 184
Crisis, economic, 1–3, 6, 9, 15, 17, 27, 28, 41, 42, 53, 95, 100–103, 107, 110, 118, 122, 130, 144, 160–162, 167–176, 180, 184, 187, 188, 198, 217, 219, 220, 222
Cuts, cutbacks, 1, 8–11, 25, 27, 29, 31, 34, 36, 37, 41, 42, 53, 63, 66, 69, 74, 75, 78, 81, 90, 100, 102, 110, 112, 115–137, 145, 150, 153, 156, 159, 175, 176, 193, 195, 197–200, 203, 206, 208, 210, 213, 218–222, 228, 235, 237, 238

D

Debt
ceiling law, 196
to GDP, 201
Decentralization, 34, 51, 78, 79n5, 95, 105, 111, 116, 146, 158, 160, 168–170, 173, 174, 184, 185, 188, 189, 196, 204–206, 208–210, 223
De-institutionalization, 134–137, 234
Delegated functions, 205
Demographic mobility, 212

E
Economic adjustment program, 78, 79
Economic policy, 58, 100, 118, 198
Economic recession, 112, 175, 198
Economies of scale, 117, 119, 129, 134, 135, 176, 210
Efficiency, 11, 26, 35, 76, 78, 84, 85, 148, 149, 176, 177, 182, 184, 188, 207–209, 228, 239
  gains, 36, 153, 180, 186, 209, 210, 213, 227
EU enlargements agenda, 204
European economic authority, 100, 101
Europeanization, 16, 18, 26, 27, 39, 51, 141, 142, 158–161, 223, 225, 234
European Stability Mechanism, 9
Eurozone, 1, 2, 4, 8, 73, 96, 101, 142, 196–198, 221
EU standards, 168, 175, 181, 195, 208, 221
Excises, 200, 229
External pressure/shock, 4, 6, 13, 17, 18, 28, 30–32, 43, 67, 137, 147, 159, 160, 162, 175, 176, 186, 188, 194, 195, 208, 220, 222, 224, 226, 232

F
Fiscal amnesty, 202
Fiscal autonomy, 61, 88, 169, 173
Fiscal Compact, 125
Fiscal consolidation, 1, 2, 10, 16, 18, 60, 62, 73–75, 104, 113, 119, 121, 141, 145, 147, 147n3, 148, 154, 155, 158, 159, 161, 162, 196, 197, 201, 203, 213, 218–220, 228
Fiscal federalism, 119, 124
Fiscal retrenchment, 3, 5, 18, 27, 28, 31, 102–106, 124, 160, 223, 224
Fiscal stress/crisis, 6, 28, 31, 32, 95, 99, 131, 136, 157, 193–195, 198, 213, 222
Fragmentation, 50, 76, 77, 85, 117, 167, 176, 189, 206, 223, 233

G
Golden Rule, 125, 135
Grants, statal, 36, 59, 68, 78, 85, 88, 107, 136, 144, 145, 149, 151, 153, 161, 170–172, 184, 185, 188, 206, 210, 230
Green Paper, 78, 86, 90

H
Healthcare expenditure, 184
Healthcare service, 183–188, 205
Historical continuities, 17, 141–163

I
Indebtedness
  local, 83
  subnational, 77, 91
Indexation (pensions, wage), 199
Inflation, 199, 203
Institutional Constraints, 157
Institutional environment, 189
Institutionalization, 13, 14, 38, 61, 103, 222–225, 232
Institutional reform/rearrangement, 29, 77, 146, 177, 188
Intergovernmental relations, 3, 136, 224
Inter-municipal cooperation, 88, 169, 219, 228, 230
Internal stability pact, 131

Investments expenditure, 36
Isomorphism
coercive, 39, 223, 225, 226
mimetic, 3, 7, 39, 195, 213, 225, 226
normative, 39, 225

L
Legitimacy, 6, 13, 31, 39, 40, 57, 75, 89, 92, 116, 122, 160–162, 224, 235
Lesson drawing, 16, 37, 38
Less with less, 35, 36, 113, 149, 159, 220, 227, 232, 233
Liberalization, 105, 121, 126, 130, 136, 177, 180
Local autonomy, 14, 17, 29–31, 42, 78, 98, 100, 102, 104–106, 111–113, 147, 151, 160, 161, 169, 177, 178, 226, 227
Local borrowing, 172, 205, 206
Local capacity, 111, 136, 167, 174, 182
Local civil servants, 105, 173
Local economic development, 204
Local governance, 1–4, 17, 53, 89, 136, 142, 200, 204
Local government enterprises, 74, 89–90
Local government units (LGUs), 173, 202–207, 206n9, 209–211, 214, 218
Local public service (LPS), 1–18, 26, 35, 42, 43, 63–66, 73–92, 115–137, 141–163, 167–189, 193–214, 217–240
Local self-government, 186, 204
Luxury goods, 200

M
Maastricht Treaty, 202
Mediterranean Europe, 3, 4, 7–9, 11, 12, 14, 16, 18, 217, 232, 234–236, 240
Medium term budget, 202
Memorandum of Understanding on specific Economic Policy Conditionality (MOU), 69, 75, 83, 85, 86, 89, 101, 105, 141, 142, 144–148, 150, 152, 153, 156, 157, 160–162, 219, 220, 223, 237
Migration, 208
Mimétisme administratif, 34
Modernization, 11, 68, 116, 134, 157, 171, 176, 180, 184, 199
More with less, 35, 36, 159, 210, 214, 221, 227
Muddling-through adaptation, 187
Multi-level governance, 144, 175

N
Napoleonic arrangement, 3
National account, 201
Neo-institutionalism, 14
New Public Management (NPM), 2, 9, 11, 16, 25–27, 29, 33–36, 41, 42, 67, 69, 89, 116, 210, 228, 239, 240

O
Old Southern Four, 7, 8, 15, 222, 225, 227, 228
Operational expenditure, 36, 37
Operational flexibility, 52
Organic Budget Law, 201, 213
Overlapping competences, 186, 188

P
Participation, 2, 153, 156, 157, 173, 179, 187, 188
Path dependency, 12, 53
Pay freeze, 199, 229
Policy
  design, 36, 51, 123–128, 179
  diffusion, 16, 37, 38
  implementation, 43, 50, 76, 182
  instrument, 128, 135, 183, 211
  style, 26
  window, 29, 31–33, 123
Policy transfer
  compulsory/mandatory, 225
  hard, 224
  soft, 224
  voluntary, 195, 213, 225
Political
  assemblage, 40, 41, 228
  autonomy, 144
  business cycle, 203, 212, 214
  patronage, 30, 50, 52
Post-communist, 194, 194n1, 201, 207
Price setting, 181
Primary deficit, surplus, 63, 202, 203
Priority centralize cutbacks, 36, 158
Privatization, 1, 5, 35, 38, 41, 64–66, 68, 117, 119, 125, 130, 131, 133, 134, 136, 147n3, 177, 179, 180, 184, 197, 219, 221, 228, 229, 235
Process tracing, 14
Program expenditure, 36, 37
Public
  administration, 4, 51, 53, 58, 66, 89, 96, 97, 100, 101, 104, 105, 123, 142, 146, 163, 170, 173, 175, 198, 199, 201, 207
  agencies, 11, 27, 199
  consultation, 178, 187, 188
  saving, 197, 221
  servants, 142, 198

Q
Quality of democracy, 6

R
Rate of poverty, 198
Rationalist choices, 50
Rationalization, 101–104, 126, 129, 219
Recentralization, 2, 14, 31, 42, 77, 80, 126, 127, 134–137, 145, 147, 151, 220, 223, 226, 229, 233, 234
Recession, 8, 12, 55, 73, 167, 169, 170, 172, 173, 194, 203, 211, 220, 222
Re-engineering design, 211
Referendum, 57, 76, 123, 126, 128, 130, 133, 135, 137, 219, 237
Reforms, 3, 25–43, 49–69, 73, 96, 142, 169, 194, 196–200, 218
Regulation, 3, 36, 40, 51, 101, 105, 110, 118, 125, 127, 128, 130, 133, 171, 177–179, 182, 204n5, 208
Rescaling, 5, 13, 14, 32, 36, 127, 128, 135, 152, 178, 180, 209, 218, 219, 227, 228, 230, 235, 237
Resilience, 99, 106, 113, 158, 175, 233, 235
Revenues, 55–57, 60, 77, 80, 81, 107, 108, 111, 124, 125, 143, 148–151, 158, 160, 161, 169–173, 183n7, 197, 199–202, 204–206, 210, 211, 213, 229, 230

S
Same with less, 35, 36, 158, 186, 220, 227, 233
Self-organisation, 106–110, 112, 133
Service clustering, 156

Service provider, 37, 95, 177–180, 188
Social assistance, system, 111, 200
Social capital, 50, 88
Social security, service, 199
Socio-economic development, 207
Southern question, 8
Sovereign debt crisis, 8, 13, 17, 53–68, 73, 117, 218
Stability and Growth Pact, 101, 118, 121, 155, 158, 202, 214
Stabilization, 53, 55, 58, 62, 62n1, 184, 203
Sustainability, 101–106, 116, 130, 187, 197, 204, 219

T

Tariffs, 126, 130, 132, 133, 136, 176–179
Tax, 9, 10, 36, 52, 56, 60, 76, 80, 83, 88, 123–126, 147n3, 149, 150, 153, 169, 171, 184, 197, 199, 200, 202, 203, 205, 206, 210, 221, 229, 230
Territorial consolidation, 168, 174, 209
Territorial reorganization, 85n10, 189
Training, 51, 153–157
Troika, 8, 57–59, 61, 62, 62n1, 68, 75, 78, 80, 83, 85–87, 120, 141, 145, 148, 153, 154, 158, 223

U

Users pay, 177

V

Value added tax (VAT), 10, 200, 229

W

Waste collection, services and management, 16, 145, 156, 179, 180, 229
Water provision, services, 2, 176
Welfare state, 6, 29
Window of opportunity, 11, 30, 85, 134, 149, 174, 218, 220, 226
World Bank (WB), 33, 169, 170, 173, 178, 186, 188, 197, 199–201, 213, 220, 221, 239

Kolibri 360 GmbH
Ferdinand-Jühlke-Straße 7
99095 Erfurt, Deutschland
produktsicherheit@kolibri360.de